T0193708

Feel the Way You Want to Feel ... No Matter What!

Aldo R. Pucci, PsyD

President
National Association of Cognitive-Behavioral Therapists

iUniverse, Inc.
New York   Bloomington

Feel the Way You Want to Feel ... No Matter What!

© Copyright, 2008, 2010 by Aldo R. Pucci. All rights reserved.

All rights reserved. No part of this book may be used or reproduced by any means, graphic, electronic, or mechanical, including photocopying, recording, taping or by any information storage retrieval system without the written permission of the publisher except in the case of brief quotations embodied in critical articles and reviews.

This publication is intended to be used for educational purposes. It is not a substitute for counseling, psychotherapy, nutritional, or medical treatment. If you have questions or concerns about your emotional or medical well-being, seek the services of a qualified mental health or medical professional.

iUniverse Star
an iUniverse, Inc. imprint

iUniverse books may be ordered through booksellers or by contacting:

iUniverse
1663 Liberty Drive
Bloomington, IN 47403
www.iuniverse.com
1-800-Authors (1-800-288-4677)

Because of the dynamic nature of the Internet, any Web addresses or links contained in this book may have changed since publication and may no longer be valid. The views expressed in this work are solely those of the author and do not necessarily reflect the views of the publisher, and the publisher hereby disclaims any responsibility for them.

Any reproduction of this publication, in any form, by any means is strictly prohibited without the written permission of the author. This publication is designed to provide accurate and authoritative information in regard to the subject matter covered. It is sold with the understanding that the publisher is not engaged in rendering legal, accounting, or other professional service. If legal advice or other expert assistance is required, the services of a competent professional person should be sought.

From a Declaration of Principles jointly adopted by a Committee of the American Bar Association and a Committee of Publishers

ISBN: 978-1-936236-04-6 (pbk)
ISBN: 978-1-936236-05-3 (ebk)

Library of Congress Control Number: 2010901558
Printed in the United States of America

iUniverse rev. date: 2/26/10

In deciding to whom to dedicate this book, I realized that there are several people who were instrumental in my writing it. First, I dedicate this book to my parents, Dominic and Maria Pia Pucci. My parents were instrumental in teaching me a good work ethic and in supporting me in my endeavors. I am grateful for their support and encouragement.

I also dedicate this book to my wife, Sandy, and my children, Aldo and Maria. They are my reason for many of the things that I do.

Finally, I dedicate this book to Dr. Stephen Mascio, Dr. Stanley Mannino, and Dr. Sang Park. Along with my wife (who strongly encouraged me to seek medical evaluation), these fine physicians saved my life when I was on the verge of a life-ending heart attack. Dr. Mascio demonstrated his wisdom in giving me a resting electrocardiogram (despite the fact that I was "only" thirty-nine years old) that gave the initial diagnosis of heart disease. Dr. Mannino performed the stress test and cardiac catheterization that revealed my three significant blockages, and Dr. Park performed my heart bypass surgery. Drs. Mascio and Mannino continue to provide me with excellent medical treatment, keeping me in good shape to hopefully write many more books.

Without my wife and these men, this book could not have been written. I am, and always will be, grateful for their life-saving measures.

Contents

A Special Note from the Author

Feel the Way You Want to Feel … No Matter What! will teach you very powerful and effective rational self-counseling skills. You will learn how to apply these skills to *any* situation for the rest of your life, no matter what. These are the same skills that I have taught my clients throughout the years.

It is important to note, though, that this book is not a substitute for counseling, psychotherapy, or other mental health services. If it seems as though you could use additional help beyond what this book offers, I urge you to seek guidance from a qualified mental health professional. For a referral to a Certified Cognitive-Behavioral Therapist (CCBT) in your area, please visit www.nacbt.org.

I encourage everyone to receive a yearly medical evaluation. If you have not had a checkup in a while, and especially if you have been having physical symptoms like significant weight loss, loss of hair, change in your voice, chest pain, abdominal pain, recurrent headaches, weakness, or significant fatigue, I recommend that you schedule an evaluation with your medical doctor.

With that being said, let's start learning how to feel the way you want to feel, no matter what!

Introduction

Is it really possible for a person to feel the way he or she wants to feel, no matter what? Is it possible to feel happy even if the worst possible things happen to us? After reading this book, you will conclude (without a doubt) that it is possible.

Of course, it is much easier to be happy when *no* personally undesirable events happen in our lives. However, *Feel the Way You Want to Feel … No Matter What!* will show you how to effectively overcome life problems so that you can be happy about other things. This book will show *you* how to use your brain to more calmly and effectively deal with personally undesirable situations, regardless of the severity or complexity of those problems.

The bottom line of this book is very simple. Regardless of the problem, whether you have lost a loved one, lost your job, lost your home, have been diagnosed with a terminal illness, have a disability, were in a car accident, or are experiencing a situation that you believe to be terrible, you will learn how to use that wonderful organ known as the human brain to feel better and to get on with your life. And if you have any doubt about your self-counseling abilities, this book will show you why *you* can apply rational self-counseling techniques and principles to anything that comes your way.

This book is based on the philosophy and techniques of **Rational Living Therapy**, an approach to counseling and psychotherapy that I have been developing since 1990. Rational Living Therapy is a type of cognitive-behavioral therapy (CBT). The word *cognitive* means "thinking." Therefore, cognitive-behavioral therapy focuses on how people think and helps them to think in ways that make them feel the way they want to feel and that help them to achieve their goals.

This book will teach you the rational *self*-counseling skills that Rational Living Therapists teach to their clients. You might be wondering if you will be able to counsel yourself. Believe it or not, we counsel ourselves every waking minute of every day. Sometimes we counsel ourselves in a productive, rational manner, while at other times we unintentionally counsel ourselves in an unproductive, irrational manner. Rational self-counseling is something that you already know how to do. You could not make it through a single day without some amount of good, rational self-talk. The problem, though, is that we often do not pay much attention to our self-talk, and good, appropriate reactions seem much more like accidents than intentional behaviors.

What most people do not know is how to consistently, intentionally counsel themselves rationally. Why don't they? Because people are not taught rational self-counseling during the normal course of their growing up!

Therefore, this book will teach you how to help yourself feel the way you want to feel and how to achieve your goals by teaching you and showing you how to apply rational self-counseling skills. These skills will enable you to feel and act the way you want to feel and act, *on purpose*! These counseling skills give people a great deal of confidence that they can make themselves feel good anytime, in any situation.

Besides original techniques that I have developed, *Feel the Way You Want to Feel ... No Matter What!* is based on the work of pioneers of cognitive-behavioral therapy, including Maxie C. Maultsby, Jr., MD, Albert Ellis, PhD, and Aaron Beck, MD.

How to Read This Book

Self-help books are not designed to be read in the same manner that one would read a novel. Novels are read from beginning to end, and once you know the outcome, there is little reason to read the novel again. Novels are designed to be entertaining, not educational. Self-help books, on the other hand, have no plot or storyline to follow. Their purpose is to educate, not entertain (although good self-help books try to present the material in an entertaining way). Self-help books are most effective when they are read at least twice, as most people report a better understanding of the material the second time through.

This book is most effective when each chapter is read several times before moving on to the next chapter. I recommend that you do this:

- **Spend one week on each chapter.**
- **After you have read the chapter, read it at least once more.**

- **Make a note of anything you disagree with, if that is the case.**
- **If something does not make sense to you, write it down.**
- **Think of how the topics covered apply to you.**

Feeling better takes effort. There is no way to get around that fact. As Dr. Maultsby says, "About the only thing that comes easily to us is trouble." Rational self-counseling is not hard, but it does take practice to apply the techniques to your concerns effectively. It is worth the effort!

A Simple but Important Biological Fact (and Why New Year's Resolutions Are Rarely Kept)

Did you know that you, in effect, have two brains? Your brain is divided into two hemispheres—the left hemisphere and the right hemisphere, and these hemispheres are connected by a bundle of nerves called the corpus callosum. The corpus callosum allows the hemispheres of the brain to communicate with each other.

When it comes to our emotions, each hemisphere is responsible for different functions. For most people, the left hemisphere is responsible for processing language. In other words, it understands and processes the words that we use, hear, and read. The right hemisphere is responsible for producing images. When we imagine, dream, or daydream, we are using our right brain.

Our left-brain words trigger our right-brain images, and we tend to act on those images (Maultsby, 1984). When someone says, "Imagine an apple," the left brain understands the word *apple* and sends a message to the right brain where an image of an apple is produced.

While the left brain understands and processes every word that we use, the right brain understands every word but one—the word *not*. Because of that fact, we cannot imagine ourselves "not doing something." We can only imagine ourselves *doing* something.

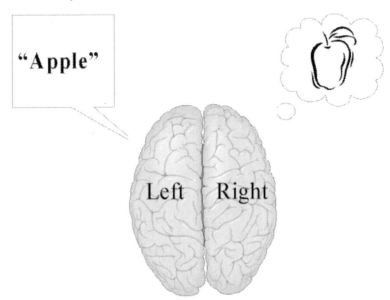

Left-Brain Words Trigger Right-Brain Images

As an example, do this experiment. Please imagine yourself *not* reading this book right now. Were you successful? If you think that you were, I will bet that you imagined yourself doing something else, like watching television or working. Notice, though, that I did not ask you to imagine yourself doing something else. I asked you to imagine yourself *not* reading this book. You cannot do it because we cannot imagine *not* doing something. We can only imagine ourselves doing something.

However, many goals are stated in negative terms. Many people, for example, make the resolution, "This year, I am not going to smoke." Have you noticed, though, that most often when a person repeats such a statement to himself, he ends up smoking anyway? At that point the person usually views himself as "weak-willed" or "too addicted."

While motivation to stop smoking is very important, the manner by which the goal is stated makes a big difference as well. What happens with this behavioral intention, "This year I am not going to smoke," is that the left brain understands the sentence, but as the sentence travels to the right brain, the word *not* is dropped, leaving the sentence: "This year, I am going to smoke." The person then unintentionally imagines himself smoking and acts on that image.

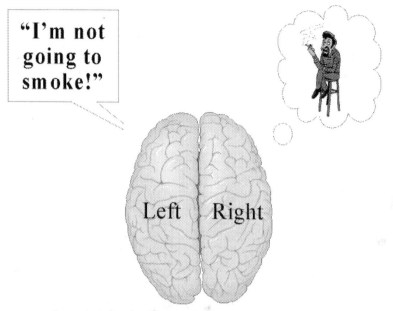

The statement, "I'm not going to smoke" becomes
"I'm going to smoke" when it enters the right brain.
We tend to act on our right-brain images.

A better behavioral intention would be, "This year, I refuse to smoke, and instead of smoking, I am going to exercise, eat well, and chew gum anytime that I get the urge to smoke until I have no more urges." A person can imagine himself doing that and then can act on those images.

Imagine that as you are walking across a tightrope doing your best to get across to the other side, someone yells up to you, "Hey, don't fall!" What would be the very first thing that you would imagine yourself doing? Falling, of course! Instead, if someone were to yell up to you, "Be careful, watch each step," you would be much more inclined to imagine yourself doing just that.

Therefore, when asking yourself or someone else to do something, phrase the request in positive terms. Rather than saying, "Do not forget your homework," say, "Remember your homework." Rather than saying, "I am not going to yell if my husband yells at me," tell yourself, "I will remain calm and rationally discuss the issue with my husband."

Phrase all of your goals in positive terms — in terms that you can visualize.

Your Goals

Please note that this book will not tell you how to live your life or what your goals *should* be. Instead, it will help you determine what *you* want out of life, and it will help you to think and behave in ways that will help you to achieve those goals.

Your goals are very important because they give you the reasons to work at feeling and getting better. For example, why would a person be concerned about feeling depressed? Because feeling depressed often interferes with achieving a goal, even if it is just enjoying an activity.

The next few pages will provide you an opportunity to write down your goals related to your physical and emotional well-being, what you want on a daily basis, and what you want out of life.

Some Tips for Successful Goal-Setting

Make your goals as specific as possible. The more specific your goals, the easier it will be for you to track your progress toward them. Rather than saying, "I want to be happier," state what you will do when you are happier, such as, "I will go bowling at least once a week, I will laugh at the comics in the newspaper (like I used to), I will sleep at least six hours a night … " In other words, these actions are a reflection of "being happier."

Separate your goals from the means by which to achieve them. People quite often confuse their goals with the means by which to achieve those goals. For example, rarely is losing weight a person's goal—it is a means by which to achieve goals, like attracting a mate, fitting in certain clothes, ending pain in the knees, or breathing more comfortably. The following are some common *goals* and what people usually actually want.

Stated Goal	What a Person Usually *Really* Wants
To lose weight.	To attract a mate, to fit in certain clothes, to have more energy for pleasurable activities, to be healthier for some purpose.
To live longer.	To spend time with grandchildren, to spend time with my spouse, to go fishing, to enjoy life after retirement.
To earn more money.	To have a nicer house, to send children to college, to more easily pay bills, to go on vacations.
To be attractive.	To have a mate, to get married, to please my mate (and maybe my mate will please me), to get a job, to get a promotion.
To have higher self-esteem.	To be more confident in pursuing goals, to attract a mate, to get a job, to be successful in certain areas of one's life.
To have the respect of others.	To have certain treatment from people, to obtain certain things that require the assistance of others, avoidance of harm from others.

This very helpful insight can make quite a difference in achieving goals. When a person has difficulty achieving a goal, he or she might begin to think hopelessly in relation to it. For example, if a woman believes that losing weight is her goal, but she has difficulty losing it due to a medical problem, she might give up on her goal. However, if her goal actually is to attract a mate, then she might look for other ways to attract a mate besides losing weight.

Set a time frame to achieve your goals. Without a time frame for your goals, it is difficult to know how hard to work to achieve them. For example, a goal of earning $5,000 in one week would require much more intensity of effort than would a goal of earning the same amount in one year.

Be realistic. Do some research to discover realistic (or healthy) expectations for achieving your goals. For example, most physicians believe that a weight-loss goal of two pounds a week is both realistic and healthy. The Internet is a great place to do that research, utilizing search engines like Google (http://www.google.com) and Yahoo! (http://www.yahoo.com). Another very good tool is Copernic Agent from Copernic Technologies (http://www.copernic.com). Copernic searches the Internet for you (including the search engines) to provide your research results.

Break your goals down into successive approximations. If your ultimate goal is to earn $100,000 a year (so that you can achieve your goals that require that level of financial resources), but you currently make $20,000 a year, break your goal down into successive steps, i.e., $30,000 this year, $50,000 next year, $75,000 the following year, and then $100,000.

A Very Special Note About Your Goals

When writing down your goals, *refuse to produce a filtered list.*

What I mean by this is that people often will only write down what they think is *possible*, rather than writing down everything that they *want*. Therefore, I am suggesting to you that you write down *everything* that you want, no matter how impossible some things might appear to be to obtain or to accomplish.

It does not matter if you want a castle overlooking the ocean, write it down! It does not matter if you are eighty years old and want to be an astronaut, write it down! Write down what you *really* want, not just what you think is possible.

As you go through this book, review your list to determine, based on the facts, what is possible and what is not. Of those goals that *appear* not to be possible, refuse to jump to the conclusion that because the goal seems impossible that it must be so. The more important the goal is to you, the more that you will want to research the topic to see if it might be possible to achieve after all.

If you have difficulty determining *life* goals, ask yourself, "Was there ever a time in my life when I wanted my life to be different than it is right now? If so, how did I want it to be?" Also ask yourself, "When I was a child and an adult asked me what I wanted to be when I grew up, how did I answer that question?"

Often, people are very happy to discover that what they thought was not possible actually is, or that what they thought would be very difficult to achieve is not as difficult as they had thought. Sometimes, though, people discover that achieving their goal will take more effort than they had thought, but that is good information to have. If you want it, go for it!

Also please keep in mind that what you are compiling when you write down your goals and desires is a "wish list" *not* a "have to" list or a "the only way I could be happy" list. This is an important fact to keep in mind because if you happen to fail to achieve a goal, your brain will allow you to be happy with something else. There are many roads to happiness.

What I Want to Change
(Underline: Example)

1. **Do this *more***	**Do this *less*** (or not at all)
— *Ask girls out on dates comfortably*	—*Bite my nails*
—*Say "no" when I mean "no"*	— *Yell/Swear*
—*Hand in assignments on time*	—*Over-eat*
—*Compliment people when they do well*	—*Procrastinate*
—*Go to grocery stores comfortably*	

2. **Emotionally Feel this *more*** (Remember, feelings are one-word adjectives, like happy, sad, excited, anxious, etc.)	**Emotionally Feel this *less*** (or not at all)
	—*Depressed*
—*Happy*	—*Angry*
—*Excited*	—*Nervous*
—*Calm*	

3. **Physically Feel this *More***	**Physically Feel this *Less*** (or not at all)
—*Energetic*	—*Pain in my knee*
	—*Headaches*

4. **Think this *more***	**Think this *less*** (or not at all)
—*That I am somebody*	—*That I'm a nothing and a nobody*
—*That I can achieve my goals*	—*That I'll never amount to much*
—*That girls will like me once they get to know me*	—*That I'm ugly and everyone who sees me thinks that, too*
—*That just because something does not go my way doesn't mean I have to be angry about it*	—*That it's the end of the world when things don't go my way*
—*That people do not think bad things about me when they see me*	—*That I'll never have what I want out of life*
5. **Know this *more***	**Know this *less*** (or not at all)
—*How to fix cars*	—*What other people are saying or thinking about me*
—*How to figure out what career I want to pursue*	—*Why my parents argue*
—*How to ask girls out comfortably*	—*The negative things that occur in the world that do not affect me*
—*How to stop feeling angry*	

What I Want to Change

1. **Do this *more***	**Do this *less*** (or not at all)
2. **Emotionally Feel this *more*** (Remember, feelings are one-word adjectives, like happy, sad, excited, anxious, etc.)	**Emotionally Feel this *less*** (or not at all)
3. **Physically Feel this *more***	**Physically Feel this *less*** (or not at all)

4. **Think this _more_**	**Think this _less_** (or not at all)
5. **Know this _more_**	**Know this _less_** (or not at all)

Life Goals (Example)

On this page, write down what you want out of life—your long-term goals. In other words, how will your life be when you take a look around and say, "I like my life because (1) I like where I live, (2) I like who I'm with, (3) I like how I generate income and how much money I have, and (4) I like how I spend my leisure time."

Remember to refuse to only write down what you think is possible. Go for it, and write what you really, really want!

What I want from life	Importance to me
	Slightly / Moderately / Very Important
Live near the beach in Florida	*Very Important*
To be able to go to the beach every day	*Moderately Important*
To have a wife and a couple of children	*Very Important*
To have a nice house with a big yard	*Very Important*
To work as a lawyer	*Very Important*
To retire when I'm fifty years old	*Moderately Important*
To earn $100,000 a year	*Moderately Important*
To do things with my family, like going on vacation, sporting events, etc.	*Moderately Important*

To what age do you want to live? _____80_____

Life Goals

On this page, write down what you want out of life–your long-term goals. In other words, how will your life be when you take a look around and say, "I like my life because (1) I like where I live, (2) I like who I'm with, (3) I like how I generate income and how much money I have, and (4) I like how I spend my leisure time."

Remember to refuse to only write down what you think is possible. Go for it, and write what you really, really want!

What I want from life	Importance to me Slightly / Moderately / Very Important

To what age do you want to live? _____

What I Want to Experience and Avoid
(Example)

On this page, write down what you want to experience as much as possible and avoid as much as possible. Spend some time with this and give it some thought as you can use this as a guide for having happy days. Write down everything that comes to mind.

What I want to experience as much as possible

Time with my wife
Time with my children
Football games / sporting events
Fishing
My favorite pasta dish
My favorite TV show
Laughing at a funny joke
Reading a good book
A good cup of coffee

What I want to avoid as much as possible

Sinus headaches
Work days longer than eight hours
Traffic jams
Tornados
Hurricanes
Icy roads
Traffic accidents
Conflict
Reality TV shows
Colds / flu
Being yelled at
Cleaning litter boxes

What I Want to Experience and Avoid

On this page, write down what you want to experience as much as possible and avoid as much as possible. Spend some time with this and give it some thought as you can use this as a guide for having happy days. Write down everything that comes to mind.

What I want to experience as much as possible

What I want to avoid as much as possible

Now Examine Your Goals, and Go For It!

Now it is time to examine your goals to determine to what degree they are possible and what it will take to achieve them. To determine possibility, utilize the following flowchart.

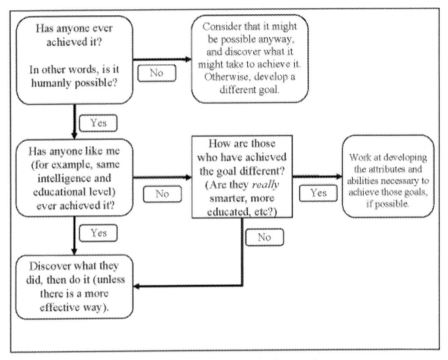

Decision Tree for Deciding Which Goals to Pursue

Rational Reminders

Now that you have set your goals, place them, and reminders of them, in places where you will see them. I am not encouraging you to obsess about your goals, just to remain mindful enough to get the job done. When I was studying for my licensing exam, I had a full-time job, and my wife and I had two very young children. The only time that I had to study was very early (4:00 a.m.) before I went to work. To make it more likely that I would get up when the alarm clock sounded,

I placed a reminder, "License and Private Practice" next to the alarm clock.

I encourage you to place such reminders in areas where it counts. If you want to lose weight, place your goals and reasons for them on the refrigerator. If you have been feeling depressed and have difficulty getting out of bed, place your reasons for getting up on your nightstand.

Pick a Role Model and Act "As If"

The next step in the pursuit of your goals is to pick a role model—someone who has the attributes and abilities that you would like to develop—someone who has achieved what you want to achieve. Study that person and then act *as if* you are that person. *Be* that person.

I remember when I was asked to teach my first college class. I immediately recalled my favorite college professor, Dr. Randy Martin. I loved the way he taught and how he conducted himself in class. So with the very first teaching day of my first class, I *was* Randy Martin. Not only did it help me to be successful as I was following a pattern of success, acting as if I were Randy completely eliminated any anxiety that I might have had with teaching my first class. It was not me teaching the class, it was Randy! Then after a while, I developed my own style that I enjoy and find to be successful.

Who will you select for your role model(s)? Write their name(s) here:

———————————————————————————

A Note About Cognitive-Emotive Dissonance and Gut Thinking

Some of the things that you read in this book might feel strange and wrong to you, especially if it is contrary to what you are accustomed to thinking. This strange, funny feeling is called **cognitive-emotive dissonance**.

Cognitive-emotive dissonance is the strange feeling that we feel in our gut (where we feel our emotions) when we do something, think something, or feel something that is the opposite of that to which we are accustomed. It feels strange. It "feels wrong."

For example, if you were to place a pen in the opposite hand than you write with and tried to write with that hand, not only would you not write well, but it would feel strange and wrong. This "wrong" feeling is cognitive-emotive dissonance.

Cognitive-emotive dissonance is *unavoidable*—we will experience it *anytime* we do something, think something, feel something, or are exposed to something that is the opposite of that to which we are accustomed.

People experience many changes that create cognitive-emotive dissonance. Examples include

- living on your own after being married for twenty years,

- eating a vegetarian diet after eating meat all of your life,

- moving into a new home,

- working for a new employer,

- feeling happy when you have felt depressed for years,

- asserting yourself when you have been accustomed to keeping quiet,

- having money when you have been accustomed to being poor,

- thinking that you are smart when all of your life you thought that you were not,

- going to a different church, or changing religions,

- someone treating you well when you have been consistently mistreated.

These are examples of situations from which we expect to experience cognitive-emotive dissonance.

Gut thinking is the mistaken idea that our emotional feelings are proof that what we are thinking is correct. According to gut thinking,

- if it *feels* wrong, it must *be* wrong;

- if it *feels* right, it must *be* right;

- if I *feel* afraid, I *must* be in a dangerous situation;

- if I *feel* depressed, my situation *must* really be as bad as I'm feeling.

However, the only thing that our emotional feelings prove is that we are thinking something to create them. Our feelings do not prove that we are right or wrong, or that our situation is good or bad. Therefore,

- just because it *feels* wrong *does not* mean it is wrong;

- just because it *feels* right *does not* mean it is right;

- just because I *feel* afraid *does not* mean that I must be in a dangerous situation;

- just because I *feel* depressed *does not* mean that my situation really *is* that bad.

Changing your behavior and emotions will feel strange and wrong. Adopting a different lifestyle or different living arrangement will feel strange and wrong. If you were to think, "Since it feels wrong, it must be wrong," you would immediately refuse it.

The only thing that this "wrong" feeling proves is that you are not accustomed to the new way of thinking, feeling, and acting. The only thing that rids us of cognitive-emotive dissonance is practice. The more that we practice the new ideas, behaviors, and feelings, the sooner they will feel "right." The more that we write with the pen in our non-preferred hand, the sooner writing with that hand will feel "right" to us.

Also consider that immediate negative reactions to new information could be the result of cognitive-emotive dissonance. Therefore, give new ideas a chance!

For example, I remember one day sitting in my living room watching television and seeing a picture of a balcony on the screen. After several minutes a man came walking out onto the balcony. It was the new pope, Pope Benedict XVI. My immediate reaction was, "I don't like him." The man had not yet uttered a single word, but I already had a negative reaction to him. Therefore, I asked myself, "Aldo, why do you not like him?" Asking myself that question helped me to realize that what I was experiencing was cognitive-emotive dissonance. For the previous twenty-six years, another man, Pope John Paul II, walked out onto that balcony. Seeing another man do so felt strange and wrong, therefore giving me the immediate impression that it *was* wrong. I therefore encouraged myself to give him a chance.

Introduction Summary

1. Human beings cannot imagine themselves *not* doing something. We can only imagine ourselves doing something. If we try to imagine ourselves not doing something, we end up imagining the very thing that we are attempting to avoid. We then tend to act on those images. Therefore, it is important to state behavioral intentions in positive terms. Rather than saying, "I am not going to punch people when I'm angry," say "If I feel angry, I will keep my hands to myself."

2. When developing goals, start with what you *want*, not with what you think is possible. Refuse to filter your list. After you determine what you really want, do research to determine if it is possible.

3. It is important to keep mindful of your goals so that you stay on track. Often people fail to achieve their goals because they lose sight of them.

4. Selecting a role model can be helpful as it will help you to follow a formula for success.

5. Thinking, feeling, or behaving in a manner that is different than that to which you are accustomed will feel strange. This strange feeling is called cognitive-emotive dissonance, and it gives you the impression that the new thought, feeling, or behavior is wrong. However, just because it feels wrong does not mean it is wrong.

1

The Good News:
Our Emotional ABCs

Before learning *how* to feel the way you want to feel, it is important to learn what causes us to feel and act the way we do. Understanding the cause of our emotions will help you to know what needs to be changed to feel and do better.

Most people have an idea of how our emotions work, but it is an incorrect idea. As a result, whenever they feel an unwanted feeling, they try to change the wrong thing. The result is that they continue to feel the unwanted feeling, and they are frustrated as well because their approach is not working.

For example, imagine that I attempt to start my car, but the car will not start. I try it again, and the car still will not start. So I tell myself, "Aldo, I'll bet there is not enough air in the tires. That is why the car is not starting." So I get out my electric air pump and place some air in the tires. I attempt to start the car, and it continues not to start. So I then tell myself, "Maybe I did not place enough air in the tires." If I continue down this path, I will have a car that does not start and that also has four flat tires. Obviously, the air pressure in the tires does not determine whether a car will start.

This is very similar to what happens when people have an incorrect idea of how our emotions work. As you will see, most people have an incorrect idea of what causes our feelings and behaviors.

Do not be surprised or alarmed if my explanation of how our emotions work feels a little strange or wrong to you. It is somewhat

1

different from what people learn growing up. After you understand how your emotions actually work, you will be glad to know that what society teaches us about our emotions is wrong.

Good News #1: Our Emotional ABCs

Whenever we feel a feeling, three things happen, and we call this the ABCs of emotions.

(A) First we become **AWARE** of something (the "A" in the ABCs). In other words, we see something, hear something, or use our senses in some way to notice a situation, event, or condition.

(B) Next, we think or **BELIEVE** something about "A," which is the "B" in the ABCs. The way that we think about this thing will be one of three different ways: positively, neutrally, or negatively. An example of a positive thought is, "This is a good thing"; an example of a negative thought is, "This is a bad thing"; and an example of a neutral thought is, "This isn't good or bad" or "It does not much matter to me."

(C) The way that we think about what we are aware of then tells our brain how to make the rest of our body feel and act. We call this reaction the **EMOTIONAL CONSEQUENCE** (the "C" in the ABCs). A positive thought causes our body to feel a positive feeling (happy, excited); a negative thought causes a negative feeling (depression, anxiety, anger); and a neutral thought causes a neutral feeling.

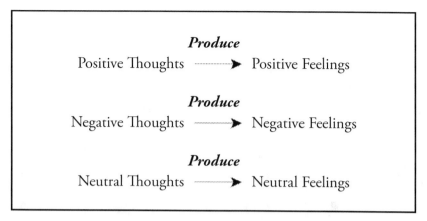

Most people do not know what a neutral feeling is because our society does not really teach this concept. The word *calm* best describes a neutral feeling. For example, have you ever sat in front of a television, not feeling particularly happy or upset that you noticed, but just kind of sat there? If so, you were experiencing a neutral or calm emotion. However, if you were to approach most people who are calmly watching television and were to ask them, "What are you feeling right now?" it is likely they would tell you, "I'm not feeling anything." However, the only time that we feel *nothing* is if there is something wrong with our brain and body (like a severed spinal cord), if we are under general anesthesia (such as for surgery), or if we are dead. Otherwise, what gets labeled as *no* feeling is usually a *calm* or *neutral* feeling.

So, contrary to what most of us were taught growing up, it is *our thinking* that causes our feelings and behaviors, *not* people, situations, things, or events!

Here is an example of the ABCs of positive, negative, and neutral emotions.

ABC's of Emotions

A. Awareness   B. Thought or Belief   C. Emotional Consequence

A. Awareness   B. Thought or Belief   C. Emotional Consequence

A. Awareness   B. Thought or Belief   C. Emotional Consequence

As you can see in this example, the way a person *thinks* about the ending of a romantic relationship determines the way that he or she feels in reaction to it. Keep in mind, though, that this is the opposite of what society teaches us. How often have you said or heard other people say, "He upset me," "It made me mad," or "She made me happy?" The reality, though, is that people, things, situations, and events *never* cause our emotional feelings and behaviors. *What causes our feelings and behaviors is what we THINK about people, things, and situations.*

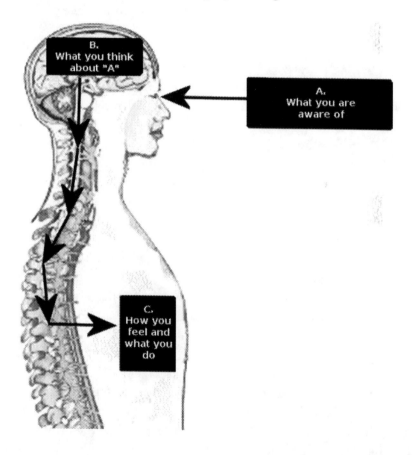

It makes sense for us to be very thankful that our emotions work the way that I am describing to you. *If in fact people, situations, things, and events really did cause our emotional feelings, we would be their emotional slaves!* Any time someone wanted us to feel upset, we would *have to* feel upset because *they would be making us feel that way.*

What this good news also means is that a situation need not change for us to change the way we feel. To change the way we feel, we can change the way we think. In fact, even if an undesirable situation does improve, we will not feel better until we change our thinking along with it.

The fact that our thinking causes our feelings and behaviors is particularly important to keep in mind when we are confronted with situations over which we have very little or no control. Thinking thoughts that help us to calmly accept a situation puts us in a better position to change it if possible.

Occasionally, someone will ask me, "Aren't there some things that are so bad that nearly everyone would feel upset in reaction to them … and if so, doesn't that mean that *the things* are causing you to be upset?" The answer to this question is, "No!" I recall a student once asking that same question. The rest of the class seemed to agree with her that there must be some things that are so bad that they cause people to be upset. So I asked her to give me an example. She said, "Nearly everyone would be upset if their house burned down, wouldn't they?" I agreed with her, nearly everyone would be upset under those circumstances. *However, that does not mean that the circumstances are what cause the upset!* I gave her and the class the following example.

Imagine that there are three houses in a neighborhood located side by side. One house catches on fire, and as it burns, it ignites the other two houses. All three houses burn to the ground. The owner of the first house says, "This is more than I can handle. I will never be able to recuperate from this. I might as well kill myself." *As a result, Owner #1 feels very depressed.*

The owner of the second house says, "Thank God! I have been trying to get out of this neighborhood for years, but no one would buy my lousy house. Now I can collect my insurance money and get the heck out of here!" *As a result, Owner #2 feels very happy.* The owner of the third house says, "My family and I really like this neighborhood, and it is going to be difficult to handle this situation, but it is important for me to do my best to calmly accept that this happened and to deal with it rationally, because if I make myself miserable over it, I will not be able to do what is best for my family." *As a result, Owner #3 feels calm or sad.*

In this example, it is clear that each homeowner's *thinking* about their house being destroyed is what caused their emotions. If it were an objective fact that the experience of one's home being destroyed *causes* emotional upset, *all three homeowners would be upset!*

We all have our own ideas about what is good, bad, and neutral. What would be the worst thing for one person could be an actual improvement for someone else. When I think of what would be one of the worst things in my life, I would say it would be losing my wife and children to death. Many people would agree with me.

When people tell me that they believe that they will never be able to change the way that they think to feel better because their situation is too bad, I think about a barber I once had. I will call him "Fred the Barber." Fred had a busy barber shop in a small town in Southwestern Virginia. About four years before I met him, he suffered a loss in his life. His wife and three daughters were traveling home from his wife's parents' home when their car collided with a tractor trailer. In a very brief moment Fred's family was gone. Imagine how he felt. Yet there he was, four years later, remarried, active in his church, and cutting my hair. He did not appear upset—to the contrary, he appeared to have an appreciation for life. I am sure he continues to miss his wife and three daughters, but he has moved on with his life. When people tell me they cannot accept personally unfortunate situations, I think about Fred and realize that the human brain allows us to accept anything that comes our way, no matter how very unfortunate it is to us.

Now that you know that your thoughts cause your feelings and behaviors, get in the habit of saying, "I upset myself … I made myself happy … My feelings are caused by my thoughts."

Good News #2: There Are Three Ways of Feeling, *Not* Two

It also makes a great deal of sense for us to be very thankful that our bodies are capable of feeling three different types of emotions—positive, neutral, and negative. Our society teaches us that there are only two ways of feeling—either positively or negatively—good or bad. So if something undesirable happens to you, like if you lose your job, you say to yourself, "It doesn't make sense for me to feel *good* about this situation, so I must have to feel *bad*" (because there are only two choices, so we are told). Thankfully, though, our bodies have always known what society has not—there are three ways of feeling. So you can have a *neutral or calm* reaction to an undesirable situation. That is precisely the goal of rational self-counseling—moving from feeling miserable to feeling along the lines of calm about a personally undesirable situation.

Feelings that are more along the lines of calm are "sad" as opposed to "depressed," "irritated" as opposed to "angry." The more along the lines of calm that we feel, the better we feel, and the better position we are in to do something to correct the undesirable situation.

Another important fact to keep in mind is that the opposite of feeling upset is *not* feeling happy. The opposite of feeling upset is *not* feeling upset, which is feeling calm. I point this out because sometimes if people do not understand this, they will ask, "Are you saying that I should be happy about my situation?" No! It would not make sense to be happy about something that you dislike. What we teach people is how to refuse to make themselves miserable over their undesirable situations—how to calmly accept them. It is very difficult, though, to be happy about anything as long as we are miserable about one thing.

Calm acceptance of personally undesirable situations frees us up to be happy about other things.

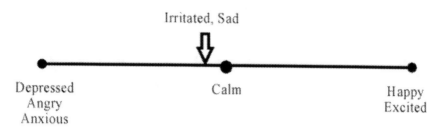

When we feel closer to "calm," we feel better,
and we are in a better position to handle most situations.

When would a person be truly, completely calm about something over which he currently is upsetting himself? Let's take the example of a man whose wife leaves him. Initially he might depress himself over the situation. If he gets to the point where he is completely calm about her leaving, it will probably be due to his no longer wanting her. Otherwise, as long as he wants her, he will feel at least "sad" at the thought that she left. Therefore, as long as he wants her, his goal would be to move from feeling very depressed to feeling sad in reaction to her leaving. The only way he would ever feel happy in reaction to her leaving would be if he found some advantage to it.

A common myth about calm feelings is that if a person reacts calmly to something, that means that he or she does not care about it. Nonsense! Calmly accepting something only means that you refuse to make yourself miserable over it. It does not mean that you do not want to do something about it.

Another myth is that cognitive-behavioral therapy teaches people that they are not permitted to feel emotionally upset. More nonsense! People have the right to feel and behave any way they choose, as long as their behaviors do not violate the rights of others. We teach people how to feel the way they want to feel without judging their emotional preferences.

Now that you understand that your thoughts cause your feelings and behaviors, I am sure that you realize the importance of paying attention to your thoughts in those situations you are currently struggling with. If you happen to upset yourself or behave in a way that is counterproductive, break your reaction or behavior down into the ABCs of emotions.

Reflexive Thoughts: Why Sometimes It *Seems* as Though "Things" Cause Our Feelings

Sometimes when people record their Emotional ABCs, they will realize what they were aware of (A), and they will know how they felt and what they did (C), but they will not know what they thought (B) about it. They will say, "It happened so quickly, I do not know what I was thinking about it." This experience will make it seem that no thinking occurred and that "A" caused "C."

However, it is important to understand that everything that we do is preceded by a thought, except for a very basic physiological reaction, such as when a doctor taps your knee and your leg jerks. We cannot do anything without somehow giving our brain the signal to do it. I am very thankful for that fact because if that were not the case, we would engage in random behaviors. Who knows what we would do if the brain did not need the signal from us to do it.

So what is this signal that the brain receives and, in this case, receives very quickly? In Rational Living Therapy we call this signal a **reflexive thought**.

A reflexive thought is a very well-learned, very practiced thought. It is a thought that is so well-learned that it no longer needs to be thought consciously—it is stored in the brain, ready for action. The second something reminds your brain of a reflexive thought, it is triggered, and you then feel the feeling that is consistent with that thought. In fact, it only takes 1/10,000th of a second for an impulse to travel through your brain. That is how quickly a person can react to something.

For example, pretend that as you are driving a little too closely behind the car in front of you, you suddenly see the car's brake lights illuminate. What would you do? Naturally, you would instantly apply your brakes to stop your car. However, before applying your brakes, would you need to say to yourself, "Gee, I see that this car in front of me is stopping suddenly, so I'd better put my foot on the brake?" Of course not! You would almost *instantly* apply your brakes and later marvel at how quickly you reacted.

What would allow you to apply your brakes quickly is a well-learned reflexive thought about what it takes to stop a car. That reflexive thought is something like, "For me to stop a car, I need to put my foot on the brake pedal." How did that thought become so well-learned? I am sure that when you were a child, you saw adults placing their foot on the brake pedal to stop the car. When you were old enough to drive, you began practicing the brake-applying belief each time that you put your foot on the brake pedal. Consequently, the belief has become so well-learned that it is stored in the brain, ready for action. The instant the reflexive thought is triggered, the foot goes on the brake pedal.

Remember that the ABCs of emotions are

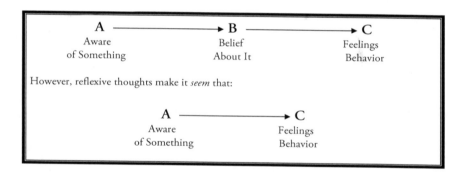

Reflexive thoughts are very helpful to us when they help us to protect our life and health. Reflexive thoughts can be a problem when they are well-learned *irrational* beliefs that produce instant unwanted emotions and behaviors.

Remember, though, that we must identify our thoughts to be able to change them. But with reflexive thoughts it appears that we have not thought anything. Maxie C. Maultsby, Jr., MD, suggests asking the following question to uncover reflexive thoughts:

"I'm *acting* as if I believe what about this situation?"

Reflexive Thoughts

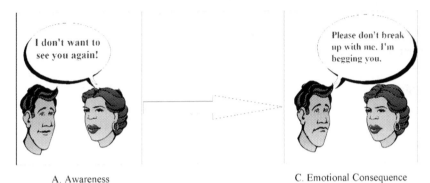

A. Awareness

C. Emotional Consequence

A Reflexive Thought is a well-learned thought, so well-learned that a person no longer needs to think it consciously. It is stored in the brain ready for action.

Unless there is something wrong with it, your body will always provide the logical reaction to what you think. Your body is a reflection of what you think. The only time when this is not the case is when there is something wrong with the body, such as depressive symptoms that are the result of a thyroid condition. In that case, how a person thinks and how they feel might be inconsistent.

The more that you learn about the different thoughts that cause the different emotions, the better you will be at uncovering reflexive thoughts. Chapter 5 discusses the common mental mistakes associated with problematic emotional reactions.

Incomplete Thoughts

When breaking down reactions into the Emotional ABCs, a common mistake that people make is to omit the part of the thought that causes the emotion, which usually is the most important part to dispute. For example:

<u>A</u>	<u>B</u>	<u>C</u>
(What you are aware of)	(What you thought about it)	(How you felt)
My husband came home at 4:00 in the morning.	He's having an affair.	Angry Anxious

To say, "He's having an affair" is not enough because that does not tell us *what you think about the idea that he is having an affair*. Unless we assume what one thinks about the possibility that a husband is having an affair, we could only guess what the reaction would be at "C"—how she felt and acted. To demonstrate:

A	B	C
(What you are aware of)	(What you thought about it)	(How you felt)
My husband came home at 4:00 in the morning.	He's having an affair, **and the rotten S.O.B. shouldn't treat me this way after I gave him the best years of my life. Now what will I do? I'm going to be alone, and that will be terrible!**	Angry Anxious
My husband came home at 4:00 in the morning.	He's having an affair, **and that's wonderful, because now I can divorce him and really cash in!**	Happy
My husband came home at 4:00 in the morning.	He's having an affair, **but it really doesn't matter because I'm divorcing him anyway.**	Calm

As you can see, the underlying belief determines the emotional reaction experienced. Therefore, as you break down your emotional reactions into the ABCs, make certain that you complete your thoughts.

Identify Your Thoughts

So the first goal is to discover what you are thinking whenever you upset yourself or engage in behaviors that you wish to eliminate. The next step will be to determine whether your thinking is rational or irrational. If your thinking *is* rational, you will want to keep it because it is helping you. However, when people experience significant, unwanted emotions or engage in problematic behaviors, they usually are mistaken in their thinking for one reason or another. If your thinking is irrational, you will want to eliminate it and to replace it with rational thoughts. This book will show you how to do so.

People often ask me, "Is it possible for a person to change the way he or she thinks? If so, how can a person learn how to think differently?" Actually, not only is it possible for us to "change" our thoughts, we do it virtually every day. For most thoughts we think on a daily basis, we do not have to "learn" how to change them. If I were to place money into a soda pop machine, I would be acting as if I believed, "This machine is going to give me a can of soda pop." However, should the machine be broken and not give me the pop, I would very quickly and easily change my mind about this machine.

However, well-learned, important thoughts often take a little more work to change. Keep in mind that we do not waste our time thinking thoughts we know are not correct. But just because we believe something to be true does not mean that it is a fact. This book will help you to determine for yourself whether your thoughts are worth thinking. It then will teach you how to replace old, problematic thoughts with new, healthier thoughts.

We learn thoughts the same way that we learn how to type, drive, read, and so on. It is the same process. What makes a new way of thinking a habit for us is practice. There are several effective methods to practice new thoughts and behaviors. You will learn about those methods in Chapter 12. It really is not hard at all. It just takes practice.

A New Habit to Develop

Rather than saying, "He upset me …, she made me mad …, it made me nervous …," get in the habit of saying, "I upset myself …, I make myself happy …, I create all of my emotions by the way that I think."

Some people make the good-sounding, but problematic statement, "I let someone upset me." To say that we let people upset us is to imply that they have the power to upset us, and that we have allowed them to do so. As you have learned, though, people *do not* have the power to upset us. They say and do things, and *our thinking about what they say or do* then upsets us. Therefore, rather than saying, "I let him upset me," say, "I upset myself over what he said."

An Important Note

People often confuse the idea of "upsetting oneself" with "choosing to upset oneself." Our thoughts do cause our emotions and behaviors. This is not to say that we are always happy with the way that we think, or that we are simply choosing to feel miserable because we have nothing better to do. People *unintentionally* make themselves miserable or act in otherwise problematic ways.

People, even when they understand and practice rational self-counseling, sometimes upset themselves because they do not know any other way to think about the situation at hand. They direct themselves to feel upset, but they would not do this if they knew another way to think. That is what this book is all about—learning how to think rationally consistently, which, in turn, makes you feel and act rationally.

Another Important Note: Our Emotional Feelings

Remember that emotional feelings are one-word adjectives, such as happy, sad, depressed, anxious, and angry. If your feeling statement is a sentence, and especially if it contains the words *feel that* or *feel like*, what you really mean is, "I think that …" This is an important point to keep in mind because human beings do not dispute feelings, we only dispute thoughts.

For example, imagine that you wake up in the middle of the night one night and you realize that you are thirsty. So you decide to go to your kitchen to get a glass of water. As you walk in the dark through your home, you do not realize that a box was left on the floor, and you stub your toe on it. Ouch! As you stand there in your home in the dark, would you debate with yourself whether or not your toe hurts? Of course not! You would know that your toe hurts because you would feel it. That is precisely what happens when we mislabel a "thought" a "feeling"—we do not attempt to dispute it any more than we would our toe hurting.

People often make statements like, "I feel that if I get on this plane it will crash." There is no such emotional feeling. This statement actually is a thought—"I *think* that if I get on this plane it will crash." Since it is a thought, we can dispute it to determine if there is any evidence that it will crash. If so, I am not getting on it either! The problem with saying, "I feel that it will crash" is that a person will take the same approach to it as they would stubbing their toe—"Well, if I *feel* it, it must be true."

However, just because your feeling statement is one word does not mean that it is an actual emotional feeling. There are many "feeling words" used is psychology that are not actual feelings, but rather are *evaluations*. Examples of "feeling words" that actually are evaluations include these:

Examples of "Feeling Words" That Are _Not_ Feelings but Evaluations

Inadequate	Alienated	Humiliated	Unloved
Worthless	Confused	Deserving	Unwanted
Hopeless	Arrogant	Disillusioned	Insecure
Betrayed	Belittled	Empowered	Optimistic
Satisfied	Embarrassed	Desperate	Inferior
Vindicated	Ashamed	Forgotten	Superior
Justified	Approved	Helpless	Confident
Liberated	Used	Hopeless	Misunderstood
Rejected	Satisfied	Justified	Persecuted
Accepted	Phony	Trapped	Restricted

For example, people do not *feel* inadequate. They *think* of themselves as *being* inadequate. Their actual emotional feeling will be consistent with what they think about being inadequate. Therefore, if being inadequate is thought to be a terrible, horrible thing, a person might feel *anxious* as a result of this thought. If a person does not understand this, he likely will conclude, "If I *feel* inadequate, I must be inadequate." Since "inadequate" is an evaluation, we can examine it to determine if in fact a person's attributes or abilities are inadequate in relation to his goal.

As you probably are concluding, there are very few actual emotional feelings—happy, depressed, anxious, angry, and calm, and variations of them based on degree. For example, "sad" is a variation of "depressed"; "irritated" is a variation of "angry." To be more accurate in distinguishing between thoughts and feelings, ask yourself, "Is this how my body feels, or is it an evaluation of myself, someone else, or a situation?"

ABC Situations

A (What I was aware of)	**B** (What I thought about A)	**C** (How I felt / What I did)

ABC Situations

A	**B**	**C**
(What I was aware of)	(What I thought about A)	(How I felt / What I did)

Chapter 1 Summary

1. Unless there is something wrong with those parts of our body that are responsible for our emotional and behavioral control (such as anemia, hypothyroidism, or an adrenal problem), it is our thinking that causes our feelings and behaviors, not people, things, or situations.

2. There are three emotional options—positive, neutral, and negative.

3. Sometimes thoughts are so well-learned that we no longer need to think them consciously. These well-learned thoughts are called reflexive thoughts.

4. To uncover reflexive thoughts, ask yourself, "I'm acting as if I believe what about this situation or circumstance?"

5. It is important to get into the habit of saying, "I upset myself" and "I make myself happy," rather than "It upset me" or "She made me happy."

6. People unintentionally make themselves miserable because they think misery-producing thoughts and believe that those thoughts are correct. If they knew that they were mistaken, they would not waste their time thinking that way.

2

Thoughts and
Underlying Assumptions

In Rational Living Therapy, we make the distinction between thoughts and underlying assumptions.

Underlying assumptions are beliefs that usually are pervasive, which means that they affect more than one area of a person's life. The more basic the underlying assumption, the more areas of one's life it will affect.

For example, an underlying assumption, "My husband doesn't love me," would affect a woman's relationship with her husband. A more basic underlying assumption like, "People do not love me," would affect many relationships, not just with her husband.

We have underlying assumptions about ourselves and the world around us. For example, when people drive down a two-lane road, they do so with the assumption, "I am going to remain in my lane, and the people coming toward me are going to remain in their lane." If people did not assume this, they would either never drive on a two-lane road, or there would be chaos when they did.

Underlying assumptions primarily are non-conscious, which means that when a person asks you, "What do you think about that?" it is not likely that you will express an underlying assumption. What you likely are to state is a thought.

A **thought** is specific to a situation. It is an interpretation of a situation. It is how you "see" it, and often the reason for this interpretation is that an underlying assumption feeds it. For example, let's say that a wife has the following underlying assumption about her husband: "He doesn't love me!"

So it is Valentine's Day. On the way home from work, her husband buys her a dozen roses, gives them to her, and says, "Happy Valentine's Day, dear!" During their next marital therapy session, he tells the therapist, "You know, doc, I just can't figure her out. It was Valentine's Day, so I bought her some roses and gave them to her, and she told me to shove them." What might she have *thought* about the fact that he gave her the roses since she has an *underlying assumption* that he does not love her? Possible thoughts might include these:

- He must want something from me.

- He must be feeling guilty about something.

- He only bought me those flowers because he had to.

The day after Valentine's Day, he does something to help her in some way, and her thoughts again are something like this:

- He must want something from me.

- He must be feeling guilty about something.

- He only helped me because he had to.

Each time he does something "nice" for her, her immediate interpretation or thought would be something along this line of thinking.

Now let's say that she has an even more basic underlying assumption like, "I am not loveable. There is something wrong with me. So I am sure *people* would not like me if they really knew me." I am certain that you can see how many areas of her life that underlying assumption would affect. Not only is this why she assumes that her *husband* does not love her, but this is why she tends to avoid *other people* as well.

Let's look at how this appears if we diagram it.

Why We Focus on Underlying Assumptions in Rational Living Therapy

The previous example illustrates how sometimes it appears to us that we have more problems than we actually do. If we were to ask her how many problems she had, it is likely that she would say, "three." However, if the underlying assumption, "He doesn't love me" is incorrect, then she actually has one problem (the mistaken assumption) that gives her the impression that she has three.

Focusing on underlying assumptions *speeds the process of getting better.* By focusing on underlying assumptions, you can deal with several problems with one effort by working on a common thread that might be causing the problems.

Focusing on underlying assumptions also *helps to produce long-term results* because it is addressing and correcting the *cause* of the symptoms, not just the symptoms themselves. For example, a person walks past a group of people and they begin laughing. Most people in that situation assume that they are being laughed at. Good (but incomplete) therapy sounds like this:

> Therapist: "Was there anything about you that they mentioned that would give us any indication that they were laughing at you? Did you hear them mention your name, or something that you were wearing, or anything like that?"

> Client: "No, they just laughed."

> Therapist: "So it very well could be that it was a coincidence, that they were not laughing at you at all. There is no point in assuming that they were laughing at you, so you might as well just forget about it."

This looks like good therapy, but it is incomplete therapy. I would wonder why the person was still upset about it a week later to discuss it with me. I would take it a step further with the client.

Me: "Let's pretend for a moment that in fact they were laughing at you. As far as you are concerned, why would that be a bad thing?"

Client: "Because I hate being laughed at. I can't stand it."

Me: "While it is very common for people to think that they are being laughed at in these situations, is there any particular reason why you assumed that they were laughing at you? Do you think there is a reason for people to laugh at you?"

Client: "Well, I've always thought of myself as being too short and kind of unattractive."

If a therapist only focused on helping the client refuse to "jump to conclusions," it is likely that the client would continue to have problems in similar situations due to two problematic underlying assumptions: "To be laughed at is a terrible thing that I cannot stand"; and "I'm too short and unattractive."

To help the client to obtain long-term results, it would be important to help him correct these two problematic underlying assumptions. Without doing so, they would lie dormant, waiting to be activated by situations, like walking past a group of people that starts laughing.

To uncover underlying assumptions, ask yourself questions like these: For me, why would that be bad? If that were the case, what would that mean?

Chapter 2 Summary

1. Underlying assumptions are beliefs about ourselves and the world around us. The more basic the assumption is, the more pervasive it will be, thus affecting many different situations. For example, the assumption, "The world is basically a dangerous place" would lead a person to be uncomfortable entering many different situations.

2. Underlying assumptions are beliefs that primarily are non-conscious, meaning that if someone were to ask you, "What do you think about that?" you probably would not express an underlying assumption.

3. A thought is specific to a situation. It is an interpretation of a situation or how you "see" it. Often, the reason we think a thought about a situation is because that thought is fed by an underlying assumption.

4. Irrational underlying assumptions are very important to correct. If we only correct thoughts, we might feel better, but we will not get better.

5. To uncover underlying assumptions, utilize the suggestions in this chapter.

3

About Problems

Rational Living Therapists agree with Dr. Albert Ellis (1988), the originator of Rational Emotive Behavior Therapy, in that "problems" can be categorized into two types— practical and emotional.

Practical problems are situations and circumstances that make it difficult for us to achieve our goals. For example, if your car were to break down on the way to work, the broken car would be a practical problem because it would make it difficult to achieve your goal of getting to work, which would make it difficult to earn money that day, which would make it more difficult to pay your bills.

Emotional problems usually are reactions to practical problems. An emotional problem is the unwanted "upset" that you feel when upsetting yourself over practical problems. In this example, if you felt angrier than you wanted, your anger would be considered an emotional problem. (Please keep in mind, though, that the term *emotional problem* in this sense does not imply abnormality.)

If your car were to break down on the way to work, and you felt miserable in reaction to it, it is likely that you would view yourself as having one problem—your broken car. In fact, though, you would actually have two problems—your car (a practical problem) and your misery (an emotional problem).

Would you agree with me that most humans like to have the fewest number of problems possible at any given time? Certainly! Now, if you had your choice between having your car broken and feeling miserable, or having your car broken and feeling calm, which would you pick? Also consider this fact—*the car does not care how you emotionally react to it.* The car will be just as broken whether you are happy, calm, or miserable in reaction to it. Therefore, if there is no requirement that you make yourself miserable in reaction to the car being broken, why not learn how to react more calmly to it and cut your problems in half?

This is the essence of what is known as **stoicism**—that reality does not care how we emotionally react to it. Since reality does not care, we might as well learn how to react calmly to our personally undesirable situations. This realization itself has helped many people effectively deal with personally difficult and challenging situations and daily living disappointments. Therefore, an excellent rational self-statement that can be applied to any situation is this: "I'm going to have my problem whether I'm miserable or not, so I might as well give up the misery!"

Actually, there *is* a third type of problem—an **imagined problem**. Sometimes we think that we have a practical problem when in fact we do not. Or we might be mistaken in terms of to what extent our situation is problematic. We might think that our car is broken when in fact it is not. Or we might think that the cause of it not working properly is more serious and complicated than it actually is.

No matter the circumstances, you can find a rational way to feel better!

That is a pretty bold but accurate statement. Why? Because when people make themselves miserable or act in personally problematic ways, they make one of two correctable mistakes. Either they (1) are mistaken about the facts of their circumstances, so that they are upset about something that is not, or are reacting to something that is not, or (2) they are correct about their circumstances. Their situation really is the way that they think it is, but they think that being upset is either necessary, important, unavoidable, or that there would be something wrong with them if they were to react differently. Often, though, it is simply a matter of a person not knowing how to react any other way.

Being mistaken about the facts of one's circumstances is problematic because it leads a person to act in way that is not appropriate for his or her situation. For example, a person might notice a lump on his arm and think that the lump is a cancerous tumor when in fact it is a harmless cyst. If he thinks that it is cancer and that he is doomed to die as a result, he might decide (irrationally) to commit suicide rather than to face a slow, painful death. Hopefully, someone would help him to realize that the lump is only a harmless cyst.

What if the lump really is a cancerous tumor? Now what? This is when rational self-counseling is particularly helpful in that it helps people to more calmly accept their current reality. I used cancer as an example because most people react with complete horror at the thought that they or a loved one might have it. Why? Because most people believe that horror is necessary, important, or unavoidable. Most often, people simply do not know that a concerned, calm reaction is possible. Cognitive-behavioral therapy teaches people that responding to personally undesirable situations calmly is possible and helpful.

The rest of this book will show you how to correct both mistakes.

Chapter 3 Summary

1. There are two types of problems—practical and emotional. A practical problem is any situation that is an obstacle to achieving a goal. An emotional problem is usually in reaction to a practical problem. It is the "upset" you feel in reaction to the practical problem.

2. Most people want the fewest number of problems possible at any given moment.

3. If given the choice, most people would rather have their practical problems without being significantly upset about them.

4. As long as a person will have a practical problem whether or not he or she is upset about it, he or she might as well give up the misery (or at least learn how to).

5. Regardless of the situation, a person can feel and do better because either he or she will be upset about something that is not, or he or she will think that it is necessary or important to be upset about it. Sometimes people do not know how to feel any other way.

4

The Three Rational Questions

Now that you know that our thinking causes our feelings and behaviors, you know that it is important to take a good, critical look at the thoughts that lead to our unwanted feelings and behaviors. We want to keep our good, rational thoughts because these thoughts help us to feel good and to do well. Conversely, we want to get rid of irrational thoughts because they make us feel bad and perform not so well.

How do we distinguish between a **rational thought** and an **irrational thought**? One way is to apply the **Three Rational Questions** to our thoughts. These Three Rational Questions are an adaptation of Dr. Maxie C. Maultsby's Five Criteria for Rational Thinking.

The Three Rational Questions

1. Is my thinking based on fact?

2. Does my thinking help me to achieve my goals?

3. Does my thinking help me to feel the way that I want to feel?

Three "yes" answers means the thought is rational.

Dr. Maultsby was the first cognitive-behavioral theorist to develop criteria for rational behavior. His questions remain a major contribution to the field, as they have enabled people to objectively identify problem thoughts on their own. While I have narrowed the rational questions to three, Dr. Maultsby's other two questions, "Does my behavior help me to protect my life and health?" and "Does my behavior help me to avoid unwanted conflict with others?" are clinically useful. For a complete description of the Five Criteria for Rational Thinking, read *Coping Better, Any Time, Any Where* by Maxie C. Maultsby, Jr., MD.

Let us now look at each of the Three Rational Questions in detail.

Rational Question #1:
"Is my thinking based on fact?"

This question asks, "Is what I am thinking the way that things really are?" Most people assume that their thinking is based on fact, or they would not waste their time acting on it. Keep in mind, though, that when we talk to ourselves, there are three kinds of statements that we make—jokes, lies, and sincere statements.

We do not act on jokes—when we *know* that we are just kidding when we say something. We do not act on lies—when we *know* that what we are saying is not accurate. We only act on sincere statements. The problem is, though, that what we sincerely believe to be true is not necessarily based on fact. But the human brain does not care whether what we think is *accurate*. It only cares whether we *sincerely believe it*. When we sincerely believe something, the brain makes the body produce the logical emotional and behavioral response.

A good example of this is what people in Europe thought at one time. They would look out at the ocean, and it looked like it ended at the horizon. As a result, they concluded that the world was flat—that if a person were to sail beyond a certain point, he would drop off the Earth. Because they sincerely believed that the world was flat, they would not sail past a certain point and thought that anyone who would attempt to do so was not well.

However, one guy, Christopher Columbus, proved that what they had sincerely believed to be true was not based on fact. He sincerely believed that the world was round. Because of his belief, he was willing to sail beyond where others were willing to sail, until he discovered the New World.

Since most people naturally will be inclined to answer this question, "Yes, of course my thinking is based on fact," we had better have good techniques to help us to be more objective about our thinking.

The Camera Check of Perceptions

One technique to help determine whether our thinking is based on fact is the **Camera Check of Perceptions** (Maultsby, 1984). When utilizing this technique, ask yourself, "If I were to take a picture of the situation that I am describing to myself, or if I were to use a video camera to record it and played the tape back, would it show what I am saying about the situation?"

The human brain and a camera work alike in that both take in information and produce a visual image. However, a camera will take a picture *only* of what is in front of it. A camera does not add anything to the picture, take anything away, or distort the image unless there is something wrong with it or it (nowadays) is designed to do so. The human brain, on the other hand, does not have that limitation. The human brain can add to, subtract from, and otherwise distort the image based on what we already think or believe about what we are seeing.

As a practical example, someone might ask me, "Was Suzie at the party the other night?" If I know that Suzie *usually* goes to parties, I might think for a minute (trying to visualize the party), and say, "Yes, I believe she was." In fact, though, she was not there, but I inadvertently placed her in my mental picture of the party.

When our description of a situation is not what a camera would show, our description is not accurate. When our description is not accurate, our reaction will be inappropriate for the situation.

Let's say a person is feeling somewhat depressed because he is thinking, "My wife always yells at me. She is always yelling at me." Utilizing the camera check of perceptions, I would ask him this:

Me: "If we had video cameras positioned throughout your home recording the events of this past week, and now you and I were to sit down and watch this tape, would it show your wife *always* yelling at you? I hope not, because what does the word *always* mean?"

Client: "Well, I guess *always* means constantly, twenty-four hours a day, seven days a week."

Me: "That's right. Now, is that what a camera would show?"

Client: "No, it sure wouldn't."

Me: "Good. What would a camera actually show?"

Client: "It would show her yelling at me Tuesday, and, uh, Friday."

Me: "Obviously, there is a difference in how you feel when you say, "My wife always yells at me," as opposed to, "My wife *sometimes* yells at me, certainly more than I wish she would.""

The camera check of perceptions not only helps us to make certain that we have our facts straight, but it also helps us to make certain that we say what we mean and mean what we say to ourselves.

Sometimes people will say, "That is not what I *meant* when I said that my wife always yells at me, that she yells at me twenty-four hours a day, seven days a week." However, the human brain does not care what we mean—it cares what we say. For example, imagine that as you are driving down the road a police officer pulls you over and tells you that you were traveling ten miles per hour over the speed limit. He then tells you, "I am going to have to give you a ticket for $1,000." You say, "One-thousand dollars, that is outrageous. Why so much?" The officer responds by saying, "Oh, I am sorry. Did I say $1,000? I meant $10." To you, until he corrected himself, would it have mattered what he said or what he meant? Obviously, what would matter is what he *said*. The same is the case when we talk to ourselves.

To think accurately, our verbal thoughts must be accurate. Our verbal thoughts are composed of sentences, and each sentence is made up of words. Each word in a sentence is important as is described in the following example.

A Quick Psychology Lesson

The Russian research physiologist, Ivan Pavlov, studied the digestive system of dogs by conducting experiments. He had machines that collected gastric juices connected to their stomachs. As most people who have owned a dog know, dogs salivate at the sight of food. Dogs do not need to learn to salivate at the sight of food. They are born that way. However, Pavlov accidentally discovered that the dogs began salivating to other stimuli associated with their receiving food (i.e., the sound of him getting the food). Through experiments, he discovered what is known as **classical conditioning**, that is, that when something that *does* presently produce a response is paired enough times with something that *does not*, eventually the thing that did not produce the response does. Here's an example:

Food ------------------- **Salivation**
(Food triggers salivation.)

Bell + Food ------------------- **Salivation**
(Bell is sounded right before presenting food.)

Bell ------------------- **Salivation**
(After a while, the bell alone triggers salivation.)

The continual pairing of the bell and the food led the dogs to salivate *to the bell alone* after a while.

As Maxie C. Maultsby, Jr., MD, has noted, "Words are to humans as the bell was to Pavlov's dog." Words are conditioned to having meaning, and we begin being conditioned to the meaning of words very early in life. The words that we use when we think produce conditioned emotions in us. Therefore, it is very important that we think and speak to ourselves accurately—that we say what we mean and mean what we say.

To demonstrate that words are conditioned, take my mother as an example. My mother was born and raised in Italy and moved to the United States when she was twenty-one years old. Although she has been in the United States for many years, she continues to report that Italian swear words seem worse than American swear words to her, although they essentially have the same meaning. She was conditioned as a child to believe that the Italian swear words were very bad and should never be spoken. She did not receive quite the same threatening message about the American words; thus, her reaction to them is less negative, though they are equivalent in meaning to their Italian counterparts.

So when it comes to our emotions, the words that we say to ourselves are *all important*.

Obviously the camera check of perceptions can be helpful in assisting us to say what we mean and mean what we say. As an example, one of my first clients years ago said to me, "My husband is a dirty rat!" She then went on to describe the things that he did that she did not like. After we talked for a while, the following occurred:

Me: "Okay. Do you remember last week we talked about the rational questions?"

Client: "Yes, I do."

Me: "Good. As you might recall, the first rational question is, "Is my thinking based on fact?" Now, if I were to take a picture of your husband and take it downstairs to the secretary, what would she see in the picture?"

Client: "She'd see my husband."

Me: "Okay. Let's pretend she doesn't know your husband. What would she see in the picture?"

Client: "She'd see a man."

Me: "Right. And if I were to show the picture to the rest of the therapists in the office, what would they see in the picture?"

Client: "A man."

Me: "Right. Now what did you call your husband a few minutes ago?"

Client: "Oh yah. I called him a dirty rat, but that's just an expression!"

Me: "Not really. You see, I know you are not psychotic and do not actually see him as being a dirty, furry little rodent. But when you call him a dirty rat, you feel just as bad as you would if in fact he were a dirty rat. Tell me, what do you think of dirty rats?"

Client: "They are disgusting!"

Me: "So you see you probably have thought they were disgusting for a long time, so that the mere mention of the words *dirty rat* conjures up disgusting feelings, right?"

Client: "Exactly!"

Me: "So as if your upset over what he does to you weren't bad enough, you unintentionally make matters worse for yourself simply by calling him, to yourself, a dirty rat."

Client: "I see!"

Me: "Now tell me ... Is your husband 'a man who does things you do not like' or a dirty rat?"

Client: "He is a man who does things I don't like."

Me: "And which way of thinking makes you feel better?"

Client: "That he is a man who does things I don't like."

Me: "Right. Now that doesn't take away from what he actually does to you, but having a more accurate description of him makes you feel better. It also helps you to act differently toward him, which might encourage him to treat you differently."

Do your best, therefore, to say what you mean and mean what you say to yourself.

The Common Mental Mistakes

Another fact-finding approach is to determine if you are making one of the common mental mistakes people make. These mental mistakes are described in detail in the next chapter. After reading the next chapter, you will learn how committing these mistakes makes your thinking inconsistent with fact.

Therefore, I strongly encourage you to act like a detective with your thinking. You do not need to examine all of your thinking, just thinking related to areas or things you are concerned about. In those situations, refuse to take for granted that your thinking is accurate. To do so, ask yourself these questions:

- Do I have proof that my thinking is correct?

- Do I have proof that my thinking is incorrect?

- What are other possible explanations?

- What is the evidence?

Sometimes you will not know whether your thought is based on fact without some investigation. You might need to turn to someone who is knowledgeable about the circumstances you are concerned with. For example, a person develops a lump on his arm. His immediate thought is, "This must be cancer." At this point, does he know that he has cancer? No. On the other hand, does he know that it is not cancer? No. It is important for him to acknowledge that he does not know either way and to get the lump examined by a physician.

More Help with Rational Question #1

Have you ever hoped that something that you thought was incorrect? Sometimes we hope and pray that our thinking is incorrect. On the next chart, write down any thoughts that have been troubling you that you hope are incorrect. At this point, I am not encouraging you *actually to believe* that they are incorrect, but only to acknowledge that there could be advantages to being wrong.

Thoughts That I Hope Are Incorrect!

Distressing Thought	Why do I hope it is incorrect?
Example: *"No girl would ever want to go out with me."*	*If I'm wrong, I'll end up with a girlfriend!*
Example: *"I'm a nothing and a nobody."*	*If I'm wrong, I'll feel much better!*

Rational Question #2: "Does my thinking help me to achieve my goals?"

Any thought that does not help you to achieve your goals or is contrary to them would not pass the second rational question. The belief, "I know that I am not going to pass the test tomorrow, so I am not going to study," certainly would not help a person achieve his or her goal of passing the test. Therefore, this thought would not pass the second rational question.

Sometimes a thought *indirectly* interferes with achieving a goal. Imagine that while a college student is studying one evening for an exam to be taken the following day, her boyfriend telephones and tells her that he cannot keep his date with her that they had planned for the weekend.

"Darn him, he should not treat me this way," she exclaims. Because of her belief and resultant upset, she decides to quit studying for the exam. Her performance on the test the next day is not as good as she had hoped that it would be. While her belief about her boyfriend's behavior had nothing to do with the test, the upsetting thoughts did, nevertheless, affect her performance on it.

Rational Question #3: "Does my thinking help me to feel the way that I want to feel?"

If you are feeling unwanted emotional feelings, the thinking that causes those feelings would not pass the third rational question. Keep in mind, however, that this rational question encourages us to feel the way that we want to feel, *without* alcohol, drugs, or by engaging in otherwise dangerous behavior.

So, What *Is* Rational?

For a thought to be considered *rational*, it must pass all three rational questions (for a total of three "yes" answers). If your thought is rational, you want to hold onto it because it serves you well. If you answer "no" to one or more of the three questions, your thought is an *irrational thought*. If your thought is irrational, you will want to learn how to refuse to think it any longer, to develop a new, rational thought to replace it, and to practice this new thought until it feels comfortable to you and becomes your way of thinking. You will learn how to do this in the following chapters.

A Special Note

Ideally, any self-help method would be most beneficial if it could be implemented *during* a personally difficult event. Rational self-counseling can be implemented in such a manner with practice. Your diligent practice of the techniques and concepts presented in this book will do the following for you: (1) enable you to analyze your upset over a situation rationally after it has happened, thus helping you to determine effective measures for avoiding future upset over similar situations; (2) enable you to counsel yourself rationally during personally difficult situations to minimize upset; and (3) enable you to prevent upset by rationally predicting problems and appropriately preparing yourself.

No matter how well you know the techniques described in this book, you will encounter new situations in your life that you have not rationally dealt with, and, consequently, you will upset yourself. However, you are learning skills to avoid repeatedly upsetting yourself over the same and similar issues.

As you continue to break down your unwanted emotions and behaviors into the ABCs, begin applying the rational questions to the thoughts related to those situations.

Now that you know the Three Rational Questions, the next chapter discusses the common mistakes that people make in their thinking. Remember, understanding the common mental mistakes will help you to more accurately determine whether your thinking is based on fact.

Aldo R. Pucci, PsyD

Positive, Optimistic, and Rational Thinking

In Rational Living Therapy, we make a distinction among positive, optimistic, and rational thinking.

- A positive thought is believing that something is good or seeing an advantage to it. For example, I love squid, so when my wife makes it, I see that as a very positive thing.
- An optimistic thought is a wishful belief that something will turn out as a person hopes. For example, I might think optimistically that my wife will make squid sometime this year.
- A rational thought is based on fact, helps a person to achieve a goal, and helps a person feel the way he or she wants to feel.

The only thought that requires fact is the rational thought. For example, I might think that it is a positive thing that the world is flat, but it is not flat (whether or not it would be a positive thing if it were flat is a matter of opinion). An optimistic thought is something that someone thinks to make himself or herself feel better or that keeps him or her motivated, but it does not require fact. For example, I might be optimistic in thinking that if I jump out of an airplane without a parachute, I will land on my feet. That thought might make me feel good on the way down, but not so good when I land!

Optimistic thinking sometimes is helpful and not particularly problematic. For example, before a championship fight boxers often are asked in interviews about the possibility of losing. The boxers usually respond by saying, "I am not even thinking about losing. I am going to win." They can afford to have this approach because losing will not be the end of them. The consequence of losing will not be so significant that it is in their best interest to consider it.

Rational Living Therapy very much emphasizes the importance of rational thinking. Rational thinking will help you to be in the best position to achieve your goals because it encourages you to deal with reality, not with a fantasy.

Chapter 4 Summary

1. In Rational Living Therapy, we define a rational thought as one that is based on fact, that helps a person to achieve his or her goals, and that helps a person to feel the way that he or she wants to feel (without alcohol or other drugs).

2. What is rational for one person is not necessarily rational for the next.

3. Words are to humans as the bell was to Pavlov's dog. It is just as important that we say what we mean when we talk to ourselves as it is when we talk to others.

4. The Camera Check of Perceptions is an outstanding technique for helping people to say what they mean and mean what they say when they talk to themselves.

5. In Rational Living Therapy, we do not promote positive or optimistic thinking. We promote and recommend rational thinking.

5

The Common Mental Mistakes

The human brain is a fascinating organ capable of much more than we may ever know. The brain plays a very active role in controlling the organs of the body. It monitors and controls nearly all of the body's activities. Your brain gets concerned when your temperature is too high or too low. It gets concerned when you have not had enough sleep or enough to eat. And your brain attempts to regulate your temperature, appetite, and sleep accordingly.

However, the human brain *is very passive* when it comes to your emotional feelings. Your brain does not care what you think. It does not care if you think a rational thought or an irrational thought. Furthermore, the brain does not have a built-in mechanism that makes us think only good, rational thoughts. The brain does not have a built-in nonsense filter that filters out mistaken, irrational thoughts. I wish that it did! However, your healthy brain will make your body feel the way it should feel based on how you think.

We do not sincerely hold a belief that we know to be incorrect. This is why we usually do not stop to evaluate the accuracy of our thoughts. *So your doubts, worries, fears, shoulds, musts, and have-tos have gotten a free ride for a long time! They have, for the most part, gone unchallenged ... completely free to make you miserable! Now it is time to refuse to give these potentially problematic thoughts a free ride and, instead, to learn how to dispute them rationally.*

One goal of learning rational self-counseling is to (in effect) build a nonsense filter in your brain. With this imaginary filter, you will be able to detect problematic thoughts and, therefore, to avoid thinking them. You will build the nonsense filter by learning the common mental mistakes listed next.

You do not have to memorize the name of each mistake. The important thing is to understand the concept of the mistakes and to have them understood well enough to be able to recognize if you are thinking in those terms. It is likely that you will begin noticing others making these mistakes as well.

The Common Mental Mistakes

A variation of the first ten mental mistakes was first described by Dr. Aaron Beck (1976) and later by Dr. David Burns (1980). I have expanded this list to twenty-six.

(1) All-or-None Thinking

People unintentionally cheat themselves out of a great deal of happiness when they think in all-or-none terms. All-or-none thinking is the mistake of viewing things in black-or-white, everything-or-nothing terms. It is viewing things as only one way or another. When a light is connected to a conventional on/off switch, the light is either on or off. Most things in life have a middle ground, like a light connected to a dimmer switch. There are degrees to which the light is on.

Few aspects of our lives have no middle ground. Examples of all-or-none thinking include phrases like this:

"A person is either *ugly* or *good looking*."

"A person is either *dumb* or *intelligent*."

"A person is either *fat* or *skinny*."

"Either you *trust* someone or you *don't*."

So a person might look at herself and say, "I am not pretty, so I must be ugly," "I am not intelligent, so I must be dumb," "I am not skinny, so I must be fat," "My boyfriend crossed me one time, so he is completely untrustworthy." Actually, though, there are degrees of attractiveness, intelligence, and size.

Degrees of Attractiveness

Totally -- Totally
Ugly   Beautiful

Degrees of Intelligence

Totally -- Totally
Dumb   Intelligent

Size

Totally -- Totally
Skinny   Fat

Degrees of Trust

Totally---Totally
Distrust   Trust

All-or-none thinking often interferes with setting goals and achieving them. People often say, "If I cannot earn $100,000 a year, I am not working at all" (as if it would not be worth the effort of working to earn $50,000 or $25,000) or "If I cannot get an A on this test, I am not going to study" (as if it would not be worth the effort of studying just to pass, like passing would not be better than failing) or "If I do not find a woman that will treat me exactly the way I want to be treated, I am not getting married" (as if having a wife who treats him mostly as he would like to be treated is not beneficial nor better than having no wife at all).

I sometimes hear all-or-none thinking from people trying to lose weight. A very common scenario goes something like this:

> "I started my diet plan on a Monday. My plan called for me to avoid all sweets, including cookies and candies. I did really well until Thursday. That's when my husband came home with a dozen doughnuts and stuck them on the counter. I looked at those doughnuts and decided that eating one wouldn't hurt me. So I ate one. But then I felt really upset because up to that point I was on my diet, but eating that doughnut meant that I was off the diet. I blew my diet. So I just went ahead and ate the rest of the doughnuts."

Rather than putting the one doughnut into perspective and realizing that there are degrees to which a person can stray from a diet plan, people often take this type of all-or-none approach.

Perfectionism is an excellent example of all-or-none thinking. "If I cannot do it perfectly well, I am not doing it at all" or "If every blade of grass in my yard is not the same length, my yard is unacceptable."

Words and expressions that imply all-or-none thinking include these:

- "That was a waste of time."
- "It's completely ruined."
- "I blew it."
- "It was destroyed."
- "She is perfect."
- "They completely messed up."

Avoid making the all-or-none mistake by considering the possibility of a middle ground.

(2) Overgeneralization

To overgeneralize is to exaggerate unintentionally. The two words most often used when people overgeneralize are *always* and *never*.

These two words are not a problem when they *accurately* describe a situation. For example, if I were to say that as long as my wife and I have been married she has never served me raw fish for dinner, that would be an accurate statement, because she has not. However, if she had served it one time in twenty years, the word *never* would not be accurate.

Some people might say, "What is the difference between saying 'one time in twenty years' and 'never'?" You might as well say 'never.'" The difference is that the word *never* can imply inability. For example:

Client: "I never do my job right at work."

Me: "Never?"

Client: "I work on an assembly line, and the other day I put the panel on correctly just once out of a hundred times!"

Me: "It sure would have been nice if you had done it correctly more often."

Client: "Yah."

Me: "Well, it sounds like you are exaggerating to yourself, though. You said that you *never* do your job right at work. The fact is that you did do it correctly once."

Client: "What's the difference between one time out of one hundred and zero times out of one hundred? I might as well say *never!*"

Me: "The difference is in what saying *never* implies to you. Your perception that you never do the job properly implies to you that you do not have the potential to do it correctly. If you do not think you have the potential to do well, you will stop trying. However, what does that one time that you got it right prove to you?"

Client: "That I can do it."

Me: "That's right! Now what's important is to see how many more times out of one hundred you can do it properly."

Overgeneralization is the *inaccurate* use of the words *always* and *never*. An example of the inaccurate use of the word *always* is this:

Client: "My boss always yells at me, and I'm darn mad about it."

Me: "Are you sure that he *always* yells at you?"

Client: "Yep. He always yells at me."

Me: "Okay. Well, how often and how long would he yell at you if in fact he *always* yelled at you?"

Client: "Well ... I guess he'd yell at me twenty-four hours a day, seven days a week."

Me: "That's right! You and your brain have known since you were very young that *always* means constantly, without stopping. *Always* does *not* mean sometimes or occasionally or every now and then. Let me ask you. How many days a week does your boss yell at you?"

Client: "Four to five days a week."

Me: "Okay. And how many times a day does he yell at you?"

Client: "Usually just once."

Me: "Is this an all-day yelling?"

Client: "No. He yells at me for about two minutes each time. I guess I was exaggerating to myself, huh?"

Me: "Yes. There is a big difference between twenty-four hours a day, seven days a week and two *minutes* a day, five days a week … Is there a difference in how you would feel if you thought, "My boss yells at me much more than I wish he would" and "He always yells at me?"

Client: "There sure is!"

Therefore, it is very important to make certain that you use the words *always* and *never* accurately. If you do not, you will have an exaggerated response to what is going on.

Another way people overgeneralize is when they take a small sample of something and assume that it reflects everything with similar characteristics. Overgeneralization causes prejudice. "All African Americans are bad because *one* beat me up." "All Catholics are boozers because *the ones that I know* are." "All whites hate anyone who is not like them because *the ones that I know* are like that." These are obvious overgeneralizations that cause us to develop an opinion of someone or something before we have gotten to know them.

Avoid overgeneralizing by taking people and things on a case-by-case basis.

(3) Mental Filter

Mental filter is a mental mistake that affects everyone on a daily basis to some degree. Mental filter is the mistake of only seeing or acknowledging information that is consistent or "fits" with what you already think or believe. It is like having blinders on. If information that is contrary to one's belief is seen or acknowledged, it will need to be modified to make it fit.

Have you ever wanted to go to Paris in the Spring? I have never been to Paris, but I understand that it is lovely, especially in the Spring. Ah, Paris in the Spring. How wonderful it would be to experience that.

Is that what is written in the triangle, "Paris in the Spring"? That is what you likely saw if you are familiar with the expression. However, what it actually says is "Paris in the *the* Spring." If you failed to "see" the extra *the*, it is because this familiar expression created a mindset that then led you to overlook information that is contrary to it.

If a person had a lifelong tendency of thinking of herself as being stupid, she would likely either not be aware of, or forget, evidence that shows that she is intelligent (i.e., she files her own taxes, she graduated from college), or she would modify this information to make it consistent with her belief (i.e., "A moron could do their taxes" and "My professors were easy on me ... I went to an easy school").

Mental filter plays a role when we fall "in love." When two people meet and fall in love, they develop a mental filter (or blinders) for each other. The female in the heterosexual relationship might think, "He's outstanding, wonderful, and fantastic. There is no one like him. He can do no wrong." So a friend tells her, "Don't date that guy, he is an axe murderer!" She responds by saying, "Oh no, not my Johnnie. There is no way that he could be an axe murderer."

After being together for a while, they move from a romantic love to a more "mature" love. The partners might love each other even more than they had previously, but the excitement has toned down a little (thankfully, or we would never get anything done!). It is during this time that the partners are likely to say, "You've changed. You are not like how you used to be."

While it is true that people do change their behavior over time, what also occurs is that the blinders come down, and now they see *all* of each other, not what just fit that very positive notion of each other. By the time they seek marital therapy, she might have another set of blinders that supports the idea, "He can do nothing right!"

Sometimes mental filter is intentional in that a person refuses to acknowledge information contrary to his or her beliefs. Often, though, it is unintentional. Have you ever looked "too hard" for something? You look through a drawer trying to find something, but you do not see it despite the fact that it is right in front of you. That is an example of unintentional mental filter.

The following is a great (but unfortunate) example of unintentional mental filter. It is something that actually happened to me.

When my wife and I lived in a rural area of southwest Virginia, our best friends were Paul and Linda. They had moved to the area from Florida. Linda was originally from the area. They moved back to Virginia to retire and to build a house on her parents' farmland. They built their house approximately fifty yards from her parents' house.

While living in Virginia, we were blessed with our first child, Aldo, Jr. He was born on a Monday after my wife endured a thirty-six-hour labor. My parents came from the Pittsburgh area to visit their grandchild the following Monday. As we were visiting, my wife decided to take Aldo to the bedroom to nurse him. The phone rang shortly afterward. It was Paul. He sounded upset. I asked him, "Paul, what is wrong?" Paul said, "Linda's dead." I asked what had happened. He went on to describe that Linda was driving a tractor, and it had tipped over, landed on her, and killed her. I asked Paul if I could do anything to help him. He said that he had everything under control, so we ended the conversation.

I had the unfortunate task of telling my wife that her best friend had just died. After I told her, my father suggested that he and I go to Paul's home to see what we could do for him. I agreed. Before we left, I telephoned the church we all had attended to tell the priest that Linda had died.

On our way to Paul's house, my father and I commented on how life stinks. We figured Paul would move back to Florida. When we arrived at his home, we saw him standing on his in-laws' porch waving his arms. So we walked down to meet him, gave him a hug, and he invited us into his in-laws' house.

My father, Paul, and I stood in the kitchen talking when, much to my and my father's surprise, *Linda came walking into the room!* It was like a scene from the *Twilight Zone* television show. Our mouths literally dropped, and I could not speak.

Finally, I said, "Linda, I thought that you died!" She said, "I did not die, my *dad* died." What Paul had said on the telephone was "Linda's *dad*," but I thought that he had said, "Linda's *dead!*" So although Paul was telling me how Linda's father was on the tractor and how he was killed, I placed her on the tractor, and that is all I heard.

While we certainly were sad for Linda that her father had died, we were happy that she was still with us.

So I then *quite hesitantly* called my wife to tell her that her best friend had not died. She was ready to kill me! As we were talking on the phone, I looked out the window, and, much to my dismay, I saw a bus full of people from the church coming up the driveway all thinking that Linda had died. They continue to tease me to this day about the day that Linda died!

I wish that I had asked one very simple question, "Paul, what was Linda doing on a tractor?" I could have avoided making this mistake had I done so, as I had never known her to ride a tractor.

What Can You Do About Mental Filter?

Sometimes people tell me, "There is nothing good in my life. My life totally stinks!" This belief is usually the result of having a very narrow view of their life experience. When we ask them to look at all aspects of their life intentionally, they often come up with the following:

My Life	
<u>Bad</u>	<u>Good</u>
Job Stinks, Wife Nags Leaky Roof, Bills, Boss Yelling at Me, I'm Short & Fat, I'm Going Bald ...	Good Health, Enjoy the Children, Close Friends, Wife Is Very Attractive, Eat Well, Sleep Well, Fishing Every Saturday, Have a Nice House, Live in a Nice Neighborhood, Have a Good Education, Can Feed Myself, Have No Difficulty Breathing, Walk Well, Have All the Strength I Need, My Children Love Me, Nice Car, Have the Potential to Do a Lot of Things, Enjoy Going to Church ...

Naturally, if *all* a person looks at is the bad, he will not see the good. This is not to suggest that it does not make sense to acknowledge the bad to see what can be done to change it. It is best to look at all aspects of a situation when assessing it.

Part of the problem with the mental mistake of mental filter is that we naturally pay attention to information that supports the way we think and discard information that does not. When is the last time you woke up in the morning saying to yourself, "I think I will try to prove myself wrong today?" If you are like most people, you probably have never said that to yourself!

Amateur Attorney Technique

A key to overcoming mental filter is to intentionally, forcefully look for evidence that supports a different way of thinking.

What I call the Amateur Attorney Technique is a simple way to look for new evidence. First, develop a new belief, one that you do not necessarily completely believe yet one that does pass the rational questions. Then pretend that you are an attorney and have to defend this belief in court. It is your job to convince the jury that this new belief is accurate. You have one week to prepare your case.

For the next week, write down everything you can think of that will support your case. You need not believe that the information actually does support the new idea (attorneys sometimes say things they do not believe in defense of their clients). However, refuse to fabricate or "make up" evidence. Provide actual examples.

For example, if I am working with a client who thinks of herself as being *dumb* (she actually uses the word), but I have reason to believe that she is at least of average intelligence, I would ask her to consider adopting the new belief, "I am at least of average intelligence." I then would ask the client to pretend that she is an attorney and that she has been hired to defend this belief in court. It is her job to convince the jury that she is at least of average intelligence. She has until the next session to prepare her case. For the next week, she is to write down everything she can think of that will support her case.

I *Can Be Incorrect* in My Thinking!

Adopting this attitude also is very helpful in overcoming mental filter. Not only *can* I be wrong in my thinking, sometimes I *hope* that I am wrong. What thoughts do you think about yourself, others, and the world around you that you hope are incorrect? Hoping that you might be incorrect, and realizing that it is possible, will help you to be motivated to look for evidence to prove yourself wrong.

(4) Discounting the Positive

The mental mistake of "discounting the positive" works hand in hand with mental filter. People discount the positive to support their negative belief. (Note, however, that people also often discount negative information to support positive beliefs.)

For example, as a person depresses himself, he tends to discount the positive in his life. If this continues, he might get to the point where he believes that *nothing* in life is good. Another example is a person believing that receiving an A grade on a test means that the teacher felt sorry for him, that the test was easy, or that anyone could have obtained a similar result. This assumption helps him to continue to believe that he is stupid ("stupid people do not make As on tests").

Rational thinking is based on fact. Sometimes facts are personally positive; sometimes they are personally negative. Acknowledging *all* of the facts is important, not just those that support our beliefs.

(5) Jumping to Conclusions

Jumping to conclusions is developing an opinion about something very quickly without gathering facts. The fact that we tend to do this very quickly is the reason we call it *jumping* to conclusions. Sometimes people jump to conclusions because it is easier than gathering facts. That is why one of my favorite comedians, Stephen Wright, says, "A conclusion is what you come to when you get tired of thinking about something." There is a lot of truth in that statement. We are working at developing endurance for thinking—a willingness to gather facts.

The two most common ways people jump to conclusions are **mind reading** and **fortune telling**.

Mind Reading

Mind reading is just what the name implies—acting as if we can read other people's minds. However, mind reading is *not,* "He *might* be thinking this ..." or "She *might* be thinking that ..." Mind reading is "I *know* that he is thinking ..." and then *acting* on that so-called knowledge.

The first problem with mind reading is that we cannot read people's minds! While there are machines that show us that a person *is* thinking (an electroencephalograph), no instrument can tell us *what* a person is thinking (although one probably will be invented some day). Not even the psychics can tell us what a person is thinking. Frankly, I say, "Thank God!" Could you imagine the trouble we would have if we could read minds? We would have far more trouble than we already do.

Some people justify mind reading by stating, "When you have known someone as long as I have, you know how they think." However, no matter how well you know someone, you cannot know what they think. The more familiar we are with a person, the better we are at predicting how they will act, react, and the statements they are likely to make in a given situation. However, familiarity does not, in any way, give us the ability to see inside the person's brain to read his or her mind.

Acting on information "gathered" by mind reading can lead to trouble. For example, imagine that Bill comes home two hours late from work. As he enters his home, he notices that his wife, Sue, has a certain look on her face. He says to himself, "She looks like she is mad, and I just know that she is mad at me because I am late. I hate it when she is mad at me for being late, because she knows it is the nature of my job. Because she is mad at me, I will be mad right back!"

So Bill proceeds to yell at her. After he is finished yelling, Sue says, "Bill, I was not mad at you before you began yelling at me, but now I am! What you saw on my face was pain because my back has been hurting all day." As a result, Bill's mind reading error led to a completely avoidable argument. How could he have avoided this argument? Bill could have seen his wife's facial expression and said to himself, "Sue looks like she is mad, but I do not know for sure, so I will ask her." This approach would have given Sue an opportunity to explain her facial expression and, therefore, to avoid an argument.

We certainly do observe others from time to time and make certain assumptions of what they are thinking based on how they are acting. It is important, though, to view these assumptions as *guesses* as opposed to thoughts that necessarily are based on fact.

For those that are particularly hardheaded about mind reading, believing that they have the ability, I pose the following supposition. Suppose that I asked you to give me $100. I tell you that if you can guess which number that I am thinking that is between one and four, I will give you $200. If you do not correctly guess which number, I can keep your $100. Without my writing the number down, or telling someone else, would you take the chance that

(1) you could correctly guess which number I selected, and

(2) that I would be honest enough to tell you if in fact you had guessed it correctly?

If I told you that your guess was incorrect, there would be no way you could prove that you actually were correct or that I was lying. Would you be willing to take this chance of losing $100? I will bet not!

The second problem with attempting to read minds is that it is pointless. What other people *think* is irrelevant. It simply does not affect us one way or another. What does matter to us is how they *act, how they treat us*. A person could think as much as he wanted that he wants to shoot me. As long as he does not act on that thought, I have no problem. If he were to act on that thought, his act would probably would ruin my day! Conversely, a person could think that she would love to give me a part of her financial fortune, but if she does not act on that thought, I will not benefit from it.

If you are being treated in a way that is unpleasant to you, rather than trying to figure out what someone must be thinking, discuss the matter with them and see if they are willing to treat you differently.

Fortune Telling

Fortune telling is jumping to conclusions by predicting the future. As with mind reading, fortune telling is *not* thinking, "This *might* happen ..." Fortune telling is, "I *know* it is going to happen," then acting on that so-called knowledge.

Examples of fortune telling include, "I just know that I am going to flunk the test, so I am not going to study. If I ask my boss for a raise, he will tell me no. My parents are really going to be upset over this one."

Granted, the more familiar we are with a situation or person, the better we will tend to be at *predicting* future events. However, no future event is certain to occur (except death). There is nothing irrational about making educated predictions for personal guidance. For example, a person might extensively research market demand and determine that marketing a product would very likely produce a large profit. A rational decision to invest money into the project would take into account the significance of his research findings.

People often shape the future based on their *predictions* of it. The belief, "I just know that I am going to flunk the test, so I am not going to study," could lead to a **self-fulfilling prophecy**. A self-fulfilling prophecy is the result of people unintentionally creating the predicted outcome because they predicted it. Believing that he knows that he will flunk a test would lead a person to not study for it. After taking the test and flunking it, he likely would say, "You see, I *told* you that I would not pass the test!" It is clear to see, however, that his not studying *might have been what led to his flunking the test!* Had he made a guess that he would not pass, but decided to study nevertheless, the outcome *might* have been different.

Here is an example of a very common scenario involving fortune telling.

Client: "I got a low grade on my math test the other day. I sure wish I could bring up my grade."

Me: "How about asking your teacher if you could do some extra credit?"

Client: "There is no point in asking her."

Me: "Why not?"

Client: "Because I know that she will tell me no."

Me: "How do you know that?"

Client: "I just know it."

Me: (Getting out a piece of paper and marker, I draw a crystal ball with the word *no* in it.) "You see, what you are telling me is that you have a crystal ball that can tell you exactly what will happen in the future. Now I'm sure that you'll agree that you do not have a crystal ball showing us that she will say no, and I do not have a crystal ball showing us that she will say yes. Would you agree with that?"

Client: "Yes."

Me: "Okay. Now, what makes it seem to you that she is likely to say no?"

Client: "Because she has said no to everyone I know who has asked her, and that's about everyone in the class."

Me: "Okay, so if we had to bet a lot of money whether or not she will tell you no when you ask her, given what you have told me, we probably would bet that she would tell you no, right?"

Client: "Yah."

Me: "However, since we do not have a crystal ball to tell us for certain that she will say no, no matter how many times she has denied other students in the past, let me ask you. What do you have to lose by asking her, anyway?"

Client: "She might yell at me."

Me: "Okay. Well, I do not know of anyone who enjoys being yelled at. How important is it to you that you bring your grade up?"

Client: "Very important."

Me: "Okay. Then let me ask you this. Have you ever been yelled at before?"

Client: "Sure."

Me: "Did you survive it?"

Client: "I didn't like it!"

Me: "I'm sure, but did you survive it?"

Client: "I guess so. I'm still alive."

Me: "That's right. Now might it be worth taking the chance that you might get yelled at to see if your teacher would be willing to give you an extra credit assignment?"

Client: "I guess so, yah."

To avoid jumping to conclusions, take your time to formulate your opinions and consider all the facts.

(6) Magnification

Magnification is the mental mistake of exaggerating the importance of a shortcoming or minimizing the importance of a good quality. For example, teenagers often take this approach when it comes to acne. "This is a *world-record-sized* pimple. Everyone at the party will look at it, so I'm not going to go" is the approach some take to their acne problem. Or a law student might minimize the importance of her intelligence and knowledge and insist that she will not be an effective attorney because she lisps. Although her law professors tell her that she has a great deal of potential, she believes that her potential "doesn't count" and, instead, focuses on the lisping.

To avoid magnifying, ask yourself:

- **Is this shortcoming really likely to interfere with achieving my goals?**
- **Does my shortcoming really affect my life the way I think it does?**
- **Might my strengths affect my situation more than my shortcomings?**

Magnification sometimes is related to the "too much/too little" problem that we will discuss later in this chapter.

(7) Emotional Reasoning

Emotional reasoning is thinking that is affected by emotions—how you are feeling at the time. For example, when a person is depressed about one thing, he or she is likely to think depressing thoughts about other things as well—things that he or she ordinarily would not think pessimistically about. This mindset can become quite pessimistic, and the more pessimistic it becomes, the more depressed the person becomes (a vicious circle).

Sometimes our physical feelings influence our reasoning as well. We certainly know how fatigue can lead us to be less tolerant of situations. We often do not deal as well with problems when we are ill, sometimes viewing them as more significant or difficult than they actually are.

To avoid emotional reasoning, first identify it as such. Because you have been paying attention to your thinking, you are becoming increasingly aware of your typical ways of thinking when you are calm (which is usually more representative of how you actually think). When your thoughts are contrary to your typical ways of thinking, determine your mood and ask yourself if your thinking is typical for you, or if it is a reflection of your mood. Ask yourself: *Do I think this way about (current situation) when I am not already upset about something else?*

If not, refuse to take seriously the thought produced through emotional reasoning.

(8) Irrational Labeling

Labeling is assigning a name to something. Labeling is necessary for communication—we could not communicate without it.

However, labeling can be a problem when a label is inaccurate and/or when it limits our view of ourselves or others. Labels can encourage the creation of a self-fulfilling prophecy. People can unintentionally create the very condition or situation that they predict because of how they label themselves or others. If a person labels himself (or accepts the label from others) "delinquent," he is likely to act out the part.

What else would a person expect from a delinquent but delinquent behavior?

Inaccurate Labels

Inaccurate labeling is assigning a word or phrase to something that does not accurately describe it. Inaccurate labels take many forms, as the following example demonstrates:

Client: "I am just a stupid idiot."

Me: "Why do you say that?"

Client: "Because I make a lot of mistakes."

Me: "Well, the first problem is that you are labeling yourself a stupid idiot. Now, if I were to take a picture of you and took it home to my wife, she would not say, "What a nice picture of a stupid idiot!"

Client: (Laughing) "No, I guess not."

Me: "That's right. She would see a person in the picture. Now I'm sure that you are aware that some dictionaries have pictures next to some words to illustrate the meaning of the word, right?"

Client: "Yes."

Me: "If we were to look up the word *idiot* in the dictionary, would there be a picture next to the word?"

Client: "No, I don't think there would be."

Me: "That's right, and the reason is that there is no objectively identifiable thing as an idiot! There are *people* that might *act in an idiotic way,* but that describes just about everyone from time to time, doesn't it?"

Client: "It sure does! But I act idiotically more often than others."

Me: "Well, we'll need to take a look at that to see if that's the case. Even if you do act idiotically more often than others, that still only makes you a *person* who has acted idiotically more often than others, not an 'idiot.' Plus, if there were such a creature as a stupid idiot, what would that creature only be capable of?"

Client: "I guess acting idiotically and that's it."

Me: "Now, do you know anyone like that?"

Client: "No, I sure don't."

Me: "Now, there are people who have very low intellectual levels. But they are *people* with low intelligence, *not idiots or retards!* So I encourage you to refrain from labeling yourself anything but an FHB. Have I described what an FHB is to you yet?"

Client: "No, I don't believe you have."

Me: "FHB stands for Fallible Human Being, meaning that you are a human being and that you make mistakes, just like everyone else. Therefore, any word or phrase that follows the words, "I am a _____" that isn't 'Fallible Human Being' just is not accurate."

People in our society tend to use many labels that do not accurately describe themselves and others. The consequences of the use of inaccurate labels include unwanted emotional upset and a limited view of ourselves and others.

A limited view of oneself and others can have a serious impact on how we treat ourselves and others. Vice President Dan Quayle was an unfortunate recipient of negative labeling. Quayle was, in effect, labeled an "idiot" by many people in our society, and the media seemed to treat him as such. Their "idiot" label so limited people's view of him that Quayle could have had the answer to all of the nation's problems, but no one would have seen it as such, because "idiots do not say intelligent things."

Narrowing Our View of Ourselves and Others

Common labels include depressed person, lucky person, fat person, angry person, alcoholic, criminal, murderer, accountant, lawyer, doctor, electrician, father, mother, and molester. Remember, though, that there is no such thing as a depressed person, but rather a *person* who has made himself depressed. There is no such thing as a doctor, but rather a *person* who practices medicine for a living.

The following example demonstrates the importance of making such a distinction.

Client: "My husband couldn't do the wiring for the house because he's an accountant."

Me: "Why would his being an accountant keep him from doing the house wiring?"

Client: "Because he's an accountant ... What would he know about wiring?"

Me: "Well, first of all, he is not an accountant. He is a person who does accounting for a living. Therefore, since he is a person, there is the possibility that he might know wiring in addition to accounting. If there were such a thing as an accountant, all this thing would know is accounting. But I imagine he knows other things besides accounting, doesn't he?"

Client: "Sure. I see what you mean. I guess I had him kind of typecasted, didn't I?"

Me: "That's right, and this typecasting is called labeling."

Remember, if the sentence, "I am a _____," or "He/she is a _____," does not end with "human being" or "Fallible Human Being," the sentence does not accurately describe you or others.

(9) Personalization and Blame

The mental mistake of personalization and blame occurs when a person inaccurately assumes the cause of something. Sometimes it is blaming someone or something for a situation when in fact they in no way caused it. Other times it is blaming someone or something *too* much when in fact other factors were responsible as well. Problems associated with making this mental mistake include these:

- **Guilt**—because you think that what went wrong was your entire fault, and that you should not have done what you did to cause it;

- **Resentment**—because you think that what went wrong was entirely someone else's fault, and that they should not have done what they did to cause it; and

- **Trying to change the wrong thing**—It is like thinking that the reason your car is stalling is because you have a bad fuel pump when in fact your camshaft is defective. Rather than changing the camshaft, you naturally will change the fuel pump, only to find that the car continues to stall.

It is important for us to accurately assess the cause of a problem to correct it. We cause our own upset and behaviors through *our own thinking*. Other people's behaviors are caused by *their thoughts*, not by us, although we might encourage them to think or act a certain way. When it comes to interpersonal relationships, rarely is conflict the fault of a single person.

Sometimes misinformation or a lack of information leads to personalization and blame. This misinformation encourages a person to jump to conclusions about what the cause of an undesirable situation *must* have been.

For example, parents tend to blame themselves for their children's problematic behavior. If a twenty-five-year-old son were arrested for drug possession, his parents might jump to the conclusion that they must have done something wrong in raising him. While they might have done things to encourage their son to commit criminal acts, he would have had to *decide to act* on those suggestions or teachings to commit such acts. Additionally, many different sources influence children growing up, including parents, siblings, teachers, friends, songs, television, and printed material. Therefore, it is quite unrealistic for parents to believe that they were, or should have been, the only influence in the child's life.

Do your best to assess the cause(s) of problematic situations accurately. You can attribute the cause of an event to someone or something *without angrily blaming them*. Usually you are more likely to receive their cooperation when you calmly express your concerns.

(10) Irrational "Should" Statements

Irrational "should" statements cause anger and guilt. When we are angry with someone or something, we are pointing a "should" outward ("You should not treat me that way"). When we feel guilty, we are pointing the "should" inward, as guilt is anger turned inward—you are mad at yourself.

Should statements are irrational when they are moralistic demands, commands, and rules, and when they imply a belief in magic.

Moralistic Use of Should

Most people use the word *should* to express a rule, demand, or command. "A husband should take out the garbage ... A wife should do the laundry ... A child should respect his or her parents ... You should not steal." These should statements are also expressed as *musts*, *have-tos*, and *ought-tos*. They usually are absolute rules, and violating them supposedly produces dire consequences.

Many "shoulds" are societal rules. Having rules is important for a society; otherwise, there would be chaos. However, many societal rules are not based on fact but are simply made up and then followed blindly. Nevertheless, we believe them because we do not know *not* to, as the following example demonstrates:

> Client: "I felt so lazy and thought of myself as good for nothing the other day."
>
> Me: "Why?"
>
> Client: "Because I didn't do the dishes immediately after I ate."
>
> Me: "Why would you think of yourself as lazy and good for nothing when you don't do the dishes immediately after eating?"
>
> Client: "Because a person *should* do the dishes after they eat."
>
> Me: "Who told you that?"
>
> Client: "My mother preached that to me."
>
> Me: "Okay. Who do you think taught your mother that rule?"
>
> Client: "I guess her mother did."

Me: "Yes, probably so. So if we kept searching for the originator of that rule, we might find people that deemed themselves experts on laziness that agreed that if one does not wash the dishes after eating, he or she is lazy. So now you, and many other people as well, blindly follow this belief as if it were based on fact."

Client: "I see what you mean."

Me: "Good. Now. Where is the evidence that a person is lazy and good for nothing if he or she doesn't do the dishes immediately after eating?"

Client: "I guess there is none, really."

Me: "Well, when does a person have to do the dishes? When there are no other clean dishes in the house, he or she refuses or is unable to buy more clean dishes, and he or she wants to eat on a clean plate. Now, there usually are advantages to washing the dishes immediately after eating, such as the chore is completed and you can focus on other, more pleasurable things. But would you say that you are good for nothing, that you serve no purpose on this earth?"

Client: (Laughing) "No, I am important to my family and friends."

Me: "That's right. So it is important to refuse to blindly accept societal rules and to sometimes challenge them by looking for the evidence."

Believe it or not, there is a society that to this day believes that a husband should never eat with his wife's side of the family. The belief is that the wife's side of the family is possessed by the devil, and the act of eating makes a person more susceptible to being possessed. Therefore, a man has a much greater chance of being possessed if he eats with his in-laws. While many men throughout the world might agree with this tribe's beliefs, obviously there are no facts to support them. However, if a man in the tribe were to eat with his in-laws, he would be viewed as seriously mentally ill.

We are taught that many things are requirements when in fact they are only preferences. You will learn more about this fact later in my description of "need vs. want." While a person has a right to his or her morals, values, and preferences, the rigid musts, shoulds, and have-tos cause problems. These rigid rules make it difficult to adapt to circumstances that do not adhere to them.

Many of these rules actually are good, *recommended practices*. It is recommended that one wash the dishes after one eats as he or she can then focus on other, more pleasurable activities. For the most part, though, the world would not cease to exist if we were not to follow these recommended practices, although it *seems* as though it would when we state them as shoulds, musts, and have-tos.

I encourage you to challenge shoulds, musts, and have-tos by asking, "*Must* it be this way? How did I come to believe that it must be this way to begin with?"

Magical Aspect of "Should"

Most people are accustomed to using the word *should* morally, such as, "You should treat others the way you would like to be treated." However, there is a way to use the word *should* scientifically, while maintaining your moral beliefs, and be far better off for it.

A key insight into magical should statements is this one: *Magical, irrational should statements do not describe reality as it is, but how we insist it be.*

Therefore, when people use the word *should* magically, they are not dealing with reality as it is. They are dealing with a fantasy. For example, if I were to place ingredients together to make a chocolate cake, put it in the oven to let it bake, then took it out of the oven only to discover that I forgot to include the chocolate, *should* the result be a chocolate cake or something other than a chocolate cake? If I were to say that it *should* be a chocolate cake regardless, I would be insisting that the cake be a chocolate cake *simply because I wanted it to be*, despite the fact that

I did not include the chocolate. If I forgot to place the chocolate in the mixture, but pulled a chocolate cake out of the oven nevertheless, that would be magic!

Everything is as it should be at any given moment, although it might not be the way that we want it to be. For a situation to occur, everything that is necessary for it to occur must be present, or it will not happen. Irrational should statements do not consider reality.

Irrational, magical should statements insist that reality conform to one's desires, demands, or ideas of right and wrong, rather than our desires conforming to reality. However, reality does *not* conform to our *mere* desires or ideas of right and wrong.

Imagine the following scenario. The NFL Super Bowl has just concluded, and the final score is Pittsburgh Steelers, 37 points, Dallas Cowboys, 36 points.

Reporters then interview both head coaches. The Steelers' coach says, "I am so proud of my boys. They played a terrific game." The Cowboys' coach says, "We should have won that game." In fact, though, the Cowboys *should have lost* the game.

Obviously, what was necessary for the Cowboys to win was not present, for if it had been, they would have won. Unless the rules of football have changed, the team with more points at the end of the game wins. If the Cowboys' coach thinks that they *should* have won when what was necessary for them to win *was not done,* his belief would imply a belief in magic. His "should" would imply, "Everything necessary for us to win was present, but somehow we magically lost. It was just a fluke that we lost."

By thinking this way, would you expect the coach to make any changes in his game plan for the next time they play each other? I would not! Instead, if he says to himself, "As much as I wish that we *would* have won, and although we had the *potential* to win, we *should* have lost because something went wrong for us to end the game with fewer points than our opponent," he would be in a much better position to calmly accept that fact, to determine what actually went wrong, and to correct it.

Accepting your current reality is difficult if you do not acknowledge what that reality is. A benefit of accepting your current reality is that doing so places you in a better position to do something about it. The irrational use of the word *should* causes us to ignore the fact that all the necessary ingredients to create our undesirable situation are present. Ignoring that fact makes it difficult to change the situation by removing those necessary ingredients.

In other words, if I say, "My boss shouldn't yell at me," I am ignoring the fact that (1) my boss has it in his head to yell at me, and (2) I am there to take it. As long as those two facts are reality, it would be magic for me *not* to get yelled at. For me to stop getting yelled at, either (1) my boss has to change the way he thinks, or (2) I need to remove myself from the situation so that I am not around him to take it.

So everything is as it should be at any given moment because all of the necessary ingredients are there to make it that way. This statement does *not* imply that it is morally right or advantageous that the situation is as it is. The statement simply acknowledges the reality of the situation. Our mere desire for a situation to be a certain way will not make it that way. However, it *should* only be the way we want it to be if all the necessary ingredients are present, *regardless* of whether we whine, cry, hold our breath, or stomp our feet.

When it comes to angering ourselves with irrational should statements, if the anger we feel serves no useful purpose, and we know that the situation will remain the same despite our anger, we might as well calmly accept it. Our calm acceptance of a situation does not mean that we like it or have no desire to change it. Calm acceptance means that you acknowledge the reality of the situation and, by doing so, are in a much better position to do what is possible to change it.

The Serenity Prayer is based on the principle of calm acceptance:

> *God grant me the serenity*
> *to accept things that I cannot change,*
> *the courage to change the things that I can, and*
> *the wisdom to know the difference.*

Work at changing irrational should statements to wish statements.

Change Irrational "Should" Statements to "Wish" Statements

Irrational "Should"	Rational "Wish"
1. He should have more respect for me.	1. I wish that he would have more respect for me, but he doesn't. Let me see what I can do to encourage him to develop more respect for me.
2. She shouldn't treat me like a baby.	2. I wish that she wouldn't treat me like a baby, but she does. Let me see what I can do to encourage her to treat me like an adult.
3. I should have known that he would not like it.	3. I wish that I would have known that he would not like it, but obviously I didn't. I'll see why I didn't know that and work at doing better next time.
4. I shouldn't have yelled at her.	4. I wish that I had not yelled at her. Obviously, though, I did everything necessary to yell at her, or I would not have. I'll work at removing those necessary ingredients.

Remember: Anger is like urinating in your pants. Everyone can see it, but you are the only one who can feel it. So refuse to should all over yourself!

(11) Confusing Needs with Wants

If I were limited to being able to write about only one mental mistake in this chapter, the confusion of needs and wants would be the mistake that I would select. It is by far the most important mental mistake of all described in this chapter.

In Rational Living Therapy, we differentiate between **absolute needs** and **wants**. Our absolute needs are those things we need to remain alive:

Examples of Our Absolute Needs
Those things that are
necessary to remain alive:

Air	Sufficient Warmth
Food	
Water	Sometimes a Certain Medication

Everything else on this earth is a want! However, when we mislabel a "want" as being a "need," we feel just as badly as if we were going without air or food. A very small sample of "wants" that people tend to mislabel as being "needs" includes these:

Some of the things that we are taught that
we "need" but actually only "want"

(1) Love from others
(2) Respect
(3) Attention
(4) Confidence
(5) To have a certain appearance
(6) To have an outstanding job
(7) To have an outstanding education
(8) To be liked by everybody
(9) To have things go our way
(10) That new car
(11) To be treated "well" by others
(12) Peace of mind
(13) Perfect health
(14) Outstanding accomplishments
(15) Perfection
(16) A specific person or group of people

"Need" Statements Cause Anxiety and Anger

Sometimes "need" statements cause anxiety and panic. Imagine how you would feel if you were trapped in a room and you knew that in the next five minutes all of the air in the room would be removed through a vent. You most likely would begin to panic, and the closer it got to the end of the five-minute period, the more anxious you would be. Why? Because you know that you *need* air to live.

Contrast that example with a situation where you discover that your local grocery store stopped offering your favorite breakfast cereal. You might feel sad, but you would not panic like in the first example, because you know that you only *want* your favorite breakfast cereal, you do not need it (although you do need food), and that is the difference between needing and wanting.

Sometimes "need" statements cause intense anger. Now imagine how you would feel if you were in a room and you knew that in the next five minutes all the air in the room would be removed through a vent. However, this time, leaving the room is easy, but I am going to do my best to keep you from getting out. No matter how well you liked me previously, you would make yourself pretty angry at me. Why? Because I would be keeping you from something that you need—air!

A technique to determine whether something is an absolute need or a want is to ask yourself: *How long could I go without this before I would die?* In other words, how long can you go without it before doing so would kill you? We know approximately how long we could survive without food, air, and water. How long could we *survive* without that new stereo, that boyfriend or girlfriend, or the respect of others? Notice that this is different than killing oneself. When a person commits suicide, *something* does not kill the person—*the person* kills himself or herself.

Conditional Need Statements

Conditional need statements are based on an assumption that for Event A to occur, Conditions 1, 2, and 3 must exist. Conditional need statements can be accurate or inaccurate. For example, an *accurate* conditional need would be this statement:

"For me to be physically present at the grocery store,
I need to travel to it."

It is impossible for a person to be somewhere without traveling to the destination. An *inaccurate* conditional need would be this one:

"For me to be happy, I need to have $1 million."

If a person believes that there is no other possible way to be happy other than to have $1 million, he or she will act as if that were the case. Obviously, there are other ways to make oneself happy.

Sometimes absolute need statements are hidden within conditional need statements. For example, an accurate conditional need statement is, "For Joe to obtain a legitimate college degree, he needs to complete a college program." However, if he does not get accepted into a college program and panics in response, he would be equating his failing to obtain a college degree with a life-or-death situation (absolute need).

But don't we need someone to love us? I am asked this question routinely, especially by therapists who attend my seminars. It is a difficult question to answer because we must first *define* love to be able to decide whether we need it. If I were to ask each reader to send to me their definition of food, water, and air, I would receive pretty consistent definitions. They would all be about the same. However, if I were to ask for definitions of love, I would receive many different definitions.

I cannot think of anything that would be included in a definition of love that is something that we need, but I can think of many things that we might want. For example, a common definition of love includes conditions such as, "when people love you, they hug you, kiss you, tell you that they love you, they take care of you when you are not feeling well, etc." These conditions or elements of the definition are wants or desires, not needs. People do not die from a lack of hugs, kisses, or verbal affection. Most (not all) people want those things, but they are not needs. Actually, that fact alone proves they are not needs. Everyone needs to have air, food, and water, but not everyone wants love, affection, and attention.

Sometimes therapists use as proof that we need love the fact that years ago babies died in orphanages, and their deaths were attributed to a "lack of love." It turns out, though, that what they likely died from was a lack of tactile stimulation—caretakers did not touch them enough. It might be that infants need tactile stimulation, but adults do not appear to have such a need. Nevertheless, a person does not need to love someone to provide tactile stimulation.

(12) Confusing Choosing to (Choice) with Having to (Force)

Anytime people have the sincere impression that they are forced to do something that they do not want to do, they resent it. The more that they dislike it, and the greater the perception of being forced, the greater the resentment.

The only time that we are ever *forced* to do something is when we are physically overpowered and made to do against our will. Otherwise, when we do something, no matter how much we dislike doing it, we are *choosing* or *deciding* to do it.

Sometimes we decide to do something because it is the lesser of two evils. For example, every time we file and pay our income taxes, we choose or decide to do so. Why? Because choosing *not* to pay them leads to a consequence that is unacceptable to us. Could we tell the Internal Revenue Service what to do with their 1040 form? Sure we could! Some people do! However, paying our taxes, as unpleasant as most of us view it, is not as unpleasant as are the consequences of not paying them.

Realizing that we are deciding to do something, rather than being forced, significantly reduces our resentment. It does not make the event or duty more appealing. It does make our experience with it more pleasant, though.

Also, realizing that we are deciding to do something rather than being forced to places us in a position to take credit for having made a wise decision.

For example, many people resent the process of dieting because they view themselves as "having to" diet and "having to" lose weight. Perhaps they *need* to lose weight to fit into a particular bathing suit or to lessen their risk of heart disease, but *they do not have to* fit in the bathing suit or lessen their risk of heart disease. Those are optional things to do. Actually, people decide to diet for many different reasons. When people realize that it is their *decision* that leads them to diet, and they also realize that at any time they can *decide* to return to previous eating habits, they feel much better about their dieting and usually are much more willing to do so.

A basic fact of life is that the *only* thing that we *have to do* is die. Ultimately, dying is absolutely *un*avoidable. Everything else is optional.

Keep yourself mindful of the difference between "choosing to" and "having to," and you will lessen your frustration and resentment level considerably.

(13) Can't Stand-itis

Can't stand-itis is an extension of the confusion of needing and wanting.

Can't stand-itis is another form of underestimating one's ability to tolerate a situation. Can't stand-itis implies a belief that one *needs* a situation to be different than it is. When we view a situation or condition as something we cannot stand, we tend to avoid it as if *not* doing so would kill us. Conversely, when we believe that we have the ability to deal with a situation effectively, we tend to be unafraid to approach it.

The following is a typical example of can't stand-itis in action and how to dispute it.

> Client: "My daughter has been hanging around the wrong crowd and getting into trouble with drugs. I want her to stop, so when she disobeys me about it, I make her stay at home, usually for one week. But every time I ground her, I end up letting her go back out after one hour."
>
> Me: "Why do you do that?"
>
> Client: "Because she starts yelling at me and calling me all sorts of names."

Me: "Okay, but why would you let her outside when you are trying to correct her behavior?"

Client: "Because *I can't stand it* when she yelled at me and calls me names."

Me: "Well, I do not know anyone who enjoys being yelled at. With that said, I'll bet you that you can stand it. I'll bet you my house, my practice, and what little savings I have because of my house and practice, I'll even throw in my children, and bet you that you can stand it when your daughter yells at you."

Client: "How can you say that?"

Me: "Because you are sitting here telling me about it. If you couldn't stand your daughter yelling at you, you would have died. Now if you were to tell me that you couldn't stand a piano falling on your head, I'd say that you probably are right. But when you tell your brain that you cannot stand your daughter yelling at you, how do you act?"

Client: "Like her yelling at me is going to kill me!"

Me: "Exactly! Beautiful! Granted, I'm sure that you do not like being yelled at. Most of us don't. But if you view your daughter's yelling at you as being what it actually is—an inconvenience—you will simply make yourself irritated and annoyed, rather than very anxious and angry. Now, if you were to be simply irritated and annoyed, what do you think that you would do when she yelled at you?"

Client: "Stick to my guns and keep her in the house."

Me: "That's right."

Unless it is something that can kill you, replace the statement, "I can't stand it" with "I don't like it, and because I don't like it, I'm going to do something about it."

A Special Note: What About the Quality of Life?

Occasionally, I am asked about the importance of the quality of life. A person might ask, "Yes, I know what is going on will not kill me, but what about being happy?" To understand the answer to this question, allow me first to explain what is known as Maslow's Hierarchy of Needs.

Abraham Maslow (1954) identified what he described as "innate needs" as needs that when fulfilled provide satisfaction and meaning to a person's life. These needs make the person experience a constant "deficit state." Just as one need is satisfied, another need "kicks in" placing the person in a position of always striving for something. Maslow demonstrated how these needs are prioritized into a hierarchy as follows:

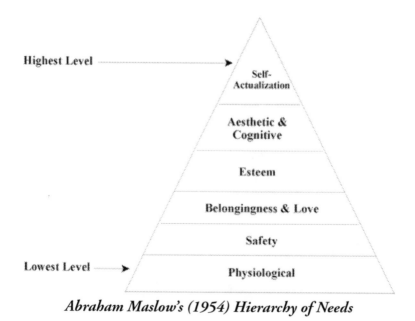

Abraham Maslow's (1954) Hierarchy of Needs

For a person to be concerned with a higher-level need, he or she must first have the lower-level needs generally satisfied. For example, if a person is starving (a physiological need to eat), she is not going to be very concerned about her self-esteem at that moment. If a person is in a war zone with bombs exploding around him (safety needs), he is not going to be concerned about his awareness of knowledge or about writing poetry (aesthetic and cognitive needs).

From a Rational Living Therapy perspective, though, the only true "needs" among those listed in Maslow's hierarchy are the physiological. To live, we need to have our physical needs met. The remainder of what Maslow describes as needs are actually wants—things we sometimes desire to make life better or to add quality to our lives.

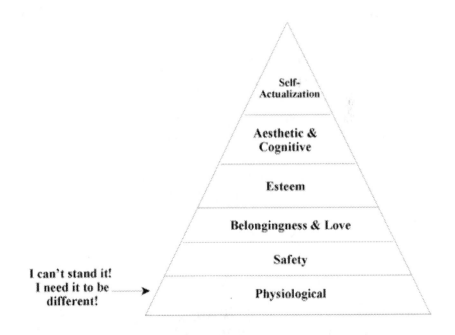

By the way, the safety needs are a *sense* of safety. People do not need to have a sense of safety, but we need to be safe to remain alive (physiological need).

When we mistakenly believe that we cannot stand something, we subsequently act as though we are going to die, as if a physiological need is not being met. So thinking or acting as though we cannot stand something or that we need a situation to be different than it is puts us on the physiological level of the hierarchy. As long as that perception exists, we are not going to care about those things that bring quality to our lives, like being loved, belonging to a group, esteeming ourselves, and so on. For example, when people believe that they "need" to be in a romantic relationship, they do not tend to be particularly selective as to who the next person in their life will be. They tend to grab the first person who comes along. Therefore, quality of life is not an issue at that point. They treat the absence of a romantic relationship as if they were lacking air, food, or water. As a result, their desperation makes quality of life irrelevant.

(14) Catastrophizing

Catastrophizing is another form of underestimating one's potential to deal with a situation effectively. This underestimation often leads us to perceive the situation as being worse than it actually is for us.

Words and expressions often used when catastrophizing are *awful, terrible, horrible, catastrophic,* and *end of the world.* Unless these words are used when joking or lying, they often are an extension of the confusion of needs and wants. When we label something as awful or terrible, we equate it with something that we *can't stand* or *need* not have. The statement, "It is *terrible* that I lost my job" tends to produce the same anxiety or anger that the statement, "I *can't stand* that I lost my job" does.

Another Brief Psychology Lesson

In the early 1900s, two researchers, Robert Yerkes and John Dodson (1908) discovered that there is an optimal level of arousal for each task. If a person is not sufficiently physically aroused for the task at hand, his or her performance on it will be poor. Conversely, if a person is too physically aroused for the task at hand, his or her performance will be poor as well. Their discovery became known as the Yerkes-Dodson Law.

The optimal level of arousal is different for each task. For example, if a mother's child were trapped under a car, she likely would have a difficult time *calmly* lifting the car off her child. For her to lift the car successfully, she would need to be sufficiently distressed (aroused). However, if she were too aroused, she might freeze and not be able to approach the car.

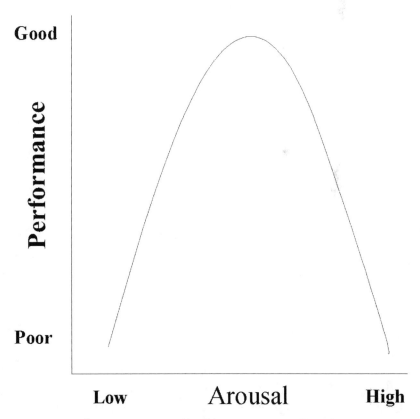

Yerkes and Dodson (1908) discovered that there is an optimal level of arousal for each task.

Imagine if she were to take into a test-taking situation the level of arousal required to lift a car. She likely would be too aroused for that task, as that level of arousal would make it difficult for her to think and to remember what she had learned.

The words *awful, horrible,* and *terrible* tend to create too much arousal. The attitude, "I do not care about this," tends to create insufficient arousal. The word *unfortunate* tends to produce an optimal level of arousal in most situations.

Dr. Albert Ellis (1988) has written extensively on the topic of catastrophizing. He emphasized that nothing is *objectively* awful, horrible, or terrible. For example, many people throughout the world viewed the events of September 11, 2001, in the United States as terrible. However, on that same day, there were people who were dancing in the streets with joy at the sight of America being harmed. If the terrorist attacks of September 11 were *objectively* terrible, everyone would have seen them that way.

Since nothing is objectively terrible, horrible, or awful, we are free to label *anything* as such and to make ourselves miserable as a result. We are also free to label *anything* as being unfortunate or inconvenient and to make ourselves feel more along the lines of calm. The question is, "Which way of labeling a personally undesirable event will work better for us?" The word *unfortunate* implies that a situation is personally *undesirable but survivable.*

Keep in mind, though, that nothing is objectively unfortunate either. That is why in Rational Living Therapy we like to add the words, *for me.* The statement, "This is an unfortunate situation for me" suggests that this situation is contrary to *my* goals, what *I* want out of life, and I *dislike* that fact.

Labeling a personally undesirable situation as unfortunate does not mean that one does not care about it or is uninterested in correcting the situation. As the Yerkes-Dodson Law demonstrates, labeling these situations as unfortunate places a person in a much better position to correct them than does labeling them terrible, horrible, or awful.

But aren't there some situations that are worse than others? For whom? This question again implies that there are objectively good, bad, and neutral situations, events, or conditions. However, what is considered good to one person might be considered bad to another, and this is determined primarily by one's goals.

Some situations interfere with our own goals more than others, thus making them *personally worse* for us. These personally worse situations often require more time, energy, and effort to correct than do other situations. Nevertheless, we are better off labeling these situations as "personally worse" and as "unfortunate for me," instead of labeling them as terrible, horrible, and awful.

(15) Magical Worry

Worry is fearful thinking. It is the act of obsessively thinking about a feared outcome.

How often does what you worry about actually happen? I will bet that unless you are very selective in worrying, your answer to this question is, "Not that often." After years of worrying about things only to have our worries not come true, sometimes we unintentionally make a connection—when we worry about things, they do not happen. This connection often leads us to believe that our worrying keeps unwanted events from occurring. We then become afraid *not* to worry. This is what Maxie Maultsby, MD, calls "magical worry."

Maultsby (1984) calls worry "civilized voodoo" because worry does not keep events from happening, as worry is *only* thinking. Worrisome thoughts cannot influence, change, or prevent a situation. *Actions* prevent situations from occurring, not worrisome thoughts. So if a person *acts* on his or her *concerns*, a better outcome might occur. Simply *worrying* about it will not change anything. Besides giving a person an ulcer, another problem with worry is that it makes it appear as though you are doing something about your situation—"At least I am worrying about it."

The basic message, therefore, is that refusing to worry is okay because worry has never protected you. We recommend that you do this instead:

- Know what you want out of life, like the well-being of your-self and your loved-ones;

- If you come across information that shows that your well-being or that of your loved ones is being threatened, be concerned; and

- Act on that concern.

Simply being concerned without acting on that concern is not any more helpful than simply worrying.

Sometimes people unintentionally set themselves up for worrying because they are confronted with a situation that seems dangerous, but they approach it anyway. A better approach is to recognize a true threat and to act on it.

For example, one January, our son, Aldo, was scheduled to make a trip from our home near Pittsburgh to Washington, D.C., with several of his classmates and our priest. I was in Los Angeles during the week preceding his scheduled trip. The day before he was to leave, my wife telephoned me and told me that the weather forecasters were predicting a significant snowstorm for the area through which our son would be traveling (a very mountainous area). She wondered if it would be best to keep him home. I asked my wife what the probability of the snowstorm was, and she said that the forecasters were estimating an 80 percent probability.

So I suggested to her, "Honey, we could either allow him to go and worry the entire time, wondering if the bus driver is going to be able to get them to Washington safely, or we could recognize that the chances of Aldo being harmed are significant enough to keep him home." We decided to keep him home.

Since we do not have a crystal ball that tells us what the future will be, we can only make a prediction based on the current facts as best as we can know them. In the situation with our son, the snowstorm did occur, and it did in fact become a dangerous situation. Thankfully, the school decided to cancel the trip. Sometimes we err on the side of caution, and in fact the undesired situation does not occur. But until someone invents that crystal ball, we can only base our predictions on the facts that are available to us. As the saying goes,

Worry is like rocking in a rocking chair...
It gives you something to do,
But it gets you nowhere!

(16) Having Irrational Definitions

Sometimes our definitions of important concepts (like love, respect, trust, and caring) can cause us problems in that they can be unrealistic and/or rigid, thus causing us to frustrate ourselves when our goals are not met. Examples of irrational definitions include these:

- If a man does not spend all of his time with me, he is *selfish*.

- A person is *lazy* if she does not wash the dishes after she eats.

- If a woman *cares* about me, she will do this for me every day.

Such definitions are limiting and self-defeating. They can be so limiting that a person ultimately does not get what he or she wants, as in the following example:

Client: "I am a failure."

Me: "Why do you say that?"

Client: "Because my career isn't going as well as I'd like."

Me: "Well, remember that you are not a failure but a person who has failed. But I'm interested in knowing what you consider failure to be. What is your definition of the word *failure*?"

Client: (Thinks for a moment) "I guess when I don't do things perfectly well."

Me: "And what happens to you when you think of yourself as a failure or that you have failed?"

Client: "I end up giving up!"

Me: "Now look at your definition of failure. What you are saying is that to succeed, you must do something perfectly well. If you do not do something perfectly, you have failed, right?"

Client: "Right."

Me: "And is failing good, bad, or neutral?"

Client: "It's bad!"

Me: "How bad?"

Client: "Very bad!"

Me: "So you see, your definition of failing is not going to work in terms of helping you to succeed and to feel good, because it is an all-or-none approach. You believe that a person either is totally successful or totally unsuccessful at something. However, there are degrees of success and failure, as there are various degrees of almost everything. So even if you have done an adequate job at something (enough to achieve a reasonable goal), if it is not perfect, then you have failed, and that's really bad, according to your definition."

Client: "Well, that is how I have thought."

Me: "Okay, then let's replace that thought with something like this: I am not a failure, I am a person who sometimes doesn't always achieve perfection at things, and even if I do, the perfection doesn't last for long. That fact only proves one thing—that I am just like everyone else, a Fallible Human Being. However, rarely is something that I do a total failure, as there are various aspects of it that I do get right. Anyway, failing is not awful, terrible, or the end of the world, it is only unfortunate! I'll use my disappointment to do reasonably, not perfectly, better."

Pay attention to your definitions of important concepts, particularly those that appear to be causing you trouble. Assess whether (or to what degree) your definitions work for you.

(17) Confusing Relying with Depending

To *rely* on someone is to trust that he or she will do something that you *could* do yourself or that you could find other means of doing it. To *depend* on someone is to count on a person to do something that you *cannot* do yourself or find other means of having it done.

We often rely on others because doing so makes life easier. The person who has lost her vision might at first depend on others to guide her around when walking because she does not know how to walk independently. However, when she has learned to walk independently, she might *rely* on others at times to make walking *easier*.

Sometimes we *mistakenly believe* that we are dependent on others because we believe that we do not have the resources to achieve certain goals (such as taking care of ourselves) on our own when in fact we do.

Sometimes people assume that they do not have the potential to be self-reliant because they have not been, at least in certain situations. However, remember the expression, "Just because you haven't, doesn't mean you can't."

Being willing to take a chance to see how well you can achieve your goals and care for yourself independently is important. If you doubt your ability to achieve your goals independently, or to only rely on the help of others, challenge your belief with the rational questions.

(18) Confusing Inability with Unwillingness

When a person is *unable* to do something, he or she does not have the skills, knowledge, and/or physical attributes to do it. A person is *unwilling* to do something when he or she has the physical and mental ability to do it, but decides not to do it and, instead, chooses a different behavior.

For example, a popular television commercial claimed that "no one can eat just one" of the company's potato chips. The basis of this claim was that the potato chips were so good that once one chip was eaten, one could not help but eat more, as if the chips somehow disabled the frontal lobe of the brain, causing a person to eat them uncontrollably. What actually happens is this:

A	B	C
(Awareness)	(Thought/Belief)	(Emotional Consequence)
Eats a potato chip	"Boy was that good, I think I'll have another one."	Happy feelings Eats another chip

This ABC sequence continues until a person either decides to stop eating (stomach is full, jaw muscles hurt, chips no longer tasty, have to go to work) or until he or she runs out of chips! Therefore, it is not that the person *cannot* eat just one; he or she is *unwilling* or *chooses not* to eat just one.

Unwillingness can be the result of different motivators, including fear and desire. A person simply might not have the desire to do something. Other times, however, he or she might feel afraid or very uncomfortable acting in a certain way.

Examples of fear-based unwillingness include the following:

- "I can't tell him no."

- "I couldn't give a speech in front of a large crowd."

- "I can't stand the sacrifice it takes to lose weight."

- "I can't ask that pretty girl for a date."

- "I can't tell the waiter that my steak is not cooked properly."

In each case, a person has the physical and mental ability to do the things he or she claims cannot be done. However, the *unwillingness* to perform these behaviors is due to anxiety or discomfort. This is an important distinction, because in each case a person does *not* need to *learn how* to perform these behaviors—he or she wants to learn how to perform them *comfortably*.

Therefore, if you find yourself believing that you *cannot* do something, ask yourself:

- "Do I have the physical and mental ability to do it?"

- "If I absolutely had to, would I?"

If you answer yes to these questions, what you really mean is that you feel uncomfortable performing the behavior. If so, it is important to rationally dispute the thoughts leading to the discomfort.

(19) Confusing Possibility with Probability

When we plan for the future, we can only make a *prediction* about the outcome because we have no crystal ball to give us absolute certainty. To make a rational prediction, it is important to ask two questions:

- Is what I am predicting possible?

- If it is possible, what is the probability of it happening?

When a person is anxious, he or she fears (predicts) that something problematic will happen in the future. To assess this fear, we first ask,

"Is it possible for the event to happen?" If it is possible, we then ask, "What is the likelihood of it happening?"

People often assume that if something is *possible*, it must be highly *probable*. This incorrect assumption, or overestimation of the probability of this feared event occurring, often leads to unnecessary concern or anxiety.

For example, I live in the Upper Ohio Valley, which is known for its many bridges. Many residents of this area avoid traveling across those bridges because of a common fear of bridges collapsing while traveling across them. When examining this fear, we first ask, "Is it possible for a bridge to collapse?" Certainly. We know that bridges have collapsed in the past, and there is nothing about any bridge that makes it *absolutely* safe. So this fear is based in reality and not on a bizarre delusion, like being afraid that Martians are controlling your mind.

Next we ask, "What is the probability that any given bridge will collapse?" In examining the bridges, we find that they have a very good safety record, with none of them ever coming close to collapsing. We also know that they are inspected regularly, and one was closed for a brief period when an examiner discovered a very minor problem (one that would not have caused the bridge to collapse).

Finally, considering the fact that thousands of vehicles travel across these bridges each day with no problem, a *very safe* bet would be that the bridges in my area will remain structurally sound when we travel across them.

Notice that we examine and gather facts when determining possibility and probability. I do not want people simply to take my word for it that the bridges are safe. I want them to see what the facts tell us. In examining the actual safety of any given bridge, if we discover that a bridge is not structurally sound, that it has not been maintained, and that a civil engineer suggests avoiding driving across it, I am going to avoid that bridge as well!

When a Low Probability Just Is Not Enough

Sometimes people tell me, "I do not care if God himself were to tell me that the airplane is not going to crash, I still would not get on it!" When this is the case, there often are underlying assumptions (as described in chapter 2) that make it difficult to benefit from a low probability of an undesirable event occurring.

The following example demonstrates how underlying assumptions make low probability irrelevant to a person:

Client: "I'm afraid of flying."

Me: "Are you afraid of flying, or are you afraid of crashing?"

Client: (Laughing) "I guess I'm afraid of crashing!"

Me: "That's right. First, let's discuss whether it is possible for a plane to crash. Obviously it is, right, because they have. Now, what is the probability that any given plane that you would travel in would crash? Did you know that as we speak there are thousands of airplanes in the air, and this is the case for most of the day, every day?"

Client: "Sure, I know all that. But it wouldn't matter to me if God himself told me that a plane that I wanted to get on would not crash, I still wouldn't get on it."

Me: "Even if God told you that there was 100 percent certainty that you would make it to your destination safely?"

Client: "Yep."

Me: "Okay. Well, this might sound like a silly question, but besides it ruining your day, what would be the problem, as far as you are concerned, if the plane were to crash and you were to die?"

Client: "That would mean that my kids wouldn't have a father."

Me: "Okay. And as far as you are concerned, what problem would there be if your children did not have a father?"

Client: "They would grow up disturbed."

Me: "And if they grew up disturbed, why would that be a problem, as far as you are concerned?"

Client: "Because they would have a miserable life."

Me: "What would it be like for you if you knew that your children had a miserable life?"

Client: "It would be terrible. I couldn't take that."

As long as the client in this example fears such a negative outcome, he will be unwilling to take even the slightest chance that the feared outcome will occur. By learning how to overcome the fear of his children necessarily growing up disturbed, he will be more willing to take advantage of the excellent safety record of the airline industry.

It is important to note, though, that sometimes people *underestimate* the probability of an event occurring and develop problems as a result. Veteran professional boxer Tommy Morrison announced in 1996 that he had contracted the HIV virus. At a press conference to announce his retirement from boxing, Morrison commented, "I thought I had a better chance of winning the lottery than of contracting HIV." While it is not particularly easy to contract HIV through heterosexual sex, the chances of contracting HIV through it are far greater than the chances of winning the lottery. Apparently, his underestimation of the chances of contracting HIV led him to engage in behaviors that increased the likelihood of contracting it.

Therefore, when making a prediction, first determine if it is possible for the event to occur. If it is possible, next assess the probability of it occurring. If you determine that it is possible, and that the probability is high, then determine the severity of the consequence. If I know that there is a high probability that I will get a paper cut while doing paperwork, I might be willing to take that chance. However, if it were very probable that doing paperwork would kill me, I would likely refrain from doing it.

(20) Projection

People often assume that because they have certain beliefs, other people must think the same way. So they assume that the motives of others are similar to their own. For example, someone who views herself as ugly might have these beliefs: "This boy is not interested in me because he thinks that I am ugly. Why wouldn't he think I am ugly? It is obvious that I am!"

While it is true that there are very common beliefs in our society, that does not mean we all think alike. No two people have the same set of wants, likes, dislikes, opinions, values, and morals. Consequently, because each of us is unique, it is a mistake to assume that others *must* think, feel, and want as you do. Some men like very slender women, while others like those who are full-figured. Some women like men with beards, and others do not. Our diversity makes it important to realize that people can have opinions that differ from our own. This is particularly true when examining our perception of ourselves. People often view us differently than we view ourselves, especially when our own opinion is very negative.

Sometimes projection occurs when we accuse others of being motivated to do something because we ourselves have that motivation. The husband who often questions the whereabouts of his wife, believing that she is having an affair, might fear this because he himself has had an affair. His own motivation to have an affair shapes how he perceives his wife's behavior.

Is My Assumption the Result of Projection?

If we...	*We tend to...*
Speak badly of others,	think that they speak badly about us.
Cheat others,	think that they are cheating us.
Have a low opinion of our own attributes,	assume that others dislike our attributes as well.

Since projection is mind reading, ask yourself, "Is my assumption of what someone is thinking influenced by what *I* tend to think in similar situations?" If so, remind yourself that just because you hold that belief does not mean that others do as well.

(21) Being Upset About the "Idea" of Something

As is the case with irrational should statements, people often upset themselves over the *idea* of something rather than the actual consequences of it. When that is the case, a person is upset because he or she thinks that it is a requirement to be upset, regardless of the actual negative consequences of the seemingly undesirable situation. The following example illustrates this point.

Client: "I hate how my nose looks!"

Me: "In your opinion, what is wrong with your nose?"

Client: "I hate that it's crooked."

Me: "How has your nose been a problem for you?"

Client: "What do you mean?"

Me: "Are there any goals that you have not achieved because of your nose? Is there anything you want that you do not have because of your nose?"

Client: "I guess not."

Me: "Really think about it for a moment."

Client: (Thinks for a moment) "I can't think of any problems that my nose has created for me."

Me: "So it seems to me that you have been upset about the *idea* that your nose is crooked instead of any consequence of it. What you are saying is that your life is the way you want it to be despite your nose. Your upset has been the result of the idea that a nose shouldn't be crooked, and if it is, you should be upset about it, *regardless of whether or not the nose actually causes you any problems.*"

Client: "I think that I see what you mean."

Me: "Great. I encourage you to apply this logic to anything that you might be dissatisfied with. Ask yourself, 'Am I dissatisfied because of a consequence or because of an idea that I should be?'"

Take a moment to think of all of the situations or conditions we have been taught that we *should* be upset about. Examples include

Examples of Situations / Conditions with Which We Have Been Taught That We Are "Supposed" to Be Upset	
Being "Too" Short	Parents Not Loving You
Being "Overweight"	Not Having a Romantic Partner
Turning 40 years old	Losing Your Hair
Having Crooked Teeth	People Thinking Negatively of You

While each of these examples could be practical problems for a person, they are not necessarily. It depends on whether a person has *goals* that these situations or conditions would interfere with. Most of us have learned, though, that these situations and conditions (and many others like them) *necessarily* are problems, that we should be upset with them, and that there is something wrong with us if we are not upset in response to them.

When considering whether you are experiencing a practical problem, ask yourself, "Do I think that the situation at hand is a problem because it is interfering with achieving my goals, or do I think it is a problem simply because I have been taught that it is?"

(22) Nonsense Arguments

Nonsense arguments are those statements that people make to themselves or others that can be totally accurate, totally inaccurate, or somewhere in between. However, accuracy of the statement is not the issue. The problem with nonsense arguments is that they distract a person from an important task at hand.

Nonsense arguments often are made in the form of a "historical if" or "if only" statement, such as:

- "If only I hadn't had that accident, I would be able to walk today."

- "If only my husband hadn't divorced me, I wouldn't have the problems that I'm having today."

- "If only my parents had worked harder, I'd have a nice inheritance today."

- "If only that car hadn't run over my foot, I wouldn't have a broken foot."

These "if onlys" are largely irrelevant. The relevant question is, "What do I do about my situation now?" The only reason to spend any amount of time thinking about personally negative events of the past is to learn from them.

As we say in the Pittsburgh, Pennsylvania, area, "There is no point in trying to shovel last year's snow. You can't shovel it, but you can't get stuck in it either."

Focus your energy on resolving any current concerns, learning from your past, and creating a happy tomorrow.

(23) Irrational Hopelessness/Helplessness

Hopeless thinking is an example of jumping to conclusions, no matter how much a person has researched the problem he or she is thinking hopelessly about.

For a person to think hopelessly, he or she must make the following assumption: "*I know all there is to know about this problem. If I do not see a solution to it, one must not exist!*"

Even after a *seemingly* exhaustive search for a solution has been conducted, to think hopelessly, one must *assume* that no solution exists beyond where he or she has looked and that no solution *could ever* exist. It is this *assumption* that can lead a person to stop searching and to fail to take advantage of a potential solution.

Why do people jump to such pessimistic conclusions? Various reasons exist, including these:

1. Previous Learning About What Is Possible or Available

As we grow up, we are taught what is possible and what is not. For many of us, we first believe that *anything* is possible. We then come to "learn" from various sources what *people* can and cannot do, and then we learn more specifically what *we* can and cannot do. Sometimes, though, what we learn is not worth learning because it is not accurate.

Sometimes we learn from others by word, by example, or both. Our father's and mother's accomplishments demonstrate to us what is possible. They might also encourage or discourage us with statements like, "You can do it" or "You will never amount to much," or statements about themselves, like, "I will never get ahead" or "It is always someone else that is successful, never me."

This learning creates underlying assumptions (refer to chapter 2) that cause us to assume automatically that we can or cannot successfully accomplish something.

When examining whether you have the potential to achieve a goal or to correct a personally undesirable situation, ask yourself, "Is it possible for a human being to do this?" In other words, have other people like you, with the same attributes and background, accomplished what you want to accomplish? A simple "not that I know of" answer will not suffice. I encourage you to do some research.

Also realize that just because others have not accomplished what you want to does not necessarily mean it cannot be done. Has anyone ever tried? If so, why were they not successful? What could you do differently?

When people say that something is impossible, I am often reminded of Coach Doug Blevins. Coach Blevins is the National Football League's most sought after kicking coach. His star pupil is Adam Vinatieri, who won two Super Bowls for the New England Patriots with last-second field goals. Coach Blevins had a dream since he was a child to coach in the NFL.

Today, he is an outstanding kicking coach despite the fact that he has never walked a day in his life. He has cerebral palsy and has been using a wheelchair since he was a young child. It is beyond me how Coach Blevins managed to (1) learn kicking technique, (2) figure out how to teach (from a wheelchair) athletes how to kick, and (3) convince professional football teams that he could coach their kickers. How many times do you think he was discouraged from pursuing his dream?

2. Impatience/Low Frustration Tolerance

People sometimes begin thinking hopelessly *because* they have given up.

Sometimes they end their pursuit of a goal because they are impatient and not willing to wait for success. The attitude is, "If I cannot have it (or fix it) now, forget it." Impatience often is the result of confusing needing with wanting, as in, "I need to have it now!" It is important to change this attitude to, "I would rather have it now, but I certainly can wait!"

At other times, low frustration tolerance causes a person to be intolerant of failing. The attitude is, "If success (or a solution) does not come easily, forget it." If a person views roadblocks, setbacks, and frustrations along the way to success as terrible, horrible, and awful, he or she will not attempt to achieve anything that requires much effort. It is important to change this attitude to, "I wish that success and solutions would always come to me easily, but I do not need them to." Remember, though, that about the only thing that comes easily to us is trouble. Everything else takes work!

3. Taking Someone's Word for It

As we will discuss in greater detail later in this book, "expert voice" is a significant factor that helps us to determine whether we believe something to be a fact. When we believe that someone is an expert, we are likely to view what they tell us as credible and, therefore, factual. Sometimes, though, the "expert" is not as knowledgeable as we think.

I remember some of my high school teachers "informing" me and my classmates that a person had to be exceptionally intelligent to get accepted into law school and to practice law. They also informed us that a student needed straight As to be accepted into law school. As young, naive high school students, we accepted what they said as being factual. We figured that if our teachers said it, it must be so. My teachers were wrong on both counts. It is hard to tell how many potentially exceptional lawyers they discouraged with their "knowledge."

I encourage you to refuse to take *any* expert's word for it. Experts only know what they know. God only knows what they do not know. Obtain a second and third opinion. Research solutions to your problem or approaches to achieving your goal. As long as your goal or situation is important to you, continue your search. Why not? What do you have to lose? However, what do you have to gain by finding a solution?

I also encourage you, though, to search *rationally*. The irrational pursuit of a goal or solution leads to a person forsaking other goals and important concerns. Keep in mind that hope does not require facts. We "hope" when we do not have facts. When we *know* that there is a solution to our problem, we do not need to hope. So a person is always free to hope that their situation will improve, regardless of the situation.

(24) Too Much/Too Little Problem

People often relate their or others' attributes or behavior to a goal without realizing it. Common examples of this include

I'm too fat!	I'm too skinny!
I'm too short!	I'm too lazy!
I'm too ugly!	I'm too dumb!
I drink too much!	I eat too much!
He sleeps too much!	She swears too much!

A very appropriate and relevant question to ask yourself or others in response to such statements is, "For what?" In other words, "What are you too fat for?" The word *too* in this case suggests "an excessive amount of." Therefore, the word *too* suggests that it is in relation to something. So if I say that I am "too fat," I am implying that I will not be able to achieve a goal as the result of how much fat I have.

If someone weighing seven hundred pounds were to say to you, "I am too fat," you might agree with him. However, this statement suggests that his size necessarily would keep him from achieving a goal. This underlying assumption often leads people to avoid pursuing a goal. The following example illustrates this point:

> Client: (Female in her late thirties who weighs four hundred pounds) "I am too fat."
>
> Me: "Too fat for what?"
>
> Client: "I'm not sure what you mean."
>
> Me: "You said that you are too fat. When people say that, they are implying that their size necessarily is a problem for them— that it is keeping them from achieving a goal. So I'm wondering what you are too fat for. How is being your size a problem?"
>
> Client: "I'll never get a boyfriend and get married. Who would want someone this fat?"
>
> Me: "Okay. Well, I won't deny the fact that in our society the thinner a person is, to a certain point, the more attractive they tend to be seen by more people. With that said, what you are saying is that it is impossible for you to attract a mate and get married because of your size. Now, do you know of anyone who is at least your size who has attracted a mate and has gotten married?"
>
> Client: "Actually, I know of three women who are at least my size that are married."
>
> Me: "Okay. Well, if you are, using your words, too fat to get married, why were they not too fat? How did these women manage to meet their husbands and to get married?"

Client: "They all three met their husbands at social events."

Me: "Do you go to social events or gatherings?"

Client: "No. I go to work then spend the rest of the evening at home with my parents."

Me: "So one possible explanation as to why you are not married like they are is that you have not placed yourself in a position for men to get to know you. Your assumption that they necessarily would not like you because of your size has kept you away from them."

Client: "I think that I see what you mean."

Me: "Now, I'm not suggesting that you not work at losing weight if that is what you want to do. It probably would increase your chances of attracting a mate. We just disputed the assumption that you *have to* lose weight to attract a mate."

This mental mistake is related to the mistake of "being upset about the idea of something." Many people believe that being four hundred pounds *itself* is a problem.

Remember that we discussed the concept of a "practical problem" earlier in this book. A practical problem is the result of something standing in the way of our achieving a goal. Therefore, one must have a goal to have a practical problem. If being four hundred pounds is a practical problem, the question "for what?" helps us to determine the goal that being that size might affect. It also helps us to decide whether it actually does present an obstacle to achieving that goal.

I encourage you to challenge any underlying assumptions that you might have that the phrases "too much" or "not enough" suggest by first asking, "for what?"

(25) Ambivalent Beliefs

Ambivalent beliefs are beliefs that a person believes just strongly enough to distress themselves over *not* acting on them, but not strongly enough *to* act on them. They usually are moralistic, but need not be.

Many people have an ambivalent belief regarding premarital sex. They believe that premarital sex is wrong. However, they believe that it is wrong just strongly enough to feel guilty after having premarital sex, but not strongly enough to keep themselves from having it. This "being on the fence" approach does not work. It sets up a person for failure.

This is one of those rare situations when I suggest all-or-none thinking. Either think that premarital sex is wrong and, therefore, learn how to stop having it, or give up the belief and have it. Of course, it is important for a person also to consider whether (in this example) premarital sex is *rational*, independent of whether or not it is "wrong."

If you do things repeatedly that you later regret, you might have ambivalent beliefs associated with those behaviors. If so, discover what those beliefs are and then apply the rational question to them. Relate those beliefs to your goals and determine how important it is either to act on them or to give them up.

(26) Correlation Equals Causation

When two things occur at the same time (correlation), sometimes people assume that one thing caused the other (causation). For example, before learning the Emotional ABCs, you might have come to this conclusion at times: If someone said something to you and you were upset in response, you may have concluded that what the person said caused you to be upset. It *seemed* that way because what they said and how you felt happened at virtually the same time.

Just because two things occur concurrently does not mean that one causes the other. For example:

> If "A" and "B" happen at the same time:
>
> "A" could have caused "B"
>
> "B" could have caused "A"
>
> "C" could have caused both "A" and "B"

Did you know that there is a positive correlation between intelligence, knowledge, and height, so that the taller a person is, the more intelligent and knowledgeable he or she tends to be? Does this mean that being tall *causes* a person to be more intelligent and knowledgeable, or does it mean that being more intelligent and knowledgeable *causes* a person to be taller? Actually, there is a third variable to consider. We begin life shorter and grow taller as we age. We also begin life less intelligent and knowledgeable and grow more so as we age. Therefore, as we age, we grow taller and become more intelligent and knowledgeable.

An example of the "correlation equals causation" mental mistake is "magical worry," which was discussed earlier in this chapter. Remember that with magical worry, people notice that usually after they worry, the undesirable outcome does not occur. After a while, the causal relationship is established, "If I worry about it, it will not happen." What is not realized is that a third factor caused the event *not* to happen. Another example of the "correlation equals causation" mental mistake is the mental mistake of personalization and blame. If a person has a stroke after being upset in reaction to something that I say, it would *seem* as though (1) I caused his distressed feelings, (2) the upset feelings caused his stroke, and therefore, (3) I caused his stroke.

One way to avoid making this mental mistake is to become knowledgeable of the subject matter at hand. Do some research into the subject. Ask questions such as, "What are other possible explanations?"

Concluding Remarks About the Common Mental Mistakes

I encourage you to become very familiar with the common mental mistakes so that you can recognize if you make them. These mental mistakes have become for me what some singing on the Fox television show *American Idol* is to my wife (we love that show, by the way). My wife has a degree in music education, and she specialized in voice. When she hears someone sing off-key (as they often do on *American Idol*), it hurts her ears. When I hear shoulds, musts, and have-tos, it hurts my ears! That is exactly what we want for these mistakes to be for us—noise.

Common Emotional Problems and the Common Mental Mistakes

While any of the Common Mental Mistakes can lead to the following feelings, those listed with each emotion are the most common culprits.

<u>Anger</u>

    Irrational Should Statements (Directed Outward)
    Confusing Needs with Wants
    Can't Stand-itis
    Catastrophizing
    Blame
    Confusing "Choosing to" with "Having to"/"Force" with "Choice"

<u>Guilt</u>

    Irrational Should Statements (Directed Inward)
    Confusing Needs with Wants
    Catastrophizing
    Personalization

<u>Depression</u>

    Irrational Hopelessness/Helplessness
    Confusing Needs with Wants
    Catastrophizing

<u>Anxiety</u>

    Confusing Needs with Wants
    Confusing Possibility with Probability
    Magical Worry
    Can't Stand-itis
    Catastrophizing

Chapter 5 Summary

1. There are at least twenty-six common mental mistakes that lead people to upset themselves.

2. These mental mistakes lead people to misperceive themselves and the world around them.

3. Understanding these mental mistakes helps a person to more accurately determine whether his or her thinking is based on fact.

4. While each mental mistake can cause emotional distress, some mental mistakes are associated with certain emotions, such as depression, anxiety, and anger.

6

Ideas that Cause Misery

Rid Yourself of These Mistaken Beliefs

Rational Living Therapy is heavily influenced by the work of Dr. Albert Ellis, the grandfather of cognitive-behavioral therapy and originator of Rational Emotive Behavior Therapy. Dr. Ellis (2006) identified common shoulds and musts that significantly distress people. He organized these shoulds into three main categories. I now will describe each that Dr. Ellis identified, as well as others that I have identified, and provide my rational suggestions for overcoming these mistaken beliefs.

I. "I must do well and win the approval of others or else I am no good."

Sub-beliefs

1. "I must have love and approval from everybody."

I am very thankful that this belief is not correct because having the love and approval of *everyone* is a very difficult, if not impossible, goal to achieve. Even Jesus Christ, considered by Christians to be the son of God, did not have the love and approval of everyone!

As a matter of fact, I maintain that if everyone likes and approves of you, you do not know very many people!

Related beliefs are, "I need someone to love me" and "I must not do anything that would cause others to think less of me." While most people do view love and approval as dire needs, they are, at best, wants and preferences.

At times, there certainly are practical reasons for seeking approval from others. For example, I spend a great deal of time conducting continuing education seminars for mental health professionals. Since I am paid on a percentage basis, the more people that attend my seminars, the greater my income. It is important for me, from a financial standpoint, to have enough mental health professionals who approve of my seminars actually attend them so that I can achieve my financial goals. However, I do not need *everyone* who attends to like them—only enough in relation to my financial goals. That is why I do consider attendees' feedback. After conducting seminars for over fifteen years, I do not know if I have ever conducted a seminar that was approved by everyone who attended. Invariably, someone who attends will have bad taste!

Therefore, it is important to replace this "must" with

> *"I prefer to have love and approval from most people,*
> *but I in no way must have it."*

2. I must be competent and successful.

To be successful at achieving a goal, one needs to possess adequate skills. However, most people have the mistaken belief that they must be competent at *something* and generally successful. They believe that they must have an important skill or talent, and when they do not, they treat this situation as if it were a catastrophe.

If the motivation for this belief is to gain love and approval, I recommend asking oneself, "Do I really want to associate with people who love me only because of my skill or success? What will happen if I am no longer successful?" Keep in mind that we all run the risk of losing our skills at some point, whether due to illness, injury, or the aging process.

Therefore, replace this "must" with

> *"I prefer to be competent and successful, but I do not need to be.*
> *If people do not like me because I am not successful, forget them!"*

3. I must successfully avoid unpleasant or undesirable situations.

Who would not *want* to avoid personally unpleasant or undesirable situations? I just returned from my cardiologist's office where I had a stress test and cardiac imaging. This was not a particularly pleasant activity, but one that is important for me to help me to achieve my goal of living a long, healthy life.

A related belief is, "Unpleasant and undesirable situations upset me. I cannot control my emotions in difficult situations." You remember from chapter 1 (The Good News: Our Emotional ABCs) that this belief is complete nonsense. First, there is no such thing as an *objectively* unpleasant or undesirable situation, only *personally* unpleasant ones. Second, situations never upset us; we upset ourselves because we think upsetting thoughts *and believe every word of them*.

Therefore, replace this "must" with

"I prefer to avoid personally unpleasant situations,
but sometimes it is important for me to face them!"

4. I must think, feel, and act the same as I always have.

The basic idea with this belief is that one's past has such a strong influence on a person that it is impossible to change. However, there is no evidence whatsoever that behavior, emotions, and thoughts cannot change. One's past only represents his or her learning and experience. This is not to suggest, however, that a person cannot *unlearn* what he or she has learned in the past. This book is all about unlearning and learning anew.

Therefore, replace this "must" with

"It does not matter how I came to have my problems.
What matters is discovering what I can do about them now!
Regardless of what has happened in my past, I can
change the way I feel and act!"

5. I must find order, certainty, and predictability in life.

This belief usually is the result of a low confidence level in relation to being able to handle problematic situations as they come. Everyone *wants* to have order and predictability. It is what helps us to be effective in our daily lives. However, believing that one must have certainty to function is mistaken, especially given the fact that there is no way to guarantee *any* outcome. An *assumption* of safety and stability (based on experience) makes rational sense. In the absence of any evidence that conditions will change, one could continue to make this assumption. However, an insistence on certainty often will make it difficult to achieve one's goals.

For example, when selecting a marital partner, most people base their decision on a prediction, "This person will be with me, love me, and care about me for the rest of our lives." These criteria make rational sense in relation to selecting a partner for life. However, it is problematic to believe that one must have absolute certainty that an intended spouse will meet these criteria. *Every* marriage has the potential for failure. *No* job is absolutely secure. *Every* college student runs the risk of selecting a career that years later they dislike.

The key is to develop confidence that you can handle problems as they come—that if something that you were counting on does not work out, you will find a solution to the problem. Also develop the attitude that it would not be the end of you if you were to never find a solution. It would only be unfortunate.

Therefore, replace this "must" with

"I prefer stability and some degree of predictability in my life,
but I do not need it!
If something in my life does not work out,
I will seek a solution to the problem.
If there is no solution, too damn bad!
No amount of misery will change that fact!"

6. I must depend on other people because I can't depend on myself.

In chapter 5 (The Common Mental Mistakes) I described the difference between relying and depending. For a reminder, please refer to chapter 5.

7. I must understand the secrets of the universe.

How did the universe come to exist? How did God come into existence? Why am I here? These are questions that have been with human beings for centuries. Most people find them to be quite interesting questions. However, some believe that they cannot be happy unless they have the answers. One's happiness does not depend on discovering the answers to these questions, and that is a good thing. Some questions about the universe may never be answered with accuracy. Some answers seem to be beyond human comprehension. For example, when asked, "How did *God* come to be?" many theologians respond by saying, "God always was. In heaven, there is no beginning or ending." This is a difficult concept for most humans to grasp.

While these questions are interesting, it is important to accept the difficulty in answering them and to realize that one's life does not depend on it. There is nothing about our daily living or life goals that requires discovering the secrets of the universe.

Therefore, replace this "must" with

"It would be nice to know the secrets of the universe to satisfy my curiosity, but none of my goals depends on acquiring this knowledge."

8. I must rate myself as either "good" and "worthy" or "bad" and "worthless."

A central aspect of Rational Living Therapy (and most cognitive-behavioral therapies) is the emphasis on the importance of separating *person* from behavior, thoughts, and feelings. In other words, we are not what we do, what we think, or how we feel. We are *human beings* who do, think, and feel. Rational Living Therapy also emphasizes that it is foolish to rate oneself as good or bad for several reasons.

First, the ratings of "good" or "bad" are global, meaning that they are an overall rating—"I am *totally* good or bad." Second, this rating game leads a person to rate himself or herself based on thoughts, feelings, and behavior. If a person accomplishes something outstanding, then he or she is "good." If a person fails at something, then he or she is "bad."

There might be reasons at times to rate behaviors. Michael Jordan was very good at playing basketball, much better than most other professional basketball players. However, that fact does not make *him* good and *them* bad.

Finally, rating yourself in terms of how good you are at being a person is irrational. Human beings cannot be anything other than human beings. We cannot be a plant, dog, chair, or car. Therefore, we need not *do* anything to be human. To say, "He is a good person" is to say he is good at being a person. Everyone is good at being a person because it is impossible to be anything else! "He is a person who tends to do good things" more accurately describes objective reality.

It is equally foolish to rate people in terms of how *worthy* they are. Since we are all the same, human beings, we all have the same worth. As a result, human worth is largely irrelevant. But why do people want to think that they have worth? Because they think that having worth entitles them to something. Obviously, though, the vague concept of human worth is not enough. If a person were to think that he is entitled to a pay raise because he has human worth, he would have to rely on his boss agreeing with that philosophical point of view. However, the boss does not care about the employee's human worth. He is interested in the worth of the employee's *performance*.

Therefore, replace this "must" with

> *"I am a human being who thinks, feels, and behaves.*
> *I refuse to rate myself as being "good" or "bad," and, instead,*
> *I will rate my behavior in relation to my goals."*

9. I must never feel depressed, anxious, or enraged.

In addition to feeling upset about a situation, many people end up feeling upset about the fact that they are upset! Dr. Albert Ellis (2002) called this "symptom stress." Examples of symptoms stress include

- Being depressed about being depressed,
- Being anxious about being depressed,
- Being depressed about being anxious,
- Being anxious about being anxious,
- Being afraid that you are going insane,
- Being afraid that you are going to have a nervous breakdown,
- Being afraid that you are losing your mind,
- Being afraid that you will need to be hospitalized,
- Being afraid that you will always have your problem,
- Putting yourself down for not having resolved your problem,
- Putting yourself down for being the only one with your particular problem.

There are three main reasons why Rational Living Therapists and other cognitive-behavioral therapists concern themselves with symptom stress. First, we do not have an endless supply of energy (although many of us have much more energy than we think we do). If we use a significant amount of our energy being upset about the fact that we are upset, that does not leave much energy to deal with the original reason for being upset!

Second, symptom stress can distract a person significantly. I have met many people who were so caught up with the fact that they were upset that they actually forgot the original reason they were upset!

Third, symptom stress puts undue pressure on a person, giving him or her the impression that relief must be obtained immediately. This insistence on immediate relief often leads people to engage in very irrational behavior (drinking alcohol, taking drugs, and excessive gambling) to obtain that "needed" relief.

The most common belief that causes symptom stress is, *"I can't stand how I feel!"*

When people tell me that they cannot stand feeling depressed, anxious, angry, or otherwise upset, I know that their belief is incorrect. Obviously they *can stand it* because if they could not, it would have killed them.

When I mention this fact to therapists that I train, sometimes they tell me, "Oh Aldo, that's just playing with words. When people say that they can't stand how they feel, they really do not mean that it will kill them." However, when it comes to our emotions and behavior, it is not just semantics (words), it is all semantics (Maultsby 1984).

Keep three important facts in mind. First, in relation to our emotions and behavior, the human brain is our humble servant (Maultsby 1984). It does not care what we think. It allows us to think whatever we want, whether the thought is accurate or not.

Second, the human body does not lie (if it is working properly). In other words, the human body will provide the logical response to what is thought in the brain. If a person thinks a depressing thought, the body will respond with depression. If a person thinks a fearful thought, the body will react with anxiety.

Third, there are three types of statements we make to ourselves— jokes, lies, and sincere statements. If a person is just joking or lying when making the statement, "I can't stand how I feel," that statement will not have much of an emotional effect.

However, how do we react when we have the *sincere* belief that we cannot stand how we feel? We react as if we were in a life-or-death situation, like being in a burning building. That is the reaction I see in people when they sincerely believe that they cannot stand their emotional feelings. Since the body does not lie, we know that this reaction must be the result of equating feeling upset with something that could kill the person.

Since no person has ever died as the direct result of being upset, I encourage my clients to change the statement, "I can't stand how I feel," to

*"I do not like how I have been feeling,
and since I do not like it, I am working to make myself
feel the way I want to feel.
Until then, I can stand feeling this way."*

Emotional distress is unpleasant, uncomfortable, and unfortunate, but it is something that we all can tolerate or "stand." Realizing this makes people feel much less pressure to get better and actually speeds their progress.

If you have concerns about your condition, discuss them with a mental health professional. Keep in mind that being upset about your emotional condition serves no useful purpose and actually makes it harder for you to feel better. Realize that you are in the process of learning to feel better, and through time and diligent practice, you will feel better. *Refuse* to distract yourself with unproductive thoughts about how you are feeling. Instead, work on imagining how good you will feel when you are feeling the way you want to feel. Also, realize that

- Most people are not in need of psychiatric hospitalization (and it is not the end of the world for those who do);

- No person has ever lost his or her mind;

- There is no such thing as a nervous breakdown (if there were, you would need a neurologist, not a psychiatrist!);

- People with healthy brains (the overwhelming majority of people) have control over their emotions. Because of that fact, we need not worry that we will be "stuck" uncontrollably in a depressive or anxious state;

- The reason most people fear they will always have their problem is because it *seems* that way given the fact that they do not know how to rid themselves of the problem. Just because it seems that way does not make it so;

- Most people's problems are a matter of degree, not kind. What they are experiencing is not unique or different from what everyone experiences, but it might be more severe. For example, everyone experiences depression at times, but maybe not to the degree that would require hospitalization. However, most people do not experience hallucinations (seeing or hearing things that are not actually there). When people experience hallucinations consistently, that is a problem that is different in kind from what most people experience;

- You cannot fix something if you do not know how to do so. We do not expect ourselves to know how to perform brain surgery, yet we expect ourselves to be able to counsel ourselves rationally about a particular situation before we have actually learned how. Society does not teach us how to think properly. Our parents do not teach us how to deal with situations in a rational manner (because they do not know themselves). Rational self-counseling is not taught in school. Therefore, it is highly unrealistic to expect that you would know how to make yourself feel better when you are feeling down. Actually, I wonder how people do as well as they do given what they learn growing up;

- People do not walk around with signs saying, "I suffer from severe depression," or "I abuse my children," or "I worry about everything," or "I had an abortion two years ago." Because people can act "normally" although they are quite upset "inside," it makes it seem as though no one else has your problem but you.

Therefore, replace this "must" with

"I prefer to feel at least calm or happy, but I do not need to feel that way. Emotional distress is only unpleasant and inconvenient, not terrible, horrible, or awful!"

10. I must achieve perfection with everything I do.

To know whether a person must achieve perfection with something, it is first important to define "perfection," keeping in mind that this definition will vary from goal to goal.

For example, the belief, "I must have the perfect body," leaves one wondering, "What would a perfect body look like?" What is perfect to one person is imperfect to another. The definition of perfection in relation to one's body would not work in relation to building a cabinet. The more specific the definition, the easier it will be for you to determine whether perfection was actually achieved.

However, achieving perfection is one thing. Maintaining it is quite another. Because we all are imperfect creatures, Fallible Human Beings, we have an incurable tendency to make mistakes. No matter how skilled we are at something, sooner or later we will make a mistake. Therefore, it is virtually impossible to maintain perfection for very long.

For example, during the 1998–1999 NFL football season, the Minnesota Vikings kicker, Gary Anderson, had been perfect all season long. He never missed a field goal, making thirty-nine straight. Anderson also never missed an extra point, going sixty-seven-for-sixty-seven, making him the first kicker in NFL history to go an entire season without a miss. The Vikings faced the Atlanta Falcons in the NFC championship game that year. The winner of this game would go to the Super Bowl.

With a chance to win the game in overtime, Anderson missed a relatively easy thirty-eight-yard field goal. "There are no words to describe how I feel," Anderson said after Atlanta beat Minnesota 30–27 in overtime in the NFC championship game. "Six inches one way or another makes a difference," said Anderson. That day, Gary Anderson proved that he indeed is human. As a Vikings fan, I wish that he had confirmed that fact *after* the game, but that is the way it goes.

While perfection (however it is defined) might be viewed as desirable, it rarely is required to achieve a goal. This is wonderful given the fact that we cannot maintain perfection for very long. If you believe that something in your life must be perfect, ask yourself, "What are the *actual* consequences of not achieving or maintaining perfection?" In most situations, what is required to achieve a goal is not perfect but adequate performance.

There are advantages to perfectionism. Perfectionism will lead to higher standards, which sometimes will lead to a better outcome. Most often, though, perfectionism causes a great deal of anxiety, which then interferes with achieving a goal. Because of the pressure a person puts on himself or herself, perfectionism often creates the opposite outcome.

Therefore, replace this "must" with

"I like, prefer, and sometimes enjoy something turning out perfectly. However, in no way do I need to achieve perfection. Thank goodness! Even if I do achieve perfection, that will only last so long. Rarely do goals require perfection, just adequacy!"

11. If a loved one dies, I shouldn't ever feel happy again.

The most common reason for this belief is the underlying assumption that misery over the loss of a loved one signifies love. Therefore, it is assumed that the more miserable a person is at the passing of a loved one, the more the person must love the person who has died. Conversely, if the person stops making himself miserable over the loss, it is believed that he has stopped loving the deceased.

This belief is very common in Western cultures. The fact that it is common does not make it accurate—far from it. It is a belief that was completely made-up. The only thing that misery proves is that a person is making himself miserable over the loss. A person can more calmly accept the loss of a loved one and love that person just the same.

Anyone can come to the conclusion that no amount of misery will bring the deceased back, regret that the person is gone, and feel at worst sad when thinking about the loss. This approach in no way diminishes a person's love for the deceased. It is not as though the person would not continue to be willing to give her right arm to have the loved one back in her life. It simply is facing facts.

Therefore, you can laugh at a joke, enjoy a movie, look forward to the future, and still very much love the person you have lost. Refusing to do so will not make the loved one suddenly appear. The loved one most likely does not benefit from your misery. If the loved one is somehow aware of your misery, it is unlikely that he or she wants you to feel that way.

Therefore, replace this "should" with

"Whoever decided that a person must not be happy ever again after a loved one dies must not have been too interested in happiness. The only thing that misery proves is that a person is making himself or herself miserable. It in no way proves love. Granted, if I did not love the person, I probably would not be upset about his or her passing. It would not matter to me. However, I can love that person and find happiness in life at the same time. My brain allows it, and that is what I am deciding to do now."

II. Other people must do "the right thing" or else they are no good and deserve to be punished.

Sub-beliefs

1. Everybody should treat everyone else (especially me) in a fair and considerate manner.

In chapter 5 (The Common Mental Mistakes) I presented information on the irrational use of the word *should*. People often convert strong preferences into "shoulds." They then use those shoulds magically—"Because I want people to treat me fairly, they should." "Because it is morally right and fair for people to treat each other in a considerate way, they should." If all it took for people to treat each other in a considerate manner was for people to hold such beliefs, there would be very little conflict in this world. Obviously, though, the world does not conform to our mere ideas of right and wrong or to our desires. Just because we treat others kindly does not mean that they will reciprocate.

Related beliefs include, "If people act unfairly or inconsiderately, they deserve to be punished." The first problem with this belief is that "fairness" and "consideration" are a matter of opinion. As a result, others are free to view their treatment of us as being fair and considerate. Who is correct? Second, since such terms can be defined however a person chooses, people are free to view our treatment of them as being inconsiderate. Therefore, if we believe that people should be punished for inconsiderate and unfair behavior, that some natural or supernatural force should intervene to dish out the punishment, then we had better be prepared to be punished ourselves.

Therefore, replace this "must" with

"There is no law of the universe that entitles me to fair and considerate treatment from others so that I will receive it 100 percent of the time. I prefer to receive such treatment, and I will encourage others to treat me that way. I will start with myself by treating people the way I would like to be treated. That approach will not guarantee that they will treat me

well, but it might increase the chances that they will. If not, I will be okay."

2. Other people must not act incompetently or unwisely.

Related beliefs include, "If they act incompetently or unwisely, they are worthless idiots." "If they act incompetently or unwisely, they should be ashamed of themselves." "If they act incompetently or unwisely, they should expect none of the good things in life."

This belief leads to intolerance of the fallibility of human beings. We all are Fallible Human Beings (FHBs). As a result, every one of us will act "incompetently" or "unwisely" at times. No matter how expert you are at rational self-counseling, you will counsel yourself *irrationally* at times.

Expecting perfection from others leads us to be shocked and surprised when they prove that they are not perfect. Expecting imperfection leads us to be more rationally tolerant of people's incompetence.

Developing empathy (understanding) for others can be helpful for them and for us. Each of us has shortcomings. We have our strengths and weaknesses. We all have problems at times. We all have bad days.

As a psychotherapist, I have heard my clients express many fears, concerns, and problems. Practicing psychotherapy really opens one's eyes to how much people struggle at times. For example, *many* people have a fear of driving. As a result, when they do drive, they often maneuver their vehicle very slowly. Therefore, whenever I am driving around town and I get behind someone driving much more slowly than I wish they would, I remind myself of the possibility that the driver might be afraid, or maybe the person is elderly and not able to see well. It is not likely that they are driving slowly just to inconvenience me.

Therefore, replace this "must" with

"We all are Fallible Human Beings. Therefore, I refuse to demand perfection and complete competence from others. Just as I would hope that they would have understanding for my imperfections, I will work at developing understanding and rational tolerance of others' imperfections."

3. Talented people must use their talent.

Related beliefs include, "Everyone must reach their potential" and "People who do not live up to their potential have little or no value as human beings."

Given the fact that "potential" is a vague concept, how does a person ever really know if he or she has reached it? A young man might fulfill his potential to be an NFL professional football player and maybe even be inducted into the Professional Football Hall of Fame. Despite that fact, one could make the case that he had the potential to play five more years or to score fifty more touchdowns. Does the fact that he did not pursue those additional achievements negate his accomplishments? Of course not!

There is no objective evidence that a person must fulfill his or her potential in any area of life. Most people seek happiness and satisfaction. That is what seems to matter most. Sometimes attempting to fulfill one's potential leads to *un*happiness and *dis*satisfaction because a person is not pursuing happiness but rather the satisfaction of a societal rule.

Sometimes people impose this belief on others because they are envious of their potential. Statements that reflect this philosophy include, "If I were that tall, I'd play basketball. It is stupid that he isn't" and "If I were that smart, I'd be a doctor. It is stupid that he wants to be a (*plug in the profession*) instead."

Therefore, replace this "must" with

"Who am I to say what people should and shouldn't do? It is their business how they decide to live their lives. What people decide to do with their attributes and abilities is their business. There is no requirement that a person use his or her attributes in any certain way."

4. Other people must not criticize me.

Most people prefer to be treated in a kind, considerate manner. They prefer positive feedback and tend to dislike criticism. We tend to gravitate toward people who are supportive of our efforts, and we shy away from those who are not.

People do have a right (in most places in the world) to express their opinions. That fact does not mean that we must take them seriously.

The more time that you spend around others, the greater is the chance that you will be criticized by someone. It is a part of life, and to *expect* otherwise is unrealistic.

Everyone has goals. You probably know people who seem to criticize simply for the sake of criticizing. They seem to get a great deal of pleasure contradicting and criticizing others. However, most people criticize because their desires are not being satisfied.

For example, when I conduct continuing education seminars for mental health professionals, I realize that the attendees have different goals for the day. Some attend because they want to learn as much as possible during the six-hour period. Others attend because they want to be entertained. And still others are much more interested in the continental breakfast and the continuing education certificate that they receive at the end of the day.

Since my goal for the six-hour seminar is to provide as much practical information to them as possible, those who only want to be entertained might be critical if my seminar did not appear like a Las Vegas show. Those who were interested in the breakfast and certificate might complain that the bagels were too small. When it comes time to complete their seminar evaluation form, some attendees might decide that any criticism they had (in relation to their goals) was not significant enough to write down; whereas, others cannot wait to comment on the bagels. But the fact that we provide an evaluation form gives them the right to make critical comments.

Therefore, replace this "must" with

"People have a right to express their opinions, and they often act on that right. It is unrealistic to expect them not to. However that does not mean that I need to concern myself with their opinions, or that they should be damned for expressing them. They have goals, just like I do. I will, though, take critical remarks into consideration as I might be able to learn from them."

5. You cannot trust someone again after they have violated your trust.

This belief has a couple of irrational components to it. The first is the belief that trust is all or none—that we either trust someone or we do not. In fact, there are degrees of trust. Second, we trust a person to different degrees in relation to different behaviors. For example, a wife might have a high trust level that her husband will remain faithful to her, but a low trust level that he will take out the garbage. Therefore, the labels "trustworthy" and "untrustworthy" create overgeneralizations.

A person's violation of our trust does not make us unable to regain that trust in the future. As a matter of fact, people sometimes *irrationally* maintain higher trust levels for someone despite evidence that suggests that such a level of trust is unwarranted. While most people are inclined to base their trust levels on a person's previous behavior, it is important to base your trust levels on the facts—the *current* facts, that is. People do make mistakes. People do act uncharacteristically. Most importantly, people can and do change. Obviously you believe this to some degree, or you would not be working at changing your behavior by reading this book.

I am in no way recommending that we set ourselves up for continued mistreatment. If there is no evidence that a person has changed his or her ways, then it would make no rational sense to increase our trust to the same level that we would if he or she had changed.

Fear often motivates people to refuse to take into consideration the current facts. Sometimes people are very reluctant to increase their trust level of a person's behavior because they assume that they would not be able to deal with being betrayed once again. However, the fact that a person has lived through a previous betrayal is proof that he or she could cope with it again. The fact that one can survive being betrayed does not mean that he or she must tolerate such treatment from others.

Of course, it is rational to consider the actual offense when deciding whether to give a person another chance. If someone physically assaults you to the point that you must be hospitalized, you might want to seriously consider whether it is in your best interest to reenter that situation or maintain that relationship (unless there is considerable evidence that the person has indeed changed).

Sometimes people have a mistaken belief that if a person is capable of doing something, then he or she is likely to do it. The following scenario illustrates my point:

Client: "My husband had an affair. That proves that he is capable of having an affair (and therefore likely). Other husbands have not had affairs; they are not capable of it."

Me: "Actually, every man, except those who are not married or are not interested in women or those who are not physically or mentally able, is *capable* of having an affair, myself included! Now, I know that my wife is thankful that there are different degrees of likelihood that a man will *act* on his capability based on how he thinks. Just because a man has acted on his capability does not mean that he is likely to repeat that behavior, especially if he has learned from it and has corrected his motivation for engaging in that behavior. Therefore, the fact that your husband has acted on his capability does not make him any different than any other man, except that he did act on it. That does not mean that he necessarily will have an affair again. Of course, no one can guarantee that he will not misbehave in the future. Thankfully, though, you do not need a guarantee."

Therefore, replace this "must" with

"Just because someone betrays me does not mean that I do not have a right or the ability to increase my trust of them in the future. I will base my trust level on the facts, not on fear or previous behavior."

6. If I do something good, I should be rewarded.

A related belief is, "If I treat people well, they should treat me well, too."

This belief implies that there is objectively identifiable "good" behavior and that behaving in such a manner guarantees that it will be rewarded. However, objectively identifiable "good" behavior does not exist. Behavior can be deemed by an individual or group as being "good." However, that "determination" is only an opinion. Therefore, for someone to reward you for your good behavior, they first have to view it as such.

Sometimes "good" is meant morally, as when a person does a good deed for someone. In that case, the reward often is expected from a higher power. Other times, the word *good* is synonymous with "effective" in relation to a goal. When that is the case, the reward might be expected from a boss, spouse, teacher, or parent.

Even if someone has the opinion that your behavior is good, there is no objective evidence that he or she must or should reward it. Additionally, someone else's idea of what constitutes a "reward" might be different than yours.

Also remember the magical aspect of the word *should* discussed in chapter 5. If the necessary ingredients for you to be rewarded are not present, you will not be rewarded. At that point, it is important to examine your situation to determine the necessary ingredients that are missing and to determine what can be done to correct the situation.

If you have a contractual arrangement with someone, like an employer, and agreed-upon "rewards" are not provided to you following agreed-upon "good" behavior, then you could choose to rationally assert yourself.

Therefore, replace this "must" with

"No matter how I act, there is no guarantee that I will be rewarded for it. I can ask to be rewarded, but that will not mean that I actually will. If I do not receive the reward I hope for, I am free to consider changing my behavior or seeking rewards from someone or something else."

7. If I do something wrong, I should punish myself for it.

Sometimes people do things that they later regret, and they think they somehow must be punished for what they have done. A typical guilt-inducing belief is, "Because I have committed an evil act, that makes me a rotten person who *must* suffer, who does not deserve to be happy." This belief is irrational for several reasons, so let's examine them.

First, it is important for a person to examine how much he or she *actually* is responsible for the undesirable event that has occurred. Sometimes people blame themselves for negative situations when in fact it was not their fault. Other times a person is only partially responsible.

There is no point in attributing the cause of a negative event to oneself more than actually is the case.

Second, there is no such thing as a "rotten person." There are people who do "rotten" things. While some people are more inclined than others, we all are capable of doing "rotten" things.

Third, it is a problem to believe that one *must* suffer, even if one is completely responsible for causing a very undesirable situation. If a person were to tell me that she *wanted* to suffer, I would respond by saying, "That is your business. You are entitled to suffer as much as you care to." I might point out the disadvantages of suffering, but as long as the motivation to suffer is only a "want," who am I to tell people that they are not allowed to suffer? There is a big difference, though, between *wanting* to suffer and thinking that one *must* suffer. When people believe that they must suffer, I encourage them to look at the evidence. What evidence is there that a person absolutely must suffer for committing an act that is wrong?

Sometimes people believe that they must suffer because they believe that their religion tells them to do so. When that is the case, I refer my clients to their priest, minister, or rabbi—someone who is an expert on their approach to religion to make certain that they have the facts of their religion straight. Most people, after having met with their religious leader, learn that there is no requirement that a person damn himself or herself for eternity. However, sometimes a person's religion does require endless suffering in response to committing a "sin." In those cases, I point out to the client that he or she has every right in the world to continue practicing the religion and to make himself or herself miserable accordingly. On the other hand, I emphasize that the client also has every right in the world to look into other approaches to religion to see what they have to say about forgiveness.

People also learn that they must suffer from the teachings of others. Again, where is the evidence? Many rules simply are made up and are passed down through generations as if they were based on absolute fact. Even if a person were to believe that suffering is the "right" thing to do, who decided that this idea is correct, and based on what evidence?

When a person insists on suffering to some degree for having committed a sin, I ask them, "How long must you suffer?" Any answer given to this question will be arbitrary—in other words, made-up.

Even those who kill others do not necessarily receive a life sentence, yet many people sentence themselves to a lifetime of unhappiness until they learn that they do not need to do so.

Many people believe that suffering (damning oneself) is important to avoid repeating a problem behavior. They believe that if they punish themselves enough, they will be less likely to repeat the behavior. Punishing yourself is *not* required to avoid repeating a behavior. To avoid repeating a problem behavior, it is important to have a reason to refuse to repeat the behavior, a commitment to refuse to repeat the behavior, knowledge of how to refuse to repeat the behavior (and do something else instead), and the ability to act on that knowledge.

If you have done something you are ashamed of or feel bad about, accept that fact, learn from it, refuse to do it again, and move on with your life! Why not? You are not helping anyone or anything by refusing to be happy.

Therefore, replace this irrational belief with

"There is no absolute law of the universe that applies to everyone in every situation that requires me to punish myself or to suffer for doing something that I and others might consider to be wrong. Damning myself serves no useful purpose and does not prevent me from repeating the behavior. If I do something that I later regret, I will remind myself that I am a Fallible Human Being, realize that I made a mistake, learn from that mistake, refuse to act that way again, and act on that new belief. I will also keep myself mindful of the reasons that I have for refusing to repeat that behavior."

8. People should love you no matter how you act.

Before we determine whether people *should* love you unconditionally, it is important to develop a rational understanding of love.

In Rational Living Therapy, we categorize "love" into two types, "conceptual love" and "romantic love." Conceptual love refers to loving someone based on "the idea of it"—a rule, expectation, or the position the person has in our life. Conceptual love is more likely to be unconditional than is romantic love. Examples of conceptual love are the love we have for our children, our parents, and perhaps other relatives. Most of us love our children *because* they are our children, period. They do not need to do anything for us to love them. Sometimes we begin loving them before they are born, knowing that they are on their way. However, unfortunately, we know that conceptual love is not always unconditional, such as when a parent only shows attention and affection to a child when the child performs well in school.

Romantic love is much different. Romantic love usually is not unconditional. Romantic love is actually "strong like" with *caring* usually thrown in. We meet someone and discover that we really like how this person acts, looks, treats us, and how we feel when we are around them. When we discover this very quickly, we call it "falling in love." This is the reason why we do not "fall in love" with just anyone. However, if people no longer romantically love each other, it usually is because they have changed—they are not how they were when they did really like each other.

Sometimes there is a combination of the two. For example, a man might love his wife because of the fact that she is *his* wife and because he thinks that she is terrific. This is the exception to the rule, however.

With love now being defined, that takes us to the next issue. We do not give or hand over our love to others. We treat people in certain ways, and they determine for themselves to what degree those behaviors are "loving." An excellent example of this is the punishment that parents often administer because they love their child. The child does not see it that way! When the child is older, he or she might develop a different interpretation of that behavior.

Ultimately, because people cannot hand us their love, whether or not someone loves us is irrelevant. It is how they treat us that matters. Therefore, what this belief, *"People should love you no matter how you act"* actually means is, "People should treat me the way I want to be treated, no matter how I act." How realistic is that? Not very. Someone might "love" you, but not like your behavior. They might be unwilling to tolerate it. Love does not necessarily translate into pleasurable treatment from them. Absence of love does not necessarily mean a lack of pleasurable treatment from them either.

Are you willing to treat others the way they want to be treated, no matter how they act?

Therefore, replace this irrational belief with

133

"To insist that people agree with my definition of 'love' and to show me their love by treating me the way that I want to be treated, no matter how I act, is irrational. If I want people to treat me well, I will start by treating them well. Just because I do, though, does not guarantee that they will reciprocate."

III. "Life must be easy, without discomfort or inconvenience."

Sub-beliefs

1. Things must go the way I want them to go.

This belief is contradictory. The word *must* suggests a "need." It makes no rational sense to say, "I *need* the things that I *want*." Please refer to chapter 5 (The Common Mental Mistakes) for my description of the difference between "need" and "want."

2. I must constantly worry about life's predicaments.

Please refer to chapter 5 (The Common Mental Mistakes) for my description of the mental mistake known as "magical worry."

3. I must avoid, rather than face and deal with, life's difficulties and responsibilities.

Where is it written that life will be free of difficulties? What evidence is there that one must be free of responsibilities? Instead, there is overwhelming evidence that life does present difficulties along the way for each of us.

When we were children, most of us had parents who took care of us. They dealt with life's difficulties and responsibilities for us. Usually, the older we get, the less they do for us and the more we are required to do for ourselves.

Life has its difficulties. We decide what responsibilities we are willing to accept. That fact does not mean that we *want* to have those responsibilities, but that we *decide* to accept them for some greater purpose. Once we have made that decision, it makes no rational sense to resent it or to whine about it.

We could give up our "adult" responsibilities and say, "To hell with it, I am just having fun from now on." However, there is a price to be paid for adopting that philosophy, like potential homelessness, divorce, poverty, and illness.

Therefore, replace this "must" with

"I'd rather avoid the temporary discomfort of dealing with life's difficulties and responsibilities. However, doing so would only create long-term discomfort. Life has its difficulties. That is just the way it is. Given that fact, I will work at developing better tolerance for adversity. I refuse to make life more difficult by avoiding them."

4. Justice, fairness, equality, democracy and other "right" values must prevail. I can't stand it when my values are trodden on.

The first thing to consider in relation to this irrational belief is that many definitions exist for the terms *justice, fairness, equality,* and *democracy*. Therefore, there is no definition for these terms that is *objectively* accurate. What one person views as just and fair, another might view as complete injustice.

Also consider the fact that there is no evidence that these virtues *must* prevail. However, most of us certainly prefer to live in a world where we benefit from justice and equality. As a result of this preference, we might be willing to do what is necessary to make those virtues a reality for us. Remember from our discussion in chapter 5 on irrational "should" statements that our *mere* ideas of right and wrong do not make reality conform to them. We have to *act* on them to make a difference. However, acting on them does not guarantee that our ideals will become reality.

We live in an imperfect world, and humans are imperfect creatures. Consequently, we are faced with the possibility of being on the receiving end of injustice and inequality on a daily basis. We run that risk every time we roll out of bed. This is an important fact to face.

Therefore, replace this "must" with

"I prefer to be treated in what I consider to be a fair and just manner. This is a preference and a desire, not a must or need. However, just because I do not need to be treated in an equitable manner does not mean that I have to tolerate what I consider to be mistreatment. If I believe that I am being mistreated in some way, I will calmly accept that fact and see what I can do about it."

5. I must not die prematurely.

This belief assumes an objective definition of "premature death." What does that really mean? At what age would a person die and death not be considered premature? Additionally, the word *prematurely* implies entitlement—"I am entitled to live to a certain age, and if I do not, I will have died prematurely."

Obviously, we are not guaranteed any amount of time in this world. Some people die before they are born, others die in their childhood, middle age, or in their elder years. People anger themselves when a loved one does not live as long as they wish that they would have, often believing that the deceased person was somehow "cheated." Rather than being thankful for each day spent with the person, they damn the fact that those days have come to an end, as if a contract has been violated.

Related beliefs include, "I should be able to live forever," and "It is terrible that I will one day die and no longer exist." Many religions promote the idea that we actually do live forever, just not in this world. Whether or not eternal life actually is in store for us, it does not seem as though people have much to lose by holding onto hope for an afterlife. With that being said, if nothing exists after life, how could it possibly be terrible to be dead? In that case, death is eternal sleep. When we are asleep we do not realize that we are sleeping. If death is simply "lights out," we will not know that we are dead, let alone be in a position to make ourselves miserable over that fact.

Therefore, replace this "must" with

"I am not entitled to, or guaranteed, any amount of time in this world. However, I will do better to focus on quality of life rather than quantity. I will do what I can to remain healthy so that I can have more days than I would otherwise. But those days just give me the opportunity to do

something. Dying before I have done everything that I want to do would only be unfortunate. But if death truly is "lights out," I will not even be in a position to think of it as being unfortunate. And if there is life after death, I probably will not even concern myself with what I did or did not do in this world."

6. My life must have meaning and purpose.

The perception of having a "purpose" tends to guide us. If my purpose in life is to take care of my family (however I define that), then doing so will be a top priority for me. Most of my decisions will take my family into consideration. However, sometimes people have the belief that their "purpose" was imposed upon them, maybe by others or by a "higher power." This belief sometimes leads to resentment because a person is not happy with his or her "purpose." On the other hand, sometimes this belief leads to calm acceptance—"If this is what God wants for me, then so be it."

Some people view their "purpose" as their reason for existing. Without this purpose, there is no reason to live. This unfortunate position leads people to "put all of their eggs in one basket." Why *must* a person have a grand purpose to exist? Why not just enjoy life?

Fact is, there is no objective evidence that we must have a purpose in life. We do have things that are very important to us throughout the various stages of our life. When we transition from one phase of life to another, our goals and concerns change. For example, a mother whose life revolved around her children for years might wonder what to do with her time and energy now that they all have left home. However, people often foolishly assume that they no longer have a purpose in life when such events occur. They then depress themselves over the notion that there is no reason to live. What most people do not realize is that when such "life events" occur, the actual concern is "What do I do with myself now?"

One need not have a *single* mission in life. In addition to any obligations that you decide to take on, why not have several things to look forward to? The point is, we do not need to have a grand purpose. We can decide simply to enjoy life.

Therefore, replace this "must" with

"There is no objective evidence that I must have a central or grand purpose in life. There will be times when some things will be important to me and a focus of my life, but I do not need a 'reason' to exist. I have a right to live and to be happy whether or not I am doing something that others consider to be important or valuable."

7. If I do not see a solution to my problems, one doesn't exist.

Please refer to the next chapter to learn about hopeless thinking and why it is always a case of jumping to conclusions.

8. If I have tried to achieve a goal and failed, that means that I do not have the potential to achieve it.

This belief is based on the general assumption, *"The fact that I haven't achieved my goal proves that I can't."*

People apply this belief to many different kinds of goals. However, the only thing that a lack of progress toward achieving a goal proves is that what is necessary to progress toward achieving it has not yet been done! It in no way proves a lack of potential for achieving it.

Many clients tell me, "I do not think I will ever get over being depressed, because I have tried for years to feel better, and I just have not." After asking them the methods they have used to feel better, it becomes obvious why they continue to feel miserable—their *methods would be unsuccessful for anyone!* In other words, they do not know proven, effective methods to make themselves feel better. When they begin learning rational self-counseling skills, they quickly realize that they *do* have the potential to feel happy.

Therefore, replace this irrational belief with

"Just because I haven't doesn't mean that I can't! If a goal is important to me, I will work at determining if it is humanly possible to achieve it. If so, I will see what needs to be done to achieve it, which might take some determination and persistence. Then I will act on that knowledge."

9. Life should be fair.

As I mentioned earlier in this chapter, there is no definition for the word *fair* that is *objectively* accurate. As a result, "fairness" is always a matter of opinion. What one person views as being "fair," another might view as completely unfair.

While a person is entitled to define the word *fair* however he or she chooses, if one's definition is very narrow and rigid, "life" (people, things, and situations) might have a difficult time meeting that definition. As a result, it will be pretty easy to view situations as being unfair. "Fairness" is relative. The following example illustrates this point.

Bob has a $1,000,000 house

Maria, who owns a $500,000 house, says,
"It's not fair that Bob has a $1 million house."

Al, who owns a $250,000 house, says,
"It's not fair that Maria has a $500,000 house."

Sandy, who owns a $125,000 house, says,
"It's not fair that Al has a $250,000 house."

Tom, who owns a $62,500 house, says,
"It's not fair that Sandy has a $125,000 house."

Kathy, who owns a $30,000 house, says,
"It's not fair that Tom has a $62,500 house."

Hank, who is homeless, says
"It's not fair that Kathy has a house."

Ultimately, Bob, who owns a $1,000,000 house, says
"It's not fair that I am blind and cannot even see my house."

"Life should be fair" is another belief that leads to entitlement mentality. For example, I might think that if I were to perform exceptionally well during the week, it would only be fair that my boss give me the day off on Friday. Am I entitled to this definition of fairness? Sure I am. Wish me luck, though, in finding a boss that agrees with me!

The belief that life should be fair somewhat implies that there is a controlling force of the universe that keeps things balanced, equal, and fair. If that is the case, then apparently that controlling force's definition of fairness is much different than ours at times. This is precisely why I favor the non-magical, rational use of the word *should*. We will not obtain what we want in life unless the necessary ingredients to obtain it are present. Therefore, our mere belief that something is unfair will not magically change it. Our actions might change a situation, but our mere beliefs will not. So what is "fair" is irrelevant. If we want something, we must do what is necessary to obtain it. If we currently cannot do what is necessary, we can work at developing our ability to obtain it. If it is not possible to develop the ability, *too damn bad!* It is time to want something else instead.

When I was an adolescent, I loved basketball to the point that I dreamed of being an NBA basketball star. Then something unexpected occurred. I stopped growing at five feet, seven inches in height (my mother is only five feet tall). I dreamed of dunking the basketball, but I could not even grab the net. Other guys grew to be much taller and could dunk the ball easily. Was this fair? It certainly was not to the thirteen-year-old version of me. Did fairness matter? Not a bit. If it had, either I would have become able, or they would have ceased being able to dunk the basketball. Of course, I guess it also was not fair that I was so handsome and they were not! So what did I do? I changed my goal. I started lifting weights. I competed in the sport of powerlifting, won the state championship, and set three state records. I then went on to have a son (Aldo, Jr.), who at age sixteen won the state powerlifting championship and set four state records (he just had to outdo old dad).

Therefore, replace this irrational belief with

"What is 'fair' is largely irrelevant. Ultimately, what I get out of life and what happens to me is not the result of 'fairness.' Instead, it is the result of the necessary ingredients for it to occur being present. I might not always like that fact, but that is just the way it is. If I believe that I am entitled to something, I will work at obtaining it if possible. My mere belief will not get the job done. Acting on my belief might."

10. Loneliness is a terrible thing and must be avoided at all costs.

First, let's define loneliness. Loneliness is *not* simply being alone. If that were the case, no one would ever enjoy time relaxing in solitude. "Lonely" actually means, "I am upset about being alone." This emotional distress usually is in the form of anxiety, sadness, or depression.

Remember that in chapter 5 I explained that when people label something as being "terrible," unless they are joking, what they are saying is, "This is so bad that I need it not be this way; it seems like it will be the end of me." While most (not all) people prefer to be in the company of someone most of the time, disliking the fact that you are by yourself is at worst uncomfortable, unpleasant, and inconvenient.

This belief can, and often does, lead to many irrational attempts to be in the presence of others. When people believe that loneliness must be avoided at all cost, they are willing to associate with nearly anyone and to compromise their integrity and values, which sometimes includes irrational drinking, drugging, and sexual behavior. We see this a great deal with adolescents who think that they must "fit in" with someone and will gravitate toward the group that will accept them. We also see this with adults who are lonely but know that they can have their regular social time with their "drinking buddies" at the local bar.

Many psychologists attempt to make the case that humans are social creatures and that "no man is an island." They believe that socialization is a need, like food, air, and water. What a highly irrational belief! While most people prefer social interaction, that is not the case for everyone. However, everyone needs food, air, and water. Therefore, socialization is a *strong preference* for most people. As long as it is viewed as a preference, a person might feel sad or irritated in response to being alone. When socialization is viewed as a need, a person will either feel very angry, anxious, or depressed in response to a lack of it, or they will do whatever they can to obtain it.

Therefore, replace this irrational belief with

"Just because I am alone does not mean that I must be upset about it. In the future, if I am upset about being alone, that would be unfortunate and inconvenient, but not terrible. I can stand being alone; I just do not like it most of the time. Since I can stand being alone, but do not like it, I will work at seeking companionship in a manner that is rational for me."

11. Boredom is a terrible thing and must be avoided at all costs.

As with loneliness, let's first define boredom. Boredom is *not* simply having the perception that something is dull or that there is nothing entertaining to do at the moment. If that were the case, no one would ever enjoy time simply "taking it easy." Boredom actually means, "I am upset about not being entertained at the moment." This emotional distress usually is in the form of anxiety, sadness, or depression.

Remember that in chapter 5 I explained that when people label something as being "terrible" unless they are joking, what they are saying is, "This is so bad that I need it not be this way; it seems like it will be the end of me." Obviously, no one has ever died from being bored. However, some have attempted or committed suicide because they viewed boredom as being terrible—something that they could not stand.

In my psychotherapy practice I have seen boredom at the root of many problems, especially those related to habit control—irrational drinking, drugging, eating, smoking, and gambling. People's intolerance of boredom leads them to engage in behaviors that produce some amount of excitement, regardless of the degree to which the behaviors are irrational.

Sometimes people have a more general philosophy concerning life—that *life* is too dull and boring without some help, usually in the form of a drug. They demand to be *highly entertained*, rather than, perhaps, *pleasantly entertained*. If using drugs did not come at a significant price (physical, legal, social, monetary), the use of them to make life "exciting" would not be a problem. But people often do not pay much attention to the price that they pay for the "exciting life."

Avoidance of boredom is a preference, maybe even a strong preference, for most people, but not all. Many assembly line workers, for example, seem to prefer very repetitive actions without much fluctuation. They tend to prefer the routine.

Therefore, replace this "must" with

"I prefer to have fun and interesting things to do. I enjoy entertainment. But I in no way need to be excited or entertained. If I ever am 'bored' in the future, I will remind myself that not having something exciting to do is only unfortunate and inconvenient, not terrible, horrible, or awful."

12. Everyone has to die at some point, so there is no point in taking care of your body.

This belief usually is *not* held by people who cherish living. Why do people cherish living? Because living gives them the opportunity to do things, like spend time with their family, to take care of loved ones, to enjoy favorite pastimes, and so on. Without reasons to live, life does not seem to be of much value.

Rational Living Therapy does not maintain that people "should" live as long as possible. How long you want to live is your business. However, if we have reasons to live, it makes rational sense to take care of our body to the best of our ability to increase the chances that we will live as long as our body will allow. However, without a personally significant reason to live, most people see no point in going out of their way to take care of their body (at the very least) or to *not* drink, drug, smoke, or engage in other life-shortening behaviors.

As a result, it is important for a person to assess the reasons that he or she has for living. What do you want *more* than drinking, drugging, or eating high-fat foods? What (or who) is *more important* to you in your life than those vices? Once you make that determination, taking care of your body to the best of your ability will seem like the natural choice.

Therefore, replace this irrational belief with

"Living is not a goal. Living gives us the opportunity to achieve our goals. If

I do not have goals that are particularly significant to me, I will work at developing some. While it is correct that everyone must die of something, that does not mean that it makes rational sense to speed my death in any way."

13. I should never be denied pleasure.

Most people want to maximize pleasure and minimize pain. However, *demanding* pleasure is somewhat counterproductive to actually obtaining it. It is the equivalent of saying, "I am trying really hard to sleep." Sleeping is the opposite of exerting effort. Demanding suggests necessity, and a belief that something is necessary tends to put a great deal of pressure on oneself, thus taking the fun out of it.

The belief that one is being denied pleasure implies a lack of voluntary control over whether pleasure is experienced. Pleasure, for the most part, is self-produced. In other words, if a person experiences pleasure from something, it is because that event was determined to be pleasurable—he or she likes it. As a result, a person's experiencing pleasure certainly is not completely dependent on his or her circumstances.

This is another belief that leads to entitlement mentality—"Because I want to be pleased, that makes me entitled to it. Therefore, I should be pleased, regardless of the conditions or circumstances." However, as we discussed in the previous chapter, magical, irrational "shoulds" imply that reality will conform to our mere desires or demands. Obviously, the necessary ingredients for being pleased will not magically appear simply because we want or demand them.

Therefore, replace this irrational belief with

"It is highly unlikely that I will 'be pleased' every time I want to be. There will be times when things do not work out as I would have liked. That is a fact of life. Besides, if I were pleased every time I wanted, those times that I am would not seem so special. I can hope for pleasurable experiences without demanding that I have them because I do not need to experience pleasure. Pleasure is only a want or desire."

14. If something does not come easily, then forget it.

For many people, this belief might be suggestive of a low tolerance for frustration. However, as with many topics that we have discussed so far in this book, one's definition of "easily" is important. What is considered "easy" to one person might be considered "difficult" to another.

When a goal is not important to a person, this belief is irrelevant. It is when a goal is important to him or her that this belief can interfere with achieving it.

Rational Living Therapists emphasize that about the only thing that comes easily to us is trouble. Everything else requires work and effort. The degree to which we are willing to work and to tolerate setbacks and frustrations to achieve a goal will depend on the degree to which the goal is important to us. Therefore, if a goal is not particularly important to you, you might not be very motivated to overcome obstacles to achieving it. However, if a goal is important to you, you will be willing to do what it takes to get the job done. You will stick with it.

Sometimes when people are frustrated (a practical problem occurs in relation to their goal), they respond with irritation or anger, throw up their hands, and exclaim, "I just do not care anymore." This is a coping method to attempt to deal well with giving up.

Remember, though, that you can lie to the entire world, but you cannot lie to your brain. Your brain knows whether or not you care. If you cared about it five minutes ago, why would you no longer care about it now? Of course you still care! So there is no point in trying to "bs" your brain.

While we might wish that the pursuit of all goals will proceed smoothly, it is irrational to *demand* that we never have any obstacles along the way. For most of us, the sea is not going to part so that we can cross it. It is a fact of life that obstacles will come our way. We might as well accept that fact.

Therefore, replace this irrational belief with

"Virtually nothing in life that is worth obtaining comes 'easily' to us. If a goal is important enough to me, I will tolerate setbacks and frustrations along the way and do what it takes to achieve it. Why want it if I am not willing to do what is necessary to achieve it?"

Additional Misery-Producing Thoughts

I have identified additional misery-producing thoughts that are not consistent with Ellis's three categories.

1. If people cannot see something, then it does not exist.

The mental mistake of "From Missouri-itis" is based on the attitude, "I am not going to believe it until I see it." This attitude can be (and often is) applied to many different situations.

We cannot see many things that actually do exist. Air is a good example. The fact that I cannot scientifically prove that God exists does not mean that God doesn't. Maybe our scientific methods are not so good. So just because we cannot see something does not mean that it does not exist.

On the other hand, just because you cannot see it does not mean that it does exist either. The fact that I *cannot* scientifically prove that God does not exist *does not* mean that God does. Therefore, it would not make logical sense to believe, "If you cannot see air, and it exists, God must exist because you cannot see Him either."

Those who do believe in a supreme creator usually know that their belief simply is a matter of faith. They often base their faith on an assumption—something cannot come out of nothing. That assumption is enough for them to believe that a supreme being must have created the universe.

Sometimes it is important to consider the utility of a thought—does it work for me? If the advantages to holding a belief far outweigh the disadvantages, why not believe it? Many people find comfort in believing in a higher power. They look forward to an afterlife filled with bliss. As long as their beliefs do not cause them significant difficulties, what do they have to lose if at death they discover that they were incorrect? Actually, if there is no afterlife, they will not even discover that fact!

Therefore, replace this irrational belief with

"Just because I cannot see something does not mean that it does not exist. I will keep an open mind and at least consider the possibility that it could exist. Ultimately, I will do my best to base my thinking on fact."

2. You are a victim of your childhood and past. What happens to a person affects him or her forever.

This is a very common belief that even very educated and experienced mental health professionals believe (some approaches to therapy are based on this irrational belief). Just think how silly this belief actually is. What would you say to me if I said that I am still getting wet despite the fact that it quit raining? You might ask, "How can that be if it stopped raining? You are out of the rain now?" Great question! Eventually, because it stopped raining, I would dry off. However, if I were to repeatedly throw water on myself, I would remain wet.

Our past can create our current practical problems. If I were to somehow lose an arm, that would affect any personal goals that require two arms. However, my upset over it would be maintained by *me*, not by my missing arm.

Our experiences provide an opportunity for learning. Sometimes what we learn during these experiences is helpful to us. At other times, the opposite is the case. Sometimes we learn very irrational, unhelpful thoughts through our experiences. For example, a woman who was raped might come to believe from the experience that

- "This now means that I am dirty, and no one will ever want me."

- "If no one wants me, that means I'll be lonely and miserable the rest of my life."

- "What happened to me must have been my fault. That makes me a terrible person."

- "This now means that the world is a dangerous place, and I am likely to be raped in the future."

If she had never been raped, she might not have ever developed those beliefs. However, it is *not* her past or her experience that is causing her current misery. It is what she now *thinks* about her experience that causes her misery—what it *means* to her. If it were her past that is causing her current misery, what could we do about it? Not a darn thing! We do not have a history eraser. At best, we might hope for a pill that would lessen the pain.

So we are *in no way* a victim of our past. The past is over. It is history! "It" does not affect us forever. Our thoughts about "it" are what create our emotional experience now. If we refuse to change our thoughts about it, we will continue to make ourselves miserable over it.

Therefore, replace this irrational belief with

"The past is over. It is history! There is not a darn thing that I can do about my past, except to change the way that I think about it. Today is tomorrow's yesterday. Since I want to be able to look back on at least some of my past and consider it 'good,' I will make today as good as I can. I am out of my past situation. Now it is time for me to enjoy that fact, to view aspects of my past as being unfortunate, and to focus on the present and future."

3. The best way to discover what is real is to go with what most people say.

Basing your perception of reality on the consensus of the group is a potentially dangerous strategy. A group's perception of a situation is not necessarily any more accurate than an individual's perception.

For centuries, nearly everyone in Europe thought the world was flat. If someone attempted to sail past a certain point in the ocean, people assumed that the sailor would fall off the edge of the earth. Then one man (who just happened to be Italian, like I am) proved the Europeans wrong.

The best way to gauge your perception of reality is to assess how effective you are in relation to your goals. For example, let's say you are scheduled to attend a meeting on Monday morning at 9:00 a.m. at an office on Main Street. If you show up for the meeting at the scheduled location and time, then your perception of reality was "close enough." However, if you think that the meeting is on Tuesday at 9:00 a.m. on First Street, then your perception of reality will not be "close enough," and you will miss your meeting.

It can be helpful at times to receive feedback from others to gather facts, especially when it is established that a person is particularly knowledgeable in a certain area. However, seeking a second or third opinion, especially when the issue is particularly important, can be helpful. Given the ease by which we can conduct research nowadays (particularly with the Internet), seeking a contrary opinion can be helpful as well.

Therefore, replace this irrational belief with

"The number of people who share a belief in no way validates that belief. Ultimately, it is up to me to make the best assessment of the facts that I can. The more important the issue is to me, the more time I will spend looking for the facts, rather than simply going with the consensus."

4. If I have a right to do something, then it makes sense to do it.

This attitude assumes that if we have a *right* to do something, then it makes *rational sense* for us to do it. Obviously, this is not always the case. For example, a person has the right to call his or her boss a "jerk," but that does not mean that doing so would be rational.

People *do* have a right to feel, think, or do anything they want, as long as they do not violate the rights of others. However, ask yourself, *"Is it in my best interest to feel or think the way that I do? Is my thinking correct? Does my thinking and behavior help me to achieve my goals? Does my thinking and behavior help me to feel the way that I want to feel?"*

Recently, my wife and I decided to buy a new home. In the process of doing so, we applied for pre-approval for a home mortgage to see what the banks were willing to loan to us. We were amazed at how much money they were willing to give to us for a mortgage! Immediately, we increased our standards for the home we were seeking. We found a beautiful home, and the bank was willing to loan us the money. No problem.

Then we sat down to really determine what it would take to pay the mortgage payment every month. We came to the conclusion that while it was possible to make the payment, what we would have to go through to pay that debt would be pretty excessive. Therefore, we decided against buying such a high-priced home. Did we have a right to buy it? According to the banks we did! However, it made no rational sense for us to do so.

Therefore, replace this irrational belief with

"The fact that I have a right to do something does not mean that it makes rational sense for me to do it. It is important for me to keep mindful of my goals, both short-term and long-term, and to relate my behavior to them. I will consider whether acting on my right to do something will make it difficult for me to achieve my goals"

5. I am afraid to change or succeed, therefore I had better not.

Sounds strange, doesn't it? A fear of *success*? Why would someone be afraid to succeed at something at which they want to succeed?

Usually, a fear of success is really of fear of subsequent failure. It is a concern that if one were to achieve a goal, he or she might fail to maintain that success. Sometimes it is a concern that changing will lead to a worse situation than a person has already.

Sometimes a fear of success gives others the impression that a person does not *want* to change or succeed, when in fact there is desire, but the fear of what might happen if the person were to change prevents the change.

Some common fears that I have heard include these:

- I will not know what to do with myself in the evening if I do not drink.

- I will lose my friends if I stop drinking.

- If people see me walking with a limp, they will think that something is wrong with me.

- If I start feeling happy, I am afraid that I will not be able to keep feeling that way.

- If I feel better, people might start expecting things from me.

- If I act differently, I will not really be me anymore.

- If I think that I could make it on my own, I would *have to* leave my husband, because I would be out of my mind to stay with him if I knew that I did not have to.

Many thoughts can make a person reluctant to change, even though he or she desires it. Thankfully, most often these fears are unfounded. What is feared either is not likely to happen, or a person actually could cope with it if it were to happen. If you are afraid or reluctant to change your thinking, feelings, or behavior, challenge those fears using the techniques described in this book.

Therefore, replace this irrational belief with

"A fear of change or success usually is a fear of subsequent failure. If I fear subsequent failure after achieving a goal, I will work at disputing that fear. If it turns out that the fear is based on fact, then I will work at developing other goals. However, if the fear is not grounded in fact, I will work at removing the fear and go for it!"

6. It is easier said than done.

This is one of the most self-defeating, ridiculous statements that I have ever heard! What *isn't* easier said than done? What most people really mean when they say this is that the task at hand will be (or may be) *too hard* for them to do. This perception of overwhelming difficulty quite naturally often leads them to avoid attempting to achieve the goal. We tend to run from anything that we believe to be hard or difficult.

What appears to be "hard" to do often really is not—it is simply uncomfortable. I agree with Maultsby (1975) that the only time that it makes rational sense to think of behaviors as "hard" as opposed to "easy" is when we are discussing physical behaviors, not emotional or mental behaviors (feelings or thoughts).

I am sure you would agree that it is harder (requires more energy, stamina, and effort) to carry a one-hundred-pound bag of cement fifty feet than it is to carry a fifty-pound bag the same distance. However, is it any harder, does it require any more effort, energy, or stamina to think, "I am smart" than to think, "I am dumb?" Of course not!

What makes thinking, "I am smart," appear hard to think is that it feels *uncomfortable* to think that way. It is not hard, just uncomfortable. The reason for the discomfort (cognitive-emotive dissonance) is because the new belief is contrary to what a person is accustomed to thinking.

Therefore, replace this irrational belief with

"Just about everything in life is easier to say than it is to do! Most things in life are not hard or difficult to accomplish. They might take work and effort, and it might be uncomfortable to do. However, if I have a good enough reason to do it, I will tolerate the discomfort to get the job done"

Chapter 6 Summary

1. Rational Living Therapy agrees with Dr. Albert Ellis that irrational beliefs usually fall into one of three categories.

2. The first category is, "I must do well and win the approval of others or else I am no good." This category includes beliefs that imply that social approval is a dire necessity in life and for one's self-worth.

3. The second category is, "Other people must do 'the right thing' or else they are no good and deserve to be punished." This category includes beliefs that imply that others should be damned if they mistreat you in some way or prove that they are human.

4. The third category is, "Life must be easy, without discomfort or inconvenience." This category includes beliefs that are reflective of a low tolerance for frustration and discomfort.

5. These beliefs are at the heart of many distressing underlying assumptions.

7

Developing New Rational Replacement Thoughts

Because the Human Brain Does Not Like a Vacuum

Recognizing that a thought is irrational is not enough. It is just the first step. Because the human brain does not like a vacuum, if we do not replace the old irrational thought with a new rational thought, the brain will revert to the original thought.

The rational replacement thought is an argument against the irrational thought. To argue successfully against a position, you have to know the counter position. So the more that you know *why* a thought is irrational, the easier it will be to develop a rational replacement thought.

For example, politicians often have certain beliefs that they adhere to firmly. During a political debate, if an opponent states a position that is contrary to their position, they will state their rebuttal to it. The basis of this rebuttal includes what the politician believes to be accurate. The stronger the belief, the stronger his or her response will be.

To help you develop a strong rebuttal to the old irrational thoughts, look for mental mistakes (chapter 5) and demanding or otherwise misery-producing ideas (chapter 6). Understanding the content of chapters 5 and 6 will significantly improve your ability to develop new rational thoughts.

You can include an element of stoic philosophy into any new replacement thought. Recall from chapter 3 that the essence of stoicism is that reality does not care how we emotionally react to it. Reality could not care less. So if one has a choice between having a problem and feeling miserable, or having a problem and feeling calm, it makes sense to opt for the latter.

Of course, you will then want to practice your new thoughts. Chapter 12 describes several very effective practicing techniques.

Here are some examples of irrational thoughts and rational counters to them. You will notice that there are two rational counters for each irrational thought—a "good" and an "ideal" counter. The good counter usually is easier for a person to accept, but some element of irrationality remains. The ideal counter has all elements of irrational thinking removed. The ideal counter requires more effort to become accustomed to it. However, the ideal counter will provide the best solution to your problem.

Chapter 6 has many ideal counters for the highly irrational thoughts presented. Use that chapter as a guide for developing your new rational replacement thoughts.

Irrational Thought	Good Replacement	Ideal Replacement
1. I need my wife. I can't live without her.	1. I might need someone, but I do not need my wife specifically.	1. I do not need anyone in my life, including my wife. I want her, or at least someone. However, my life is not over if I do not have her or someone else.
2. I am a bad person.	2. I am not a bad person because I do some good things.	2. I am not a bad person because there is no such thing. I might rate what I do as being bad. However, I am not what I do.
3. People think bad thoughts about me, and that's terrible.	3. I can't read people's minds to know what they think of me. I do not know what people think about me. They might not think badly of me at all.	3. It makes no difference whatsoever what people think of me. What matters is how they treat me. If they do not mistreat me, who cares what they think? If they mistreat me, I will address that with them.
4. It's not fair that I have a cholesterol problem and others do not.	4. It might be unfair, but they have problems that I do not have.	4. Fairness is irrelevant. I have a cholesterol problem whether it is fair or not. Other people's problems are irrelevant. It is important for me to focus on how to keep my cholesterol down so that I can enjoy other aspects of my life as long as I care to.
5. Life is too dull and boring without a drug to make things more lively.	5. There are other things that I could do to make life exciting that do not involve using drugs.	5. Where is the evidence that life must be so exciting that I would have to take a drug to avoid boredom? There is no evidence. I prefer to do things that I enjoy, but I in no way need to do so.

Chapter 7 Summary

1. The human brain does not like a vacuum. If a new thought does not replace an old irrational thought, a person will revert back to the old thought.

2. The rational replacement thought is an argument against the irrational thought.

3. Understanding the content of chapters 5 and 6 is very helpful when developing rational replacement thoughts.

4. You can integrate stoic philosophy into any new replacement thought.

5. There are good counters and ideal counters. It takes longer to become accustomed to ideal counters, but they are worth the effort.

8

Overcoming Depression and Hopelessness

Feel Happy and Look Forward to the Future

Special note: Although it might be tempting to read this chapter first, I encourage you to read this book from the first page forward. Many of the concepts and techniques that you will learn in the first seven chapters will help you to better understand and apply the recommendations in this chapter.

It is a good idea to get a medical exam from a physician at least once a year. If you have been feeling depressed, and especially if it seems as though you have not been reacting to any personally undesirable situations and therefore do not know why you are feeling down, I recommend that you consult your medical doctor. There are medical problems, like hypothyroidism, vitamin deficiency, and pituitary problems, as well as medications, like beta-blockers for the heart, that can create depression-like symptoms.

If you have ever had periods of extreme energy during which it seemed like you did not need to sleep for two or three days at a time, and during which you were very active and maybe did things that are uncharacteristic for you, I urge you to consult a mental health professional for psychiatric evaluation. Also, if you are in any way suicidal, I strongly urge you to consult a mental health professional. While the suggestions in this chapter can help you to overcome suicidal thinking, it is in everyone's best interest to discuss suicidal thoughts with a trained mental health professional.

It is important to note that just because a person feels depressed does *not* mean that he or she has a "chemical imbalance." *Neither the severity nor length of time of depressive symptoms experienced is necessarily an indication of a biochemical problem.* For most people, depressive symptoms are the result of an unhealthy use of a healthy brain (Maultsby, 1984). The healthy, undrugged brain was designed to make us feel very depressed when we think very depressing thoughts. Therefore, most people do not *have* depression, they unintentionally depress themselves!

If a medical doctor tells you that you have a chemical imbalance, ask him or her for evidence such as blood test results. If the physician tells you that you have a problem with your serotonin (a brain neurotransmitter) and that therefore you need an antidepressant, consider that this is only a *theoretical* cause of depression, and the physician is making an assumption. There is no practical medical test for serotonin levels.

I mention this fact because many people are told by physicians that they have a chemical imbalance. The physician makes this claim in the absence of any lab data to prove that position for a particular patient. The usual next step is to prescribe an antidepressant. While many people take antidepressants and do very well with them, there are those who do not respond well, and still others who feel and do even worse with them (Breggin, 2000). This situation then creates quite a bind for the patient. The patient was told that he or she *necessarily* has a chemical imbalance, but the medication either is not helpful or makes matters worse. This situation often leads to hopeless thinking and even more depression.

There is a huge difference between believing that taking an antidepressant is required to correct an unconfirmed chemical imbalance as opposed to taking an antidepressant to help with depressive symptoms while learning how to feel better.

When a person appears to have *no* control over his or her depressive symptoms, mental health professionals then consider the possibility of a physical problem causing those symptoms. An indication of control over symptoms can be as simple as when a person puts his mind on something pleasant he tends to feel somewhat better.

I am in no way suggesting that you not follow the advice of your physician, but you do have a right to question it.

Understanding Depression

You Cannot Be Depressed Without Having Goals

People who have depressed themselves for quite a while often get the impression that they do not have goals or that they do not care about anything. However, the fact that they are depressed *proves* that they have goals and concerns.

What does it mean for a person to be depressed? When people depress themselves, they regret the fact (or perception) that something in life is not the way they want (or need) it to be. Sometimes, though, people do not know what they want out of life. When that is the case, they usually depress themselves over not knowing what they want! Most often, though, they *do* know what they want, but because they believe that it is not attainable, they try to avoid thinking about it because it would be too frustrating to do so.

Therefore, a person cannot be depressed (unless there is a physical reason for the depressive symptoms) without having at least one goal.

People Do Not "Have Depression"—They Unintentionally Depress Themselves

Despite what psychiatry tries to get people to believe, there is not an "illness" called "depression" that a person *has* or from which they *suffer*. People do not *have* depression, they unintentionally *depress themselves*.

This is not to say that there are not biological reasons for depressive symptoms. Hypothyroidism, vitamin B_{12} deficiency, a pituitary tumor, and the use of beta-blockers can cause depressive symptoms. When that is the case, a person does not have depression, they have, for example, a thyroid problem.

This is an important point because as long as people believe that they have this thing called "depression," they will wonder how they can get rid of "it." Instead, the question is, "How do I learn how to stop depressing myself, to more calmly accept my current situation, and to make myself happy about other things?"

Depression Often Begins as Anxiety

A person is confronted with a personally undesirable situation. At first, she is uncertain whether she will be able to effectively cope with it, so she attempts to correct the situation. However, she fears the consequences of not being able to correct it; therefore, she feels anxious. If she is met with failure and starts to think hopelessly, she will begin feeling depressed as a result.

Hopelessness by Itself Cannot Cause Depression

For hopeless thinking to cause depression, one must think hopelessly about something that he or she considers to be a need. When people think hopelessly about something that they realize they only *want*, they feel sad. For example, if I were very pessimistic about my favorite team winning the championship, I might feel *sad* at that thought because I realize that their winning the championship is only a want or desire.

However, if someone were to ask me, "You know, Aldo, I have always wanted to know how to be suicidal, but no one has ever shown me how. Could you show me how?" I would say, "Okay. Well, first think that you absolutely need something, that you cannot live without it, and that you will just die if you do not have it. Then swear that you will never get it." That is an outstanding formula for suicidal depression.

Therefore, one key to overcoming depression is to recognize that what one is depressed over is a *want* and not a *need* (unless it is air, food, or water, for example). Please refer to chapter 5 for a detailed description of the difference between wants and needs.

Overcoming Hopeless Thinking

As I mentioned in the previous chapter, hopeless thinking is necessarily a case of jumping to conclusions. Hopeless thinking is based on the assumption, "I know all there is to know about this problem, and if I do not see a solution to it, one must not exist." This is a very arrogant assumption. A person does not intend to be arrogant when thinking hopelessly, but it is a very arrogant assumption.

However, no one knows all there is to know about anything. The so-called experts know what they know; God only knows what they do not know. Therefore, we *cannot* prove that there is no solution to a problem. To believe that we know a solution does not exist is to believe that we know all there is to know about the universe (at least this world). Obviously that is not the case. We can only prove that we *do not know* of a solution. Therefore, what do we have to lose by researching the problem area? Nothing. However, what do we have to gain by discovering that there is a solution to the problem? Possibly a great deal.

"Hopelessness" and "hopeless thinking" are incorrect terms for what occurs. We are *always* free to hope. As a matter of fact, I am not certain how we ever came to believe that hope requires fact. The entire purpose of hope is to deal with the absence of positive facts, as in, "I sure hope that I will be able to overcome this problem." What gets labeled hopelessness is actually *irrational pessimism*. There is no evidence that a solution does not exist, only evidence that we are not aware of one.

I have outlined fourteen steps to take to overcome consistent, hopeless thinking. These steps can be applied to hopelessness concerning any area of a person's life.

1. **Base your thinking on fact.** One key to ridding yourself of hopeless thinking is to realize that you can be wrong. By entertaining the possibility that you could be wrong about your hopelessness, you give yourself a better chance to be aware of the facts. On the other hand, if you have a tendency to think hopelessly, you probably do not

give yourself reasonable credit for what you do know. Overlooking assets and abilities helps people to think hopelessly because they do not believe that they have what it takes to take care of their problem.

2. **Give yourself a chance to see.** When we believe something strongly, we have a tendency to only see or accept information that supports our belief and to reject information that doesn't. Remember from chapter 5 that this tendency is called "mental filter," and it causes us to not recognize all of the facts. So to overcome hopelessness, it is important to allow yourself to look at, and give consideration to, all evidence, not just evidence that seems to support your pessimistic belief.

Accurately assess your assets and abilities. I have had many patients who did not realize they had the potential to achieve their goals. For example, some patients believe they are "too unattractive" to find male companionship despite the fact that they often get positively noticed in grocery stores, shopping malls, and similar public settings. If they were too unattractive to those men, they would not receive positive feedback from them.

3. **Check it out.** How do you look for the facts? Today, the acquisition of information has become relatively easy due to advancements in technology, especially the Internet. If you have Internet access, do a search with the popular search engines (Google, Yahoo, AltaVista) about the topic you are concerned with. In a positive way, Internet searches can give you an indication of how much you really do not know.

Ask experts in the field related to the topic over which you are concerned. One place to search for local experts is your telephone book. You might also find people with related knowledge at your local college or university.

Ask around and simply talk about your concern with others. You might stumble upon someone who knows something about your concern. One middle-aged professional was depressed about the fact that he had never earned his PhD and believed that obtaining it was impossible for him given the fact that he had a business and a family. How could he possibly attend class with his busy schedule? He happened to bring up his frustration with a colleague one day who informed him about regionally accredited short-residency PhD programs that would basically allow him to study at home and visit the campus for meetings only twice a year. He had never heard of such a program! It just so happened that his colleague had at one time worked for a university with that type of program.

Go to the library to see what books or journal articles have been written about the subject. Ask the librarian for help. One New Jersey couple was faced with a dilemma. Their son, suffering from severe epilepsy, was to have brain surgery to remove part of his brain. The son's physicians had told the parents that this was appropriate action to take as all other treatment options had failed. Not wanting to see their otherwise healthy son lose part of his brain, the parents searched through many medical journals at a university library until they finally discovered an article written in the early 1900s about a diet that successfully treated their son's form of epilepsy. They placed their son on the diet, and he improved significantly, thus avoiding surgery.

See if others have resolved a problem similar to yours. Ask yourself, "Is there any real reason for me to believe that they can do it, but I cannot?" If you have the same attributes that they have (related to the problem), then why could you not do just as well? Common responses include, "Well, she is smarter than I am. He has more determination than I do. She has more energy. He is better looking. " It is important to take a close look at those beliefs (possibly excuses) to determine if in fact they are accurate. If not, then go for it! They did!

4. **Get your body in good working order.** It is well established that physical health influences emotional health. Think about how well you tolerate situations when you are energetic and feeling good as opposed to when you are tired or sick. Situations are more likely to appear to be problematic when we are tired. Fatigue, whether due to a lack of sleep, poor eating habits, or an excessive workload can make it appear as though we do not have the ability to effectively handle situations. Therefore, fatigue and physical illness foster hopeless and pessimistic thinking.

Eat well, sleep well, exercise, and maintain a regular schedule as much as possible. Also, consider vitamin supplementation (consult your physician) to help your body deal with stress. For more information on vitamins and other natural health supplements that can help with stress and depression, read chapter 15 of this book. If you find that you often are tired or simply do not feel well, get a check-up from your medical doctor.

5. **Refuse to give up.** Most people stop pursuing a goal when they either (1) no longer want what they were pursuing, (2) believe they cannot achieve the goal, or (3) become tired of pursuing the goal.

If you find that you truly no longer want what you have been pursing, then it makes no rational sense to be upset about the fact that you have not obtained it. Also, be certain to challenge any ideas you might have that lead you to believe that you "should" want it.

It certainly is easy to have doubts about achieving a goal or solving a problem, particularly when you have tried many approaches and have failed. Keep in mind that *"just because you haven't, doesn't mean you can't,"* and, *"if you always do what you've always done, you'll always get what you've always gotten."* Evaluate past failures to determine if in fact your method of solving the problem or achieving the goal was sound. Apparently you thought it was, or you would not have used it (unless you knowingly were taking the "easy way out"). Do your research, which includes asking experts.

One word of caution when seeking advice from experts. Experts are not all-knowing. They only know what they know. Also, experts often follow popular wisdom. Cholesterol is a great example. Most physicians follow the popular wisdom that excessive blood levels of cholesterol lead to heart attacks. They believe that high cholesterol is very predictive of heart attacks, and that anyone who has a cholesterol level more than 200 must lower it. However, what they do not know (or will not tell you) is that one-half of all people who suffer heart attacks have a cholesterol level below 200. Also consider that cholesterol level predicts approximately 29 percent of heart attacks while low levels of vitamin E predict approximately 70 percent!

The medical community finally began releasing information recently on the heart-protective characteristics of vitamin E and that it helps to keep cholesterol from causing artery blockages. However, I personally have known this since 1989, and it has been in the literature for at least thirty years. All the more reason to keep looking and to refuse to give up. By the way, it turns out that what likely is the culprit for coronary artery disease is artery inflammation, to which high blood cholesterol can contribute. So it is helpful to reduce blood cholesterol levels, but for a reason that is different than what the medical community believed.

Make it easier on yourself to solve your problem or to achieve your goal. Many women lament over the fact that their husbands refuse to ask for directions when traveling in a new area. Why not ask someone who knows the area, rather than attempt to find your intended destination through trial and error? If you try to pound a nail into a piece of wood with a pair of pliers, you might eventually succeed, but it will take you all day. Use a hammer, and it will take you seconds. When you have the proper tools, correcting the problem is not as difficult. If you do not know which tools to use, do your research.

Finally, remember that about the only thing that comes to us easily is trouble. If your goal or problem is important to you, be willing to do what is necessary to achieve or resolve it. Otherwise, it makes no rational sense to be upset about not achieving your goal.

6. **Overcome cognitive-emotive dissonance.** Whenever we come across information that is contrary to what we are accustomed to believing, we feel a strange feeling in our abdomen. This strange feeling makes it seem as though the new information is wrong. Remember that this strange feeling is called cognitive-emotive dissonance.

The good news is that just because something "feels wrong" does not mean that it is incorrect or wrong for you. Take the metric system, for example. If Americans were to once again attempt to convert completely to the metric system, they would experience a certain amount of cognitive-emotive dissonance—it would feel wrong to them because they are accustomed to using the English/American system. However, if they were to give up learning the metric system because it felt wrong, they would give up a better, more consistent system of measurement.

Believing that you could overcome your problem might feel strange and wrong to you. But if those thoughts are factually accurate, it does not matter how it *feels*. The only way to rid yourself of cognitive-emotive dissonance is to practice your new way of thinking and behaving.

7. **Practice your new belief.** Write down your new, rational belief about your situation and read it at least once every day. If you want faster results, read it more often. Visualize yourself achieving your goal

or solving your problem and being happy about your accomplishment. Practice your new thought daily for at least one month.

Act "as if" you believe your new thought by pursuing your goal or looking for a solution to your problem.

8. **Write a list of potential benefits from thinking that there could be a solution.** Even if you do not believe that there is a solution to your problem, what benefits are there (or could there be) from *believing* that a solution *could* exist out there somewhere? One benefit is increased willingness to look for a solution. Looking for a solution might not lead to a complete resolution of the problem, but it could lead to discovering something that will improve your situation.

9. **Keep track of evidence that supports the idea that there is a solution.** When we think a certain way, we look for evidence that supports that belief. If a person believes that his life is undesirable, he can easily tell you what is wrong with it. However, he likely will have difficulty listing positive aspects of his life.

Look for evidence daily, no matter how small, that suggests that you will achieve your goal or resolve your problem.

10. **Calmly accept what you might not be able to change.** While we cannot prove that there is no solution to our problems, the possibility exists that we might not discover a solution despite our efforts. It is important to learn to calmly accept that possibility.

One approach that helps us to calmly accept situations is to remember the difference between needs and wants. Is achieving this goal or solving this problem an *absolute need* or is it a *want*? Recall that need implies a life-or-death situation. That is why when a woman believes that she needs her husband, she panics at the thought of losing him, much like a person would if they were faced with a situation where there was no oxygen. Thinking that she merely wants him would lead to disappointment and sadness if she were to lose him, but that is it. It might be a great inconvenience to lose him, but she would not die. By her realizing that she will not die, she places herself in a much better position to find happiness with someone else or in some other area of her life.

Calmly accepting your current situation will also put you in a better position to find a solution, if there is one to be found. Desperation makes it easy to overlook solutions. If you have ever frantically looked for something for hours only to find that it was in front of you all along, you know the importance of approaching situations calmly.

11. **Develop new goals and interests if you are unwilling to continue to pursue your goal.** When all else fails, develop another goal or interest. To do this, you must give up the notion that happiness can only come from achieving a particular goal. People often relate this problematic belief to love interests: "She is the only one for me." "There is no one in this world that can make me as happy." Nonsense! If a man who is interested in women were to believe this, he would be unintentionally ignoring the fact that he *has not* met every woman on earth and assessed them to come to this conclusion. Also, if he had never met the particular woman over whom he is grieving, he would likely be saying this about a different woman.

Many sports reporters at one time aspired to be professional athletes. When they discovered that they did not have the physical attributes to achieve a high level of athletic performance, they involved themselves in sports on a different level. They often continue to wish that they could be out there scoring a touchdown or dunking the basketball, but by calmly accepting their own limitations, they find happiness by capitalizing on their skills (such as writing or reporting), and applying them to sports.

The human brain does not care how we make ourselves happy. We have the potential to be happy with many things.

12. **Be aware of emotional reasoning.** Feeling depressed or tired tends to encourage pessimism. If you find that you are unusually pessimistic, you might be the victim of emotional reasoning, meaning that the only reason you are thinking pessimistically is because you are depressed about other things. If you find that when you feel better (more energetic, less depressed) you have more optimism, emotional reasoning likely was the cause of the pessimism. Refuse to take seriously any negative thought that you think when you feel tired, sick, or depressed.

13. **Do not "try" but "do."** Trying is a proven method for failure. When people say that they will "try" to do something, they are expressing doubt that they will be able to accomplish the goal. It also gives them an out—"Well, at least I tried, but it was just too hard!" "Doing" puts you in a better position to get what you want.

The statement, "Starting Monday, I am going to eat 1,000 calories per day" will produce a much better result than will the statement, "Starting Monday, I will try to eat 1,000 calories per day."

14. **Get additional help from a professional therapist.** If after working at these fourteen steps you find that you continue to think hopelessly, it is time to consider seeking help from a counselor or psychotherapist. For a referral to a certified cognitive-behavioral therapist in your area, visit http://www.nacbt.org.

Understanding and Overcoming Suicidal Thinking

Suicidal intent often is expressed by the statement, "I want to kill myself." I consider this to be the ultimate example of the confusion of a goal with the means by which to achieve a goal.

In over twenty years of meeting people who were suicidal, I have yet to meet a single person for whom the statement, "I want to kill myself" was accurate. This statement implies that a person looks forward to *committing the act* of killing himself or herself, such as: "I cannot wait to pull the trigger, swallow the pills, or jump off of the building," as if he or she wants nothing beyond committing the act.

Actually, a person who is thinking suicidally is hoping for a *consequence* of committing the act. Very common motivators for suicidal behavior include the hope for relief, revenge, and notoriety. Therefore, people do not want *to kill themselves* or *to be dead*; they want, for example, *relief.*

Now that we have the goal straight, we can use the technique known as referenting. **Referenting** is the technique of looking at the advantages and disadvantages of two or more approaches to the same goal. To use this technique properly, we must first accurately define the goal. If we assume that the goal is to kill oneself, we will assess the advantages and disadvantages of different approaches to killing oneself. That will not work. If the actual goal is relief, then we can examine the advantages and disadvantages of two or more approaches to obtaining relief, as the following graphic demonstrates.

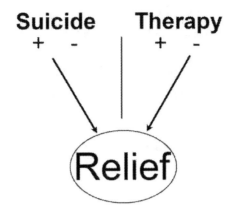

There are two distinct disadvantages to attempting to obtain relief by killing oneself. First, at best, all we can do is *assume* that relief can be obtained through suicide. I am not in a position to tell you that this is the case. I have never been able to interview someone after they successfully committed suicide for them to inform me of the result. It is understandable why a person might think that relief could be obtained through suicide, but we cannot know with any amount of certainty that relief is obtained. Also, many religions believe that the *last* thing a person obtains when they kill themselves is relief. If you follow a particular religion, what does yours say about suicide?

However, I have seen many people obtain relief with the techniques that I have described in this book. Therefore, I am in a much better position to state that a person can obtain relief through therapy or self-therapy than I am that they can obtain relief though suicide.

Second, for a person to successfully commit suicide, he or she must think that it is the thing to do up to the very last second before committing the act. If a person thinks that he or she has problems, try having the problems *along with* half of a face (because a person flinched when pulling the trigger of the gun that was in his or her mouth), or with a severely damaged liver (because a person thought that he or she took enough pills but did not think anyone would come to help), or with every bone in the body broken (because a person thought that he or she jumped off a tall enough building). While some people certainly are successful at ending their life, suicide is not the easiest thing in the world to complete successfully.

Symptom Stress

You might remember reading earlier in this book about symptom stress—being upset about being upset. Remember that while feeling depressed is unpleasant, inconvenient, and annoying for most people, it is something that everyone *can stand*. We simply do not like it, maybe very much so. There is a huge difference between believing that we cannot stand something as opposed to believing that we very much dislike it. It is the difference between thinking that your life is in danger as opposed to thinking that you are experiencing something that is unpleasant.

But what if a person were to attempt suicide in reaction to his depressive feelings? Would that not be proof that he could not stand feeling depressed? Absolutely not! His suicide attempt would only be proof that he *thought* that he could not stand how he felt.

Remind yourself of this fact if you are depressed. Repeat to yourself, "I can stand it; I just do not like feeling this way. That is why I am working at feeling and doing better. Until then, though, I will remind myself that I can stand feeling depressed."

Inaction Is Depression's Best Friend

It is very easy to hold on to a belief if we do nothing to gather new, contrary information. For example, if a man spends day after day on the couch depressed over the fact that his girlfriend ended their relationship, he makes it difficult for himself to learn that he could be happy with someone else, or that he could be happy doing something else with his time.

Inaction often is the result of people having very little to look forward to. In Rational Living Therapy, we recommend that people make themselves happy on purpose—to have a method to their happiness. Part of that strategy includes **Activity Scheduling**. Schedule something every day to which you can look forward—something that you really enjoy so that you wake up in the morning and say, "Wow, I am I glad it is Tuesday, because on Tuesdays I do ..."

It is very important to plan at least one week ahead. Many people attempt to decide when they rise in the morning what to do with their day. However, they often discover that it is time to once again go to bed and that they never did determine what to do with the day.

You might not be entirely certain what to schedule each day. A great place to start is with activities that you once found entertaining. It is also helpful to examine what others seem to find entertaining and to be willing to engage in experimentation with those activities. The following form will help you with Activity Scheduling.

Fun Things I Will Do This Week!

Day of Week	Activity	Fun Prediction 1 = Just a Little 5 = A lot!	Actual Fun 1 = Just a Little 5 = A lot!
Monday			
Tuesday			
Wednesday			
Thursday			
Friday			
Saturday			
Sunday			

In the "Fun Prediction" column, rate how much fun you anticipate having from engaging in this activity. In the "Actual Fun" column, rate how much fun you actually experienced.

Also, inaction tends to produce lethargy, which then often is labeled depression. A great way to overcome this lethargy is to become physically active through an exercise program. Now, before you roll your eyes and let out a sigh, hear me (or maybe read me) out. What I mean by exercise is any kind of healthy physical activity that keeps you in motion for at least fifteen consecutive minutes a day and that raises your heart rate. Research (Dunn et al., 2005; Babyak et al., 2000) has shown that exercise improves the symptoms of depression.

Exercise can be very beneficial to improving one's emotional state in several different ways. First, exercise helps your body release several different hormones and other chemicals that produce a sense of energy and well-being. Conversely, *not* exercising or being otherwise physically active can produce the opposite effect — lethargy, apathy, and depression. We all have had days that we spent watching television or "lying around." We often feel much greater fatigue during those days than we do during days in which we engaged in physical activity.

Second, exercise helps "burn away" the chemical byproducts of anxiety and depression that would otherwise take their toll on our organs. Third, when we make exercise fun, it gives us something to which we can look forward. I recommend light daily exercise with your physician's approval. Ask your doctor to recommend an exercise program that is best for you. Find an exercise partner or two and begin a weight-training program or join an aerobics class or simply go for a leisurely stroll. It is a great way to socialize and to take care of your body and mind at the same time.

Blumenthal (1999) and his colleagues surprised many people when they demonstrated that regular exercise is as effective as antidepressant medications for patients who are depressed. The researchers studied one hundred fifty-six older adults diagnosed with major depression, assigning them to receive the antidepressant Zoloft, thirty minutes of exercise three times a week, or both. According to Blumenthal,

> "Our findings suggest that a modest exercise program is an effective, robust treatment for patients with major depression who are positively inclined to participate in it. The benefits

of exercise are likely to endure particularly among those who adopt it as a regular, ongoing life activity."

Blumenthal (2000) and his colleagues continued to follow the same subjects for six additional months and found that the group that exercised, but did not receive Zoloft, felt better than either of the other two groups.

Exercise (especially weight training) can also enhance confidence. The increase in strength and stamina often results in a greater perception of being able to handle problems as they come our way.

Change Your Physiology and Act "As If"

The longer a person remains in a physical state or position, the more likely it will be that his or her mood will continue along with it. For example, if I am in a "bad mood" when I board an airplane in New York, since I likely would not move around much on the flight, I probably will continue to be in a bad mood when I land in Los Angeles. This phenomenon, known as "mind lock," makes it more difficult for us to think differently.

When a person has been depressed for a while, he or she will act as if that is the case by shuffling when walking, by speaking softly and monotonously, and by consistently having a frown on his or her face. If this has been the case for you, I encourage you to change your physiology by walking erect with a bounce in your step, speaking more boldly and confidently, and putting a warm, soft smile on your face, even if you have to prop up the corners of your mouth with your fingers.

Research has shown that changes in facial expressions create changes in the brain. I encourage you to *act as if you are happy* every day until you are in the habit of acting this way. Also keep in mind that you do not need to think that you have anything to be happy about to *act like you are happy*. The more that you act "as if," the more likely your brain's chemistry will change, thus giving you a greater opportunity to think, feel, and act differently.

I want to emphasize that the "acting as if" technique is *not* just a nice-sounding therapy technique. It really does work! What do you have to lose by using it?

Pick a Role Model

One way to act "as if" is to pick a role model, someone who seems to be consistently happy and acts that way. Emulate that person. Pattern your behavior after his or hers. *Be* that person.

Visualize Yourself Feeling and Acting Happy

Practice rational visualization as described in this book. Imagine yourself looking in the mirror and seeing a smile. Imagine yourself doing the things that you find enjoyable. It very well might feel strange to imagine yourself happy, but the more you imagine it, the sooner it will become comfortable to you. Repeated rational visualization will make happiness become a habit.

Refuse to Dwell on What Might Have Been

The past is over. It is history! There is nothing anyone can do to change it. However, remember that today is tomorrow's yesterday. So we can begin creating a better yesterday by making the most of today and tomorrow. Focus on what you *can* do now and in the future, rather than on what you did not do or have in the past.

A Script to Practice to Overcome Depression

I now realize that my thoughts cause my feelings and behaviors. Thank goodness! I now also realize that depressed feelings are the result of thinking that you absolutely need something, like you cannot live without it, and thinking that you will never get it. I now understand that the only things that I really need are those things that keep me alive—air, food, water, and the like. Everything else is a want or desire. I am entitled to my wants and desires. I just do not need them.

Depression is also the result of thinking hopelessly. Hopelessness is irrational because it assumes that a person knows all that there is to know about his or her problem. No one knows all that there is to know about anything!

Since I do want certain things in my life, I will first remind myself that they are only wants. Then I will remind myself that no matter how doubtful I might be that I will be able to obtain those things, it makes no rational sense to assume that there is no way to obtain them. Because I want these things, I will continue to look for ways to obtain them.

I will remind myself that, "just because you haven't doesn't mean you can't ... it only means you haven't!" This philosophy will help me to continue searching for a solution.

It is easy to be affected by mental filter—to pay attention only to information that supports hopeless thinking. That is why I will seek advice from people who know how to correct the problems that I have or achieve the goals I want to achieve.

Ultimately, if I never obtain what I want out of life, that would be unfortunate for me, not terrible, horrible, or awful because they are only wants, not needs. Therefore, since they are wants, I might feel sad—that is it. So I can be happy with other things if what I have wanted does not work out. My brain allows it.

Feeling depressed serves no useful purpose and, in fact, makes a person's situation worse. Therefore, I refuse to make myself depressed. Instead, I will focus my energy on finding a solution to my problems or a way to achieve my goals.

Chapter 8 Summary

1. Just because a person feels depressed does not mean that he or she has a chemical imbalance. Depressive symptoms could be the result of a medical problem or of certain medications. Therefore, it is a good idea to obtain a medical evaluation if you are depressed, especially if it appears that you are not reacting to something, like a loss.

2. Unless depressive symptoms are the result of a physical problem, a person cannot be depressed without having goals.

3. Hopeless thinking is based on the very arrogant assumption, "I know all that there is to know about this problem. If I do not see a solution to my problem, one must not exist."

4. Hopeless thinking, combined with the confusion of "need" and "want," causes depression.

5. Activity Scheduling can be very helpful in giving people a reason to wake up in the morning.

9

Overcoming Anxiety and Panic

Overcome Fears and Enjoy Life

Special note: Although it might be tempting to read this chapter first, I encourage you to read this book from the first page forward. Many of the concepts and techniques that you will learn in the first seven chapters will help you to better understand and apply the recommendations in this chapter.

If you have been feeling anxious or nervous, and especially if you do not appear to be reacting to something feared, I encourage you to seek a medical evaluation from your physician. There are several medical conditions that can be treated fairly easily that can cause anxietylike symptoms.

When anxiety symptoms are not the result of a physical problem, anxiety is caused by fear—a person perceives a threat. An accurate perception of threat helps us to be in a position to protect ourselves. For example, if I am driving on a two-lane road and I notice that a car is coming toward me in my lane, I had better view this as a threat and do what I can to avoid a head-on collision. However, when fear is the result of a mistaken perception of threat, that is when anxiety is unnecessary and counterproductive. The question is, "How do we recognize a true threat?"

One way to recognize a true threat is to deal with what is, *not* with what might be. For example, my son and I were trained in a martial art known as Bando. Occasionally, our Bando instructor (who certainly could inflict a great deal of pain on us) asked us to spar him. When he was across the room swinging his arms and legs, there was no problem for us. It was when he came within striking distance that a threat was present. Therefore, there was no point in us acting as though we were in danger until he was close enough to hit us.

I noticed when sparring the instructor that I would be very tired afterward, more so than when sparring my peers. I mentioned this to the instructor, and he said, "Well, Aldo, when we spar, you are so tight. You seem to brace yourself as if I am going to kill you." When he said this I realized that I was envisioning him doing things to me that he was not doing. While he could kill me, he was doing nothing anywhere near what it would take to do so. Therefore, it was time to take a much more relax approach to sparring him.

Chapters 4 (Rational Questions), 5 (Mental Mistakes), and 6 (Ideas That Cause Misery) will help you to recognize a true threat and, therefore, to deal with what *is* rather than what *is not*.

Regardless of the way in which anxiety is experienced (panic, phobia, obsessive-compulsive disorder, social anxiety) the following mental mistakes are responsible for these feelings and behaviors.

Confusing Needs and Wants

Recall from our discussion in chapter 5 on the mental mistakes that the confusion of "needs" and "wants" creates anxiety—a person is equating something with a life-or-death situation. The more one equates a situation with going without air, food, or water, the more anxious that person will be.

For example, if I believe that I need everyone's approval, I probably will be very anxious when giving a speech. Actually, I might avoid giving a speech altogether. However, if I realize that I *want* people to approve of me, but I certainly will not die if they do not, then I will be much more relaxed in giving my speech. Unless people are pointing guns at me ready to shoot me if they dislike what I have to say, giving a speech does not put your life in danger.

Can't Stand-itis

Recall also from our discussion in chapter 5 that can't stand-itis is an extension of the confusion of needs and wants. It is the belief that something is so bad that one need it not be, as if the situation will lead to one's death.

Ultimately, the only thing that we will not withstand will be the thing that kills us. Otherwise, we will have withstood everything that has come our way. Therefore, unless something can kill you, it is not that you cannot stand it, but rather that you do not like it. You might *very much* dislike it. But there is a huge difference between believing that you very much dislike something, as opposed to believing that you cannot stand it. There are many *tolerable inconveniences* in life, but not nearly as many things can actually kill us.

Magical Worry

Also in chapter 5 is a description of the mental mistake of "magical worry." Magical worry, or "civilized voodoo," leads people to become afraid *not* to worry. They are so rewarded for worrying (because what they worry about does not happen) that they come to the conclusion that their worry *prevents* negative events from occurring.

Worry is only mental activity, and mental activity does not prevent negative events from occurring. Therefore, worry has never protected you. It only has seemed that way! *Acting* on our mental activity might prevent negative events from occurring. Therefore, I very much recommend that we replace worry with concern and to act on that concern if it looks as if your well-being or that of your loved ones is being threatened.

Supplements to Help with Anxiety

There are several vitamins, herbs, and other natural health supplements that help to achieve a calm state. While these supplements certainly are considered safe, effective, and non-addictive, it is important to consult your physician and pharmacist prior to taking them. For more information on these supplements, read chapter 15.

Progressive Relaxation

Progressive relaxation is an outstanding technique for calming oneself and for getting into the habit of relaxing. To perform this technique, place yourself in a comfortable position, usually either seated or lying down. You need not be in a quiet place to perform this technique. To relax each body part, think about that part and then relax it. Allow that body part to grow nice and loose, limp, heavy, and relaxed—nice and heavy with relaxation. Once you are satisfied with the level of relaxation for that body part, move on to the next. Here is the recommended order for relaxation:

Eyelids
Forehead
Cheeks
Chin
Jaw Muscles
Back and Front of Neck
Arms (From shoulders to tips of fingers)
Chest
Waist
Legs (From hips to tips of toes)

Take your time with this technique so that it takes you at least fifteen minutes to go through the entire procedure. I encourage you to practice progressive relaxation at least once a day, with five times a day being even better. Repetition of this technique will enable you to relax more quickly in the future.

If you would like me to guide you through this technique, consider ordering my Rational Progressive Relaxation CD that is available at http://nacbt.americommerce.com.

Rational Visualization

People often think of visualization as simply being a nice-sounding therapy technique, but one of limited usefulness. However, we know that visualization, both rational and irrational, has powerful effects on a person's emotions and behaviors. We know that the human brain does not know the difference between an image that is produced from external stimuli and an image that is produced internally. That is why dreams seem so real to us.

Therefore, make use of that fact by intentionally imagining yourself feeling calm and relaxed as you engage in the behavior that you currently feel uncomfortable with. Recall our discussion in chapter 4 concerning classical conditioning. Pair relaxation with your visualization so that eventually the images will produce a calming effect for you. First relax yourself using a progressive relaxation technique as just described. Then imagine yourself in the feared situation. If you start to make yourself anxious, stop the visualization and return to the relaxation. Once you are relaxed, return to the visualization. Pair only relaxation with the visualization.

Select a Role Model and Act "As If"

A very helpful technique to overcome fears is to select a role model—someone who is calm and confident in the situation in which you wish to be the same. Once you have selected that person, act "as if" you are that person. Become that person. The more that you act as if you are that person, the sooner you will come to naturally, automatically feel calm in that situation.

For example, if you have a fear of public speaking (actually of being ridiculed), think about someone you know or have seen who is very good at it, someone who presents himself or herself as being very relaxed and confident when speaking in public. Then become that person when you speak. First imagine yourself acting like that person does. Next, begin public speaking and pretend that you are that person.

Be that person when you speak. After a while you likely will develop your own effective style.

Avoidance Is Fear's Best Friend

Fear loves avoidance. Avoidance makes it very easy to maintain a fear. For example, as long as a person does not get on an elevator, she does not give herself a chance to learn that it will not get stuck between floors or that she will not suffocate even if it does. Avoiding a feared situation then reinforces the fear. In other words, she would not avoid it if it were not dangerous. Also, by refusing to get on the elevator, her anxiety lessens. The decrease in anxiety is a reward for avoiding the elevator, and that reward encourages her to avoid the elevator in the future. Therefore, to overcome an irrational fear, it is important to be willing to face the feared situation, which takes us to the next issue.

You Do Not Have to Feel Comfortable with Doing Something to Do It

Most people believe that they must feel comfortable with doing something to do it. They make statements like, "I cannot get on this elevator unless I feel comfortable doing so." Unfortunately, many mental health professionals fall for the same belief. To get on an elevator, one must not feel *comfortable*—one must simply get on it.

This is a very important insight, because while it makes sense to prepare oneself to feel comfortable, some people will not feel as comfortable as they care to regardless of the amount of preparation. Why? Because they have a bad case of "From Missouri-itis." Missouri is known as the "show me" state. People in Missouri have a reputation for not believing something until they see it. So if a person with a bad case of "From Missouri-itis" never gets on the elevator, when will he or she believe it? Possibly never.

Overcoming "From Missouri-itis"

There are two ways to overcome "From Missouri-itis." The first is to understand that you need not experience something directly to realize that it exists. The person who is phobic of riding elevators does not need to personally ride one to see that they are safe. He or she could observe others riding them to assess their safety.

Another way to overcome "From Missouri-itis" is to face the fear—to engage in the feared behavior or to enter the feared situation. There are excellent techniques to help a person face their fear. One such technique is known as **systematic desensitization**, and it is discussed in chapter 12. Systematic desensitization helps a person face their fear gradually. Another technique is called **exposure and response prevention**. I will share that technique with you as it applies to obsessive-compulsive problems.

While not necessary, enlisting the help of family members or friends to take you by the hand and to face the fear can be helpful. Most loving family members and friends will be willing to help. If they are not, it could be that they simply do not understand what a person goes through when they have a significant fear. Explain it to them. Help them to understand.

Now let's discuss how people experience anxiety and what can be done to alleviate it.

Panic and Agoraphobia

Panic simply is a brief period of intense anxiety. During this time, a person might feel lightheaded, breathe heavily, have a rapid heart rate, have pressure in the chest, and experience confusion. Usually, panic appears to come on suddenly.

Panic often resembles a heart attack. Therefore, it is common for people who panic to be told that they have this problem by an emergency room physician. The person, believing that she is having a heart attack, goes to the emergency room. After medical evaluation, she is told that her heart is fine, that she experienced panic. Once we have medical data to show that the heart is healthy, we then help her to realize that the following cycle occurred.

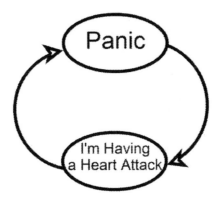

After she feels anxious, she begins to think that she is having a heart attack. Being afraid that she will die as a result, she feels more anxious, which increases the symptoms and gives her an even greater impression that she is having a heart attack. Once we have assurance from a physician that the person's heart is healthy, we stop this cycle by teaching her to remind herself, if she feels anxious, that it is *only* anxiety, not a heart attack. This reminder will help her to decrease the anxious feelings almost immediately. She then will learn how to stop panicking all together.

Fear of Panic

One of the main reason people panic is because they are scared to death to panic. Ironically, their intense fear *of panicking* makes them much more likely *to panic*. Because of this, it is important to refuse to fear panic. For most people, panic is very uncomfortable, unpleasant, and inconvenient. However, no matter how much they dislike it, they *can stand* intense anxiety. The best proof that they can stand it is that they are feeling it. If they could not stand it, it would kill them. Panic does not kill people; it is *only* uncomfortable.

This approach might sound somewhat unsympathetic. Actually, though, it is very uplifting. What I am saying to you is that if you panic, you have withstood every single panic attack, no matter how uncomfortable they have been. The best proof of this fact is that you are reading this book! *Therefore, from now on, remind yourself, maybe even forcefully, that anxiety and panic are only uncomfortable and unpleasant.*

Reflexive Thoughts and Panic

You probably recall from chapter 1 our discussion of the ABCs of emotions and reflexive thoughts. Recall that reflexive thoughts are very well-learned, very practiced thoughts. They are so practiced, so well-learned that they no longer need to be thought consciously. They are stored in the brain, ready for action. The second that the brain is reminded of the thought, it is triggered, and so is the instant emotional and behavioral response that is associated with the thought.

Panic is an excellent example of a reflexive thought in action. As far as we know, there are very few things which human beings are genetically programmed to fear. Most of what we are genetically programmed to fear is demonstrated by infants. Infants have a startle response to loud noises, for example. However, no infant that I have ever known was afraid of flying in an airplane or driving in snowy conditions or asking a person for a date. We know that a significant aspect of parenting is helping children to learn to be afraid of dangerous situations.

Therefore, panic is the result of a well-learned intense fear. The fact that it is well-learned enables a panic response to be sudden and appear to come out of nowhere. This is what gives a person the impression that they "had" a panic attack or that "it" came over them.

Panic Was Important at One Time

At one time, when people were not as safe and it was more difficult to defend oneself, intense anxiety reactions were important for dealing with threats. Intense anxiety prepares the body to deal with a potentially harmful situation. Intense anxiety leads us to fight, freeze, or flee. For example, pretend that as I am walking through a wooded area I hear a noise behind me. I turn around and see a bear behind me ready to attack me. I likely would make myself pretty anxious about the situation. The anxiety might help me to run as fast as possible, to fight the bear if I cannot avoid it, or to freeze. Interestingly, it turns out that in that situation, freezing would probably place me in the best position to survive.

The problem is, today, many people equate their daily living situations with life-threatening situations. As a result, the body responds to those daily-living situations as it would if a bear were ready to attack them.

From "I *Had* a Panic Attack" to "I Unintentionally Made Myself Panic"

Unless panic symptoms are the result of a physical problem (hyperthyroidism, an adrenal problem, mitral valve prolapse, anemia, allergies), people do not *have* a panic attack—they *unintentionally panic themselves*. They very rapidly equate something with a life-and-death situation, as if their life were on the line.

Reluctance to Leave Home By Oneself or To Be Home Alone

People who unintentionally panic themselves sometimes are very reluctant to leave home without being accompanied by someone. They often are reluctant to be home alone as well. They believe that the person accompanying them will help them if they were to start to panic. The question is, "Help them to do what?"

Many people who panic have a fear of incapacitation. They believe that they will either lose consciousness or not be able to function well. The result of this incapacitation, they believe, will be catastrophic. However, if someone accompanies them, they are more confident that

that person will help them should incapacitation occur. I often hear clients say, "She knows how to calm me down" or "He could help me get out of the store if I start to panic."

The experience of panic, and the degree that it affects one's ability to function, is grossly exaggerated by people who panic. This exaggeration is quite unintentional. What they anticipate will occur usually does not. For example, the majority of people who panic do not pass out. Most often when people pass out, they do so because their blood pressure drops. When people panic, their blood pressure increases. They have the sensation of passing out because they are dizzy from the increase in blood pressure. If a person does lose consciousness when panicking, they might have a physical problem that panicking worsens. Therefore, it is very important to obtain a medical examination if a person loses consciousness when anxious (or any other time, for that matter).

Ultimately, unless a person does lose consciousness (at which point it would not be advisable to drive until that problem is resolved), having a companion accompany a person at home or away from home is not necessary, it has only seemed that way.

Additionally, no one can calm a person. We always calm ourselves. They might say things to us that are comforting and reassuring, but we have to *view them* as being reassuring to be comforted. The good news is that we can learn to *tell ourselves* the same comforting messages that someone else would tell us until we learn to stop panicking all together.

Many people who panic also have a fear of panicking in public as they believe that they will appear to others to be foolish or severely mentally ill. They are afraid that others will think negatively of them.

Recall our discussion in chapter 5 on the mental mistake known as "jumping to conclusions" that one way that we jump to conclusions is by "mind reading." If you were in a store and you passed out (unlikely), simply fell down, knocked something over, or started shaking, that *might* be something that usually does not occur in that store. As a result, it might attract people's attention, if they are even aware that you in the store. Most people do not go into stores to observe others—they go there to shop.

However, even if this behavior does get noticed by others, there is no way to know what others actually think about it. They might think negatively, or they might think compassionately. Ultimately, though, it does not matter what they think. It is how they treat you that matters.

Another important consideration is that people do not tend to see us as anxious as we feel. It is a common occurrence after a speech to hear the speaker say that he or she was nervous, but those attending the speech did not detect any anxiety.

Even if people witness you acting in a manner that they think is unusual or just downright "crazy," how long will they think or talk about it? They might think about it on the way home. They might tell their family about the "nut" that they saw in the store that day. They might even think about it the next morning, but then they will move on to something else.

Feeling anxious is nothing over which a person must be ashamed. Everyone feels anxious from time to time, and *everyone* is capable of panicking.

Reluctance to Drive

People who panic sometimes are afraid to drive because of anticipated incapacitation. Until you stop panicking all together, a very helpful strategy is to give yourself an out. Plan your route and determine places along the way that you could pull over if by chance you were to panic. Once you pull over, relax yourself, and then continue on your way.

Having an "out" will help you to be more comfortable with driving so that you will give yourself a chance to see that you will not panic when driving, or even if you do, you will be able to cope with it.

Practice "driving" through visualization. First relax yourself (such as with my Rational Progressive Relaxation CD), then visualize yourself calmly, confidently driving along the routes that you normally travel. If by chance you make yourself anxious when performing the visualization, stop it, relax yourself again, and then return to the visualization. Pair only relaxation with the imagery.

Specific Fears and Phobias

A phobia is an intense fear of something along with avoidance (either physically or mentally) of it. When working to overcome a phobia, it is important to first be clear about the *actual* fear. For example, most people describe their reluctance to fly in an airplane as a "fear of flying." I have yet to meet someone who is afraid of *flying*. People are afraid of *crashing*. As long as the plane remains in the air, I am just fine. If it were to crash, that would ruin my day!

After identifying the actual fear, it is important to assess whether what is feared is possible to occur. If it is possible, it is important to assess the probability of the feared event occurring. In making a determination of the probability of something feared occurring, refuse to take someone's "word for it" and gather information.

Sometimes people will not be satisfied with the low probability of a feared event occurring. When that is the case, an underlying assumption (see chapter 2) is probably influencing their thinking.

If you find that you are having difficulty finding comfort with the low probability of a negative event occurring, look for underlying assumptions and correct any that are mistaken using the rational questions (as described in chapter 4).

Systematic Desensitization

An excellent way to overcome phobias is to utilize systematic desensitization. It helps a person to gradually, relatively comfortably face their fear. For a complete description of this excellent technique, see chapter 12.

Obsessive-Compulsive Problems

An obsession in this sense is a fear that creates anxiety. A compulsion is any behavior, either physical or mental, that reduces the anxiety. Sometimes the compulsion will make logical sense as it directly addresses the fear, as when a person washes his or her hands constantly because of a fear of becoming ill from germs. Other times, the compulsion seems to be quite magical, like when a person turns on a light three times or taps three times to somehow keep her parents from dying.

A very common *misunderstanding* in the mental health field is that a person with an obsessive-compulsive problem knows that their fear is unrealistic. Actually, the person *thinks* that he or she knows that the fear is unrealistic. They believe that they *should* think that it is unrealistic. However, if the person *knew* that it was unreasonable, he or she would no longer believe it!

Dealing with Intrusive Thoughts—The Mental Hiccup

Often, people with obsessive-compulsive problems will experience intrusive thoughts—thoughts that they do not intend to think, but that simply "pop" into their mind. Sometimes people distress themselves over those thoughts because they are concerned with what they might mean. Sometimes these intrusive thoughts are violent or suggest uncharacteristic behavior.

To rationally deal with these thoughts, it is important to determine if in fact they really are reflective of how you think. For example, one client of mine was a delivery driver with the following concern:

> Client: "I'm really worried about a thought that I keep thinking. When I drive across a bridge, I sometimes ask myself, 'Gee, what would happen if I stopped this vehicle and jumped off?'"

> Me: "Do you ever answer this question?"

> Client: "What do you mean?"

> Me: "Well, you asked, 'What would happen?' So I'm wondering if you try to answer this question."

Client: "No, I guess that I don't."

Me: "Okay. Well, you probably know what would happen if you were to jump off of a bridge."

Client: "Yes. I'd probably die."

Me: "Sure. Now, do you have any intention of killing yourself or of dying?"

Client: "Absolutely not. I have a wonderful life and am happy, except for this stupid thought."

Me: "Are you sure that you are happy, or is it that you think that you should be?"

Client: "No. I really am happy with my life."

Me: "Okay. So this thought is what I call a mental hiccup. In other words, for some reason, and that reason does not matter at all, this thought pops into your head. Everyone has thoughts like this from time to time. Since you have no intention whatsoever of acting on it, refuse to take the thought seriously. If by chance you do have this thought in the future, say to yourself, 'I refuse to take this thought seriously because it is silly.' Then drive on down the road. The more that you do this, the sooner you will stop thinking it."

If you experience an intrusive thought that suggests harm to yourself or others, and you are concerned that you will act on that thought, seek assistance from a mental health professional in your area.

Two Usual Types of Compulsive Behavior

Obsessive-compulsive behavior usually is manifested in two ways—"**checking**" and "**hand-washing**."

An example of "checking" behavior is when a person repeatedly looks to see if she unplugged her curling iron. The feared consequence is that the house will burn to the ground if the curling iron were left on. Checking reduces the anxiety.

Everyone checks from time to time. There is an old saying in carpentry, "Measure twice and cut once." When my son played football, I would have him check to make certain that he had all of his equipment before boarding the bus. Checking itself is not a problem. It is when checking is to the degree that it interferes with a person's goals that it becomes important to address.

To eliminate irrational checking behavior, first work at *removing the fear*. What is the worst that will happen if you were to refuse to check? Utilize the rational questions to dispute any fears that you might have.

Also, consider how much something is likely to change before you check on it. For example, one client of mine was obsessed with the size of his Adam's apple, thinking that it was too large for him to attract a mate. He would engage in checking behavior by repeatedly (sometimes as many as one hundred times a day) looking in the mirror to determine if it had gotten larger or smaller. The question was, "How likely is it that one's Adam's apple will change in size?" Not very, especially throughout a twenty-four-hour period. Therefore, it made sense for him to assume that his Adam's apple was the same size at 8:00 p.m. as it was at 8:00 a.m.

Behaviorally, *use reminders* to reassure you. First determine your best way of remembering something. Do you tend to remember something better by hearing it, reading it, writing it down, saying it to yourself, or feeling it? Maybe you remember better by using a combination of senses, such as saying something aloud. In that case, say to yourself as you are unplugging your curling iron, for example, "I unplugged my curling iron today, November 13, 2007."

If you remember better visually, you might first make unplugging the curling iron a deliberate act (rather than having your mind on something else while unplugging it). Really pay attention to the act of unplugging it and then mark the fact that you did unplug it on a chart or calendar. You might even throw in, "I unplugged my curling iron today, November 13, 2007."

Next, after taking these steps, work at overcoming any Missouri-itis that you might have by refusing to check if in fact you did unplug it. You might do this systematically if you are uncomfortable at first. For example, you might enlist the help of others who will be home so that if by chance they smell smoke or the fire alarm sounds, they could take appropriate steps. After you become accustomed to that approach (by "seeing" that you in fact are unplugging your curling iron) you could then leave home without their assistance.

Finally, create a *reward system* for yourself, so that each day that you refuse to check (let's say) more than once, you treat yourself in some way. If you happen to check more than once, you do not receive the treat. The "treat" might be something that would help you to achieve a long-term goal. For example, for each day that you check no more than once, you save $5 toward that flat-screen television that you have been wanting. Check more than once on a given day, that day's $5 does not go into the television savings.

Irrational hand-washing behavior is the result of a fear of becoming ill from coming into contact with germs. The greater the fear, the more a person will avoid anything that *might* have germs. If they do happen to touch something that they believe has germs, they will wash their hands until they are satisfied that there no longer is a risk of becoming ill. Because they cannot see the germs (if they actually are present), they make an arbitrary decision in terms of how much hand-washing is required to remove them.

The ideal solution to compulsive hand-washing behavior is to rid oneself of the irrational fear. Germs obviously do exist in the form of bacteria and viruses. Some objects are more likely to have a higher concentration of germs than others, such as a toilet. Therefore, if coming into contact with such an object, it does make sense to wash one's hands prior to eating, for example.

However, what also exists is one's immune system that successfully deals with germs every day. Antibiotics help us with bacterial infections. Most viral infections simply run their course. Believing that one will *die* from coming into contact with germs is what leads people to phobically avoid them. One thing that you know for certain is that your immune system (maybe with help from medicine from time to time) has kept you alive. If you do have a weakened immune system, discuss with your physician ways to keep yourself healthy.

Therefore, the question is, "What kinds of germs am I likely to contact in various situations, and what will be the likely consequence of doing so?" Some people avoid small, closed-in spaces, like airplanes for fear others sharing that space might sneeze or cough. While the common cold is unpleasant for most people, it certainly is not the end of the world. It makes rational sense to weigh the potential benefits of entering a situation against the potential risks. Does it make rational sense to skip that tour of Europe because you might catch a cold on the airplane? It depends on how much you want to tour Europe.

On the other hand, public restrooms (generally speaking) are known for having potentially harmful germs. That in no way means that it is important to avoid them. It does make rational sense, though, to wash your hands after using them and to use toilet seat covers if they are available.

Hand-Washing and "From Missouri-itis"

Sometimes, no matter how much evidence people gather that a situation has a low risk of creating serious illness, they will not believe it until they see it. An outstanding technique to overcome this "From Missouri-itis" is called exposure and response prevention.

Exposure and response prevention (ERP) is a technique that allows you to gradually expose yourself to feared situations and to refrain from washing your hands for a prescribed period of time until you eliminate your fear.

This technique is very powerful, but it does require some determination on your part to implement on your own. If you are not confident in your ability to implement it on your own, seek the help of family members. If you have difficulty enlisting their help, it might be in your best interest to seek professional help. For a referral to a certified cognitive-behavioral therapist, visit the National Association of Cognitive-Behavioral Therapists' Web site at http://www.nacbt.org.

Implement ERP by taking the following steps:

1. Make a list of everything that you fear touching, things that you believe are contaminated with germs.

2. Arrange your list into a hierarchy with the least feared thing to touch at the bottom of the list and the most feared at the top.

3. Touch the least feared thing on your list for ten minutes. During this time, allow yourself to feel any anxiety that you might feel.

4. On a scale of 0 to 10, with 0 indicating no anxiety at all, and 10 indicating as anxious as you can be, rate how you felt touching the feared item during the ten minutes.

5. Refuse to wash your hands for at least one hour after touching the object. When you do wash your hands, limit the time you take to thirty seconds.

6. Repeat this technique once more during the day.

When you can touch the least feared object on your list for ten minutes with no anxiety, move to the next object on your list. Implement this technique for each item on your list until you have completely removed the irrational fear of germs.

If the ERP technique seems too intensive for you, you could take a preliminary step by imagining yourself touching each object. First relax yourself, then imagine touching the least-feared object and feeling calm. If you start to feel anxious, stop the visualization and return to the relaxation. After you are once again relaxed, create the image again. Pair only relaxation with the visualization of touching the object. Once you can imagine touching the least-feared object without feeling anxious, move on to the next object. Repeat this process until you can imagine yourself touching every object without anxiety.

Aldo R. Pucci, PsyD

A Script to Overcome Anxiety

It is important for a person to be apprehensive if he or she is in danger—to be afraid enough to take action. However, recognizing a true threat is important. Sometimes it seems that we are in danger when in fact we are not. If I happen to be afraid of something, I will look at whether what I am afraid of is possible. If it is, then I will look at how probable it is. Then I will look at how well I would actually be able to cope with the situation if it were to occur, being careful to avoid underestimating my abilities with "can't stand-itis" and confusing needing with wanting. The fact is, the only things that I cannot stand are those things that could kill me. Everything else is an inconvenience, maybe a very large inconvenience, but still only an inconvenience for me.

I refuse to equate anything with a life-or-death situation when it is not. I now know that worrying is like rocking in a rocking chair—it gave me something to do, but got me nowhere! Worrying itself has never changed anything. Worrying really is civilized voodoo! Worrying about something never magically influenced my environment. If my well-being or the well-being of my loved ones is threatened, I will be concerned, and then I will act on that concern. There would be no point in even being concerned if I were unwilling to act on that concern.

I refuse to make myself anxious because I do not like feeling that way. I can stand feeling anxious or nervous; I just do not like it. Feeling anxious is only uncomfortable and inconvenient, not unbearable.

Fact is, I have always handled everything that has ever come my way. The best proof of that is that I am alive. I might not always determine a solution for a problem right away, but I will figure one out eventually. I will continue to handle everything that comes my way one way or another.

Chapter 9 Summary

1. Irrational anxiety is the result of the confusion of needs and wants. The more anxious a person is, the more he or she is equating something with a life-or-death situation.

2. Magical worry is civilized voodoo. Worry does not prevent negative events from occurring. Therefore, it is okay to refuse to worry.

3. Avoidance is anxiety's best friend. Avoidance tends to confirm one's fear.

4. Comfort is not required to do something. Sometimes overcoming a fear requires enduring some discomfort.

5. The greater the fear of panic, the more likely it is that a person will panic. Therefore, it is important to consider panic as being uncomfortable, maybe even very uncomfortable, but something that a person can stand.

10

Overcoming Anger

Anger is like urinating in your pants.
Everyone can see it, but you are the only one who can
feel it.

Special note: Although it might be tempting to read this chapter first, I encourage you to read this book from the first page forward. Many of the concepts and techniques that you will learn in the first seven chapters will help you to better understand and apply the recommendations in this chapter.

Because people often believe that they are justified in being angry, it is important to have a reason to refuse to anger yourself. Very common reasons to learn to refuse to anger oneself include these:

- Being a good role model for your children

- Being more effective in certain situations

- Keeping healthy

- Improving your relationships

- Avoiding legal difficulties

What are your reasons for learning to more calmly respond to personally difficult situations? Before you proceed any further in this chapter, think of the reasons that you have, and then write them here:

Reasons That I Have to Learn to Refuse to Anger Myself	
Reason	**Importance to Me**

Keep yourself mindful of these reasons. You need not obsess about them. Just keep mindful enough to keep yourself motivated to do what is necessary to overcome your tendency to anger yourself.

What If Anger Helps Me?

Sometimes people will object to taking a calm approach to their situation. They either believe that feeling angry is necessary or helpful to achieving their goal. Their being angry gets people's attention.

An important insight that we provide in Rational Living Therapy is that you need not *feel* angry to *act* like you are. Military drill sergeants do this everyday. If displaying anger gets you what you want, simply *act* like you are angry. Of course, you might find, though, that approaching the situation calmly and kindly might result in a more favorable outcome. Just about everything that we do angrily we can do calmly. A calm approach usually is more effective.

What About Outrage over an Injustice?

Sometimes outrage motivates us. It sometimes encourages us to refuse to tolerate a situation. Most Americans were outraged in response to the terrorist attacks of September 11, 2001. This outrage has led us to take action to decrease the likelihood that this will happen to us again.

However, recall our discussion in chapter 5 concerning the Yerkes-Dodson Law that states that there is an optimal level of arousal for every given task. Being too angry can backfire, thus making it more difficult to correct the undesirable situation. The old adage, "Cool heads prevail," is very wise.

The goal is not to be angry. The goal is to correct a situation. Being mindful of that fact will help you to be more focused on doing what is necessary to correct the situation, which might very well require you to refuse to make yourself angry over it.

Shoulds, Musts, and Had-Betters

If you have been having a problem with anger, I encourage you to review the Irrational Should Statements section of chapter 5. Also, chapter 5 discusses the various "musts" that create irrational expectations and entitlement mentality.

In summary, "shoulds" are problematic in two ways—they are demands and commands, rather than preferences, and they imply a belief in magic.

Need Versus Want

Also in chapter 5 is an explanation of the difference between needs and wants. If you have a tendency to anger yourself, be certain to review that section of this book. The angrier a person is, and the more violent that she is, the more likely it is that she is thinking a "need" thought. You can see in her reaction that she is equating something with a life-or-death situation.

We see cases of road rage where, as someone is driving down the road, they get cut off by another driver. So the offended driver chases that person down, has the person pull over, and shoots him or her. Did the offended driver act as though he or she was *inconvenienced*, or did he or she act as though this was a war zone? Unless a person enjoys killing others, he or she will not do so over being inconvenienced.

How much would you be willing to fight to make certain that you and your loved ones had air, food, and water? I would be willing to fight a great deal. Therefore, make certain to remind yourself that unless you or a loved one is in a life-or-death situation, that what you are dealing with is an *inconvenience*. It might be a huge inconvenience, but it remains just that, not something that will be the end of you.

Can't Stand-itis

Can't stand-itis is an extension of the confusion of needs and wants. It is believing that a situation is so bad that a person need it not be, as if it will lead to his or her demise. Certainly, this perception makes it difficult to tolerate a given situation.

There are very common situations of which people tend to be intolerant. Examples include a child crying, someone tapping, whistling, someone making noises when eating, fingernails running across a chalkboard, loud music, whining, waiting, stupidity, disrespect, and someone ahead of you driving slowly.

What types of situations do you tend to label as something that you cannot stand? Write them down and rate them in the following table:

Things I Do Not Tolerate Well

Situation/Thing

How Much I Dislike It
(0 = I like it   to 10 =
I absolutely hate it)

Now that you have this list, work at being more tolerant of each item. First, forcefully, stubbornly remind yourself that each item in that list is an example of an inconvenient situation. Each is something that you can stand and take. You simply do not like it.

Second, visualize yourself in those situations. Even exaggerate them in your visualization. As you imagine this, also image yourself calmly reacting to them. Before you begin your visualization session, relax yourself so that you can pair relaxation with your imagery. Practice your visualization once a day for one month.

Third, intentionally expose yourself to these situations. Prove to yourself that you can take them. As you do so, remind yourself that the situation is only an inconvenience. Take pride in the fact that you are working at overcoming your intolerance for them.

Reflexive Thoughts

A very common belief among people who have a tendency to anger themselves is that "it just happens." This perception is the result of their angering themselves very quickly, *apparently* without thinking anything.

However, it cannot "just happen." Either there will be a physiological reason for a person's behavior (which is unlikely if a person is reacting to something), or the reaction will be the result of a thought that occurred so quickly in the person's brain that he or she was not aware that it actually was thought.

Recall from chapter 1 that a "very rapid" thought is known as a reflexive thought. A reflexive thought is a very well-learned thought, so well-learned that you no longer need to think it consciously. It is stored in the brain, ready for action. The second that something reminds the brain of the thought, it is triggered and off you go.

To uncover reflexive thoughts, ask yourself the following question: *I'm acting as if I believe what about this situation?* When people anger themselves, they are acting as though they are thinking two different thoughts—a "should" thought and a "need" thought. Once that is established, dispute that thought using the rational questions (chapter 4) and develop a new rational replacement thought.

Suppression

Sometimes people will attempt to deal with their angry thoughts and feelings by suppressing them. However, an important insight is this: *You can lie to the entire world, but you cannot lie to your brain!*

Your brain knows how you think. So it is pointless to tell yourself that something does not matter to you when in fact you know it does.

Continual suppression of angry thoughts and feelings tends to create a volcano within. One then gets to the point that he or she finally "erupts" over a relatively minor inconvenience.

Therefore, it is much better to work on those angry thoughts, remove the musts, shoulds, and demands, and to develop new rational replacement thoughts. Then practice those thoughts until they are "there for you" when you need them.

The Problem with Punching a Pillow

Here is another very important insight: *Every time we are upset about something, we are practicing being upset about it.*

While releasing one's pent-up angry feelings in a more acceptable way (like punching a pillow) might seem helpful, it actually becomes a practice session for being angry. Again, a much better approach is to learn how to refuse to repeatedly anger yourself about a given situation.

Fatigue/Physical Irritability

There is no doubt that fatigue, illness, and even some medications can create a physical tendency to be irritable. We tend to not tolerate things as well when we are tired or ill. Some medications, like antidepressants, beta-blockers for the heart, and antihistamines for allergies can cause fatigue. For women, sometimes irritation is the result of changes in their menstrual cycle.

Recognizing when irritation is the result of physical factors can be helpful in preventing anger. This recognition can help you to avoid emotional reasoning. Recall that emotional reasoning is thinking that is consistent with your current mood. If we are already irritated, we tend to think irritating thoughts about other things that we ordinarily would not have such thoughts about. Therefore, a helpful question is, "Do I think this way any other time about this situation, except when I am already irritated?"

Recognizing fatigue or illness as a cause of irritation in others helps us to have consideration for them. Is their behavior typical for them? If not, there is no point in treating them as if that were the case. This does not mean that you have to like their behavior. However, recognizing that "it will pass" can help you be much more tolerant of it.

Breaking Response Chains

If we look at behavior as a sequence or chain of events, the earlier in the chain we break it, the more successful we will be at preventing the behavior. Breaking response chains helps us to stop habitual, reflexive behavior and to develop a more rational alternative way of behaving.

If you habitually, almost automatically respond with anger to certain situations, breaking response chains can be helpful to you to prevent the anger reaction and to develop a new way of responding to those situations.

The first step in utilizing this technique is to recognize in which situations you are likely to respond with anger. To do this, conduct what is known as a "functional analysis" using the following form:

Functional Analysis of Anger Reactions			
Date & Time	Location	Behavior	What Was Going On

If you anger yourself, the first step is to write down the date and time. Sometimes recording the time will help you to recognize patterns that you would not have observed otherwise. For example, you might notice that you most often anger yourself late in the evening when you are tired. Next, write down where you angered yourself. Then record what you did when you angered yourself (yelled, broke something, for example). Finally, record what occurred right before you angered yourself—in other words, the "A" in your Emotional ABCs.

After recording for a couple of weeks any angry behavior that you happen to exhibit, observe your recordings to see if there are any patterns. Recognizing patterns will help you to know at what times or in what situations you are most likely to anger yourself. Recognizing these patterns will help you to "see it coming" and to take steps to prevent angering yourself.

Have a Plan

Until you stop angering yourself altogether over a given situation, have a plan of action that you can take to prevent your angering yourself. When you recognize that you are in a situation in which you are likely to anger yourself, act on your plan. Some things that you could do to prevent an angry reaction include these:

- Remove yourself from that situation and work at calming yourself.

- Change the subject if the situation involves a discussion.

- Change the activity.

- Take a temporary time out, such as going to the restroom. Once there, remind yourself that the situation is only an inconvenience, not something that is terrible or awful.

Also, if possible, you might avoid the situation altogether until you learn how to rationally cope with it.

An Important Note

People sometimes go out of their way to demonstrate their ignorance. A key insight is this—just because someone says or does something that you consider to be idiotic or offensive *does not* mean that you *must* respond to it. If your responding would only make matters worse, why bother? There is no objective need to respond to every idiotic statement made by others. There is no objective need to defend yourself verbally in most situations. If you decide to, that is your business. It is important to realize that most often verbally defending yourself is not an absolute necessity.

A terrific technique for dealing with the nonsense of others is called fogging. **Fogging** is especially helpful when someone is trying to start a debate or argument with you and you are not interested in arguing. Simply agree with them. A person might say, "Hey, the sky is green with yellow polka dots." You might say in response with a sincere tone, "Wow, you are right. I have never seen it that way before."

My mother emphasized an old saying to me throughout my adolescence. She would say, "Aldo, never argue with a fool because if you do, people will not know which one is the fool."

A Script to Overcome Anger

Everything is exactly as it should be at any given moment, although it might not be the way I want it to be. My mere wishes, desires, shoulds, and beliefs in right and wrong do not make situations magically go my way. Only behaviors influence my environment. If all it took for things to go my way was for me to want it or insist on it, I would have everything that I want. My calm acceptance of that fact helps me to make my situations more the way I want them to be.

If a situation is different than I want it to be, I will remind myself that obviously that means that all the necessary ingredients for it to be that way are present. That will open my mind to determine what those necessary ingredients are and to see what I can do to correct them.

Whenever people anger themselves intensely, they usually think that they can't stand what is going on—that they need their situation to be different than it is. Fact is, the only things that I can't stand are those things that could kill me. Everything else I can tolerate. The only things that I absolutely need are those things that keep me alive. Everything else is a want.

I am more likely to get what I want by treating others kindly and approaching them in a calm manner. I can rationally assert myself without being angry or hostile.

I will do what I can to change those aspects of my life that I want to change. But some things are either unchangeable or very difficult to change (and maybe not worth the effort). Therefore, in those cases, I will view them simply as unfortunate circumstances and/or inconveniences.

Remember that anger is like urinating in your pants—everyone can see it, but you are the only one who can feel it!

Chapter 10 Summary

1. Since people often believe that they are justified in being angry, it is important to develop personally significant reasons to learn how to refuse to make yourself feel angry.

2. Irrational "shoulds" cause people to anger themselves. These come in the form of demands and commands, as well as magical beliefs.

3. Equating anything with a life-or-death situation causes either significant anxiety or significant anger.

4. Identifying situations in which you tend to anger yourself will help you to break response chains.

5. Identifying and correcting irrational reflexive thoughts can be very helpful in overcoming anger.

11

The Rational Action Planner

Putting It All Together

The Rational Action Planner (RAP) is a technique I developed that brings together what you have learned so far into a single procedure. The RAP enables you to develop a plan of action that is more consistent with your goals.

The RAP technique is performed on a two-sided prepared form (like the one here), or it can be done on a blank sheet of paper by copying the sections of the form.

The first side of the RAP form includes the old or current ABCs of the situation, including thoughts and unwanted/problematic feelings and behaviors. It also includes a section to place your goals for the situation, a Camera Check section for the description you gave in the "A" section, and a section to record which thoughts pass the rational questions.

The second side of the RAP form is where you develop your *new* ABCs for the situation, including a Camera-Checked "A" section, new rational beliefs, and the desired emotional/behavioral response (how you want to act and feel in the situation).

The following is an example of a properly completed Rational Action Planner. Use it as a guide for your RAPs.

- Notice that the *first step* is to write down that of which you were aware or to which you reacted (the "A" in the ABCs of emotions).

- The *second step* is to write down your beliefs about it (the "B" in the ABCs). You might have one thought or one hundred thoughts. If you have more thoughts than the space provided allows, write the remaining thoughts on another sheet of paper.

- The *third step* is to write down how you felt and what you did (the "C" in the ABCs).

- The *fourth step* is to record what your goals were in that situation, either goals that you were aware of at the time (conscious goals) or those that you probably had in that situation (implied goals).

- The *fifth step* is to do a Camera Check of what you wrote in the "A" section and to record what a camera would actually show.

- The *sixth step* is to apply the rational questions to each thought that you listed in the "B" section. Write down whether or not a thought is rational under each thought in the "B" section. If any of the thoughts are irrational, you will need to complete the next side of the RAP, the "New ABCs."

Rational Action Planner™

Old ABCs

A (What you are aware of)	B (Thoughts or Beliefs about it)	C (Emotional & Physical Reaction)
My girlfriend told me that she wants to break up with me, and I fell all to pieces.	*1. I need her because I'm nothing without her! (Irrational)*	*Very nervous*
		Begged her to not break up with me
	2. It's terrible that she wants to break up with me. (Irrational)	*Told her that I'd kill myself if she broke up with me*
	3. I'll never be happy again, and that's terrible! (Irrational)	

What were (are) your goals in this situation (Conscious or Implied)?

	Achieved?
1. *Remain calm*	*No*
2. *Tell her what I really meant*	*No*
3. *Do things to encourage her to stay*	*No*
4.	

Camera Check of "A" Section (What Would a Camera Show)	Rational Questions
It would show her telling me that she wanted to break up with me, but it would not show me falling to pieces, like a pile of body parts!	Apply the Rational Questions to Each Thought in the "B" Column and Write Down Whether They Are Rational or Irrational. 1. Is my thinking based on fact? 2. Does my thinking help me achieve my goals? 3. Does my thinking help me feel the way I want to feel? **Keep any thoughts that pass the rational questions and replace any that do not.**

Rational Action Planner™ © Copyright, 1996, by Aldo R. Pucci All Rights Reserved.
Side 2

New ABCs

A (Camera Checked) *Whenever I'm in this situation:*	**B** (New Thoughts to Practice) *I'll think this:*	**C** *As a result of my new thinking, I'll feel and do this:*
I'm around her, think of her, or see her	*Anything that is physically present is "something." Therefore, it is impossible for me to be a "nothing." What I am is a human being. I need no one or nothing for me to be a human being. I was born with the same human worth as everyone else, and no one or nothing can take that away from me!* *I didn't need my ex-girlfriend — I only wanted her. Therefore, I'll feel appropriately sad as I think of losing her as a disappointment, not something that is terrible or that I can't stand. Certainly I can stand her breaking up with me, because I am!* *The sooner I calmly accept the fact that we ended this relationship, the sooner I will find happiness in another relationship or with something else.*	*Feel calm* *Treat her kindly*

Do these new thoughts pass the rational questions?

Practice imagining yourself in the "A" Section, thinking the "B" Section, and reacting like the "C" Section. Act as if you believe the new thoughts until they feel comfortable to you.

217

How do we produce the new thoughts in the "B" column of the new ABCs? We base the new thoughts on the reasons the old thoughts were irrational. The new rational replacement thoughts are a response or rebuttal to the old irrational thoughts. **Apply the rational questions to those new thoughts to make certain that they are in fact rational.**

What Do I Do Now That I Have Completed the RAP?

After completing the new ABCs, *read aloud the thoughts in the "B" column* at least once every day for one month. Why read the new thoughts aloud? Reading them aloud uses two senses, visual and auditory, therefore making it more likely that you will remember the new thoughts.

Also, *practice imagining* yourself in the situation you described in the new "A" section, while thinking the new thoughts in the "B" section and feeling and acting like the "C" section. Practice this visualization at least once every day for one month.

Finally, *begin acting "as if"* you believe what you wrote in the new "B" column by acting out your "C" column whenever you are in the "A" situation. As you will see in the next chapter, practicing your new thoughts, feelings, and behaviors is very important.

The following is a blank Rational Action Planner. Feel free to copy it for your personal use so that you can use it as often as you wish.

Rational Action Planner™

Old ABCs

A (What you are aware of)	**B** (Thoughts or Beliefs about it)	**C** (Emotional & Physical Reaction)

What were (are) your goals in this situation (Conscious or Implied)?

Achieved?

Camera Check of "A" Section
(What Would a Camera Show)

Rational Questions

Apply the Rational Questions to Each Thought in the "B" Column and Write Down Whether They are Rational or Irrational.

1. Is my thinking based on fact?
2. Does my thinking help me achieve my goals?
3. Does my thinking help me feel the way I want to feel?

Keep any thoughts that pass the rational questions and replace any that do not.

Rational Action Planner™ © Copyright, 1996, by Aldo R. Pucci All Rights Reserved.
Side 2

New ABCs

A	**B**	**C**
(Camera Checked)	(New Thoughts to Practice)	*As a result of my new thinking, I'll feel and do this:*
Whenever I'm in this situation:	*I'll think this:*	

Do these new thoughts pass the rational questions?

Practice imagining yourself in the "A" Section, thinking the "B" Section, and reacting like the "C" Section. Act as if you believe the new thoughts until they feel comfortable to you.

12

The Importance of Practice

Practice is something that everyone does on a daily basis. We may go to basketball practice, dance practice, band practice, or play rehearsal. School children practice the "fire drill," their multiplication tables, and their ABCs. Police officers practice firing their guns. I could go on all day!

Why do we practice, and why is it important? It is often said that "practice makes perfect." Well, almost so, anyway. Practice helps us in three ways:

(1) It helps us learn the proper way of performing a behavior;
(2) It helps feel comfortable with a behavior; and
(3) It helps to make a behavior more automatic.

For example, if I were to ask you to take a pen or pencil, place it in your non-preferred hand, and write with that hand for the next month, you would likely experience three things:

(1) Your handwriting would not be as good as it is with the preferred hand;
(2) Writing with the opposite hand would seem strange and wrong to you because you are accustomed to writing with your preferred hand; and
(3) You likely would forget sometimes and begin writing with your preferred hand until you "caught yourself."

The only remedy for these three problems is practice, practice, and more practice! The more you would practice writing with the opposite hand (and refused to write with the preferred hand), the better your penmanship would be, the more comfortable it would feel to you, and the more automatic it would become.

When you first learned to write, it did not feel "funny or wrong" because you were not accustomed to writing a different way. So you had no previous writing experience interfering with learning how to write. You did not have to *un*learn an old way. With emotional change, we usually are in a position to unlearn an already established way of thinking and behaving and to replace it with a new way. This process is what Maultsby (1984) calls "emotional re-education." In other words, we must re-educate ourselves if we are to react differently.

The **stages of emotional re-education** (which are adapted from Maultsby) are:

Stages of Emotional Re-Education

(1) **Intellectual Insight**
(2) **Practice** (Mental and Physical)
      Cognitive-Emotive Dissonance Experienced
(3) **Emotional Insight**
(4) **Personality / Trait Formation** (Habit)

Let's use as an example a person who believes that she is unintelligent. Her belief is, "I am dumb. There is no one any less intelligent than I am." After giving her an intelligence test, we discover that her IQ is 135 (the average is 100). She is very bright. We then point out the many things that she has accomplished in her life that are a reflection of her high IQ. Next, *we develop a thought* for her to practice (to read aloud to herself every day) that is something like this:

"I now have objective evidence that my intellectual level actually is above average. And I now also realize that many things that I have accomplished in my life are the result of my intelligence, not luck. I am not used to thinking of myself as bright, but the more I practice this thought, the sooner it will feel right to me."

Next, we *ask her to practice this thought* every day by reading it aloud and by visualizing herself accomplishing things she had previously thought were impossible for her to accomplish. We also ask her to begin acting as if she believes these new thoughts by actually pursuing her goals, therefore acting as if she is intelligent. As she practices her thought and visualizes herself accomplishing her goals, she tells us that doing so *feels strange and wrong* to her. If she were to think with her gut, she would say to herself, "Because this new thought feels wrong, it must be wrong." This gut thinking would lead her to abandon the thought. Let's say, though, that she thinks with her head and not her gut and decides to practice the new thought. After a couple of weeks, she tells us that it is beginning to *feel right to her.* After a couple of months, she tells us that thinking of herself as intelligent is becoming *automatic* to her.

The first stage of emotional re-education is **Intellectual Insight.** It is achieved when a person understands at the very least that there is a different way to do something. Hopefully, though, the intellectual insight will involve the discovery of an effective, better, or appropriate way to accomplish something. In the preceding example, she achieves intellectual insight when she realizes that the new thought that we developed for her is an accurate and rational way for her to think.

The second stage of emotional re-education is **Practice.** Practice refers to the actual mental and physical rehearsal of the new behavior. In the preceding example, the mental practice would be her reciting the thought and practicing her visualization daily. Physical practice would come from her working at achieving those goals that require an intellectual level that she thought she did not have. As she practices her new belief, she experiences *cognitive-emotive dissonance.* You might remember from the Introduction of this book that cognitive-emotive dissonance is that strange, "funny" feeling of wrongness that occurs every time we do, think, or feel something that is the opposite to which we are accustomed. Because it *feels* wrong, it gives us the impression that it *is* wrong. Cognitive-emotive dissonance is normal and unavoidable. It feels wrong for her to think of herself as intelligent because she is accustomed to thinking of herself as "dumb."

After enough practice (usually about one month's worth) she will move to the third stage of emotional re-education—**Emotional Insight**. Emotional Insight means that not only does she know in her head that the new thought is correct, but now it also feels right to her.

With enough practice, she will proceed to the final state of emotional re-education—**Personality/Trait Formation**. Personality/trait formation simply means that she has developed a habit. Now she is likely to automatically think of herself as intelligent and capable of achieving her goals.

So What Do These Stages of Emotional Re-Education Have to Do with Me?

Understanding the stages of emotional re-education helps you to realize *(1) the importance of practice, (2) the fact that cognitive-emotive dissonance is normal and to be expected, and (3) that they can serve as a guide for where you are in the process of changing.*

Practice is important for two reasons. First, it helps to remove cognitive-emotive dissonance, thus making new thoughts, feelings, and behaviors "feel right." Second, practice helps make the new thoughts and reactions automatic and "there for us" when we need them. So it is incorrect to believe that we can think a new thought just once and expect it to be there for us when we need it.

For example, my son and I participated in a martial art called Bando. Our Bando instructor regularly implored us to practice our kicks and punches between lessons. If we were to spend only four hours per week (two, two-hour lessons) practicing them, it is likely that the kicks and punches would not be automatic enough for us if attacked. If we had to think about what our instructor taught us to do when attacked *as we are being attacked*, we would likely get hurt. We want our new thoughts, feelings, and behaviors to be automatic as well.

It is important to understand that cognitive-emotive dissonance is normal and to be expected. This understanding helps people to avoid thinking with their gut—it helps people to give what they are practicing a chance, instead of giving up on it because it feels wrong.

How Do We Change Our Thoughts, Feelings, and Behaviors?

To produce long-lasting cognitive, emotional, and behavioral change, a person must do this:

How to Change Our Thoughts, Feelings, and Behaviors

(1) Realize that the old way of thinking, feeling, or behaving is irrational or otherwise not appropriate;

(2) Develop a new, rational replacement thought;

(3) Refuse to think, feel, or behave the old way;

(4) Practice the new way of thinking, feeling, and behaving;

(5) Tolerate the cognitive-emotive dissonance felt while practicing;

(6) Continue practicing the new thought, feeling, or behavior until it becomes automatic.

Step One, or realizing that the old way of thinking, feeling, or behaving is irrational, is achieved by applying the rational questions to the thoughts, feelings, or behaviors. Understanding why the thought is irrational is important because this understanding will help motivate you to avoid thinking that way.

Step Two, or developing a new, rational replacement thought, is achieved by examining the reasons the old thoughts were irrational and basing the new thought on those reasons.

Step Three, or refusing to think, feel, or behave the old way, is not as difficult as it might seem, particularly if you have done a good job with Step One. Refuse to think in the old terms, and if you happen to find yourself doing so, tell yourself, "*STOP! I refuse to think this way any longer.*" Then recite your new, rational thought to yourself.

Step Four, or practicing the new thoughts, feelings, and behaviors, is done both mentally and physically as was mentioned earlier. Specific practicing techniques are discussed later.

Step Five, or tolerating cognitive-emotive dissonance, involves refusing to take the "funny" or "wrong" feelings as proof that the new way of thinking and behaving is wrong. Additionally, while cognitive-emotive dissonance is not terrible or awful, it can be somewhat uncomfortable. But anything worth achieving takes work and a willingness to tolerate discomfort.

Step Six, or continuing to practice the thought, feeling, or behavior to make it automatic, is important for producing long-term change.

Practicing Techniques

The following are some very effective practicing techniques. Utilize these techniques every day for at least one month.

(1) Mental Practice

1. *Simple script rehearsal* involves writing out a new, rational thought to replace the problem thought and reading it at least once a day. *Memorizing* the script is even better, as long as you pay attention to what you are saying to yourself when you recite the thought. Another good way to rehearse the script is to make an audio recording of it and to listen to it at least once a day.

Associate your thought rehearsal with different behaviors, like brushing your teeth, driving to work, preparing dinner, going to bed, and other behaviors you do routinely. This helps you to *remember* to practice your new belief.

One way to develop your new thought is to utilize the Rational Action Planner as discussed earlier.

The following is a script to overcome guilt.

A Script to Rid Yourself of Guilt

Guilt is anger turned inward. If I happen to guilt myself, I will first look at the facts to determine how much responsibility I actually have for what happened. There is no point in blaming myself if it is not my fault. There also is no point in blaming myself more than the degree to which I actually am responsible.

If I am at fault in any way, I will remind myself that I should have done exactly what I did because I did everything necessary to do it. That does not mean that I think that it was right or good for me to do it. It only means that one plus one equals two, no matter how much I want it to equal four. All of the necessary ingredients for me to do it were present, or I would not have done it. So if I want to avoid repeating such mistakes, I will seek to discover what those necessary ingredients are and work at changing them.

Fact is, I could spend the rest of my life making myself miserable about what happened, but that will not in any way make up for anything or keep it from happening in the future. What keeps me from repeating problem behaviors is actively choosing to do something different, and I do not have to feel guilty to do that!

It is also important for me to assess accurately what happened and what I did. Did I violate some arbitrary rule? I remind myself that people make up all sorts of rules that have no scientific backing to them and then act like the world is going to fall apart if someone breaks one of those rules. I now realize that I am a Fallible Human Being just like everyone else. People make mistakes!

The bottom line is that guilt is a useless emotion that did nothing but make me feel bad. If I want to change my behavior, I will learn how, and

*then I'll do it! I cannot erase history! I can make it more likely that I will
have a happy future by refusing to dwell on the past.*

2. *Rational visualization* involves practicing mental imagery of your
desired outcomes. It is rehearsing by visualizing how you want to act
and feel.

Rational Living Therapists are very motivated to encourage people
to utilize rational visualization because it works. Why does it work?
Because the human brain does not know the difference between
an image produced from external stimuli and an image produced
internally. That is why dreams are so real to us—why we wake up from
a nightmare with our heart pounding. When we have a nightmare
(or any other dream), as far as our brain is concerned, we are actually
experiencing what we are dreaming. If our brain knew the difference,
that we are not actually experiencing what we are dreaming, we would
not have the physical and emotional response to the dream that we
do.

Rational Visualization Instructions

- Develop a new rational thought to practice.

- Have a clear idea of how you want to feel and act in the relevant situation.

- Place yourself in a comfortable position and practice a relaxation technique. My CD, "Rational Progressive Relaxation,"
  provides a way to learn to relax quickly and deeply. I
  recommend that you purchase this CD (by calling 1-800-853-
  1135).

- After you have relaxed yourself to a personally desirable level,
  practice visualizing your new behaviors/reactions. Imagine
  yourself thinking your new thoughts in those relevant situations. If by chance you start to feel anxious or uncomfortable
  in any way while practicing your visualization (sometimes this

is the case if a person works at overcoming a fear), stop the visualization, relax yourself again, and resume the visualization. If you repeatedly feel anxious or uncomfortable, suspend the visualization and look for any additional thoughts that might be causing your distress. When you identify them, dispute them and develop rational replacement thoughts.

Rational visualization can help you to move beyond a sticking point. For example, if a person were concerned that she will die of heart disease in her fifties because many people in her family have, I would have her practice visualizing herself as a very healthy, vibrant eighty-year-old who takes great care of her body, especially her heart.

By the way, many people practice *irrational* visualization. They unintentionally practice their undesired behaviors and reactions by imagining them. The person worried that she will die in her fifties might actually visualize herself dying at that age. Rational Living Therapists teach that we go in the direction that we look. So if we are looking to die in our fifties, we might unintentionally create that reality. If we look to live to be eighty-years-old, we are more likely to do what is necessary to create that reality.

3. *Self-hypnosis* is another excellent mental practicing technique. See chapter 13 for more details.

4. *"Covert" systematic desensitization* involves breaking a feared situation down into parts to develop an ordered list from the least-feared aspect of the situation to the most feared. For example, if a person were afraid of dogs, the following hierarchy would be developed:

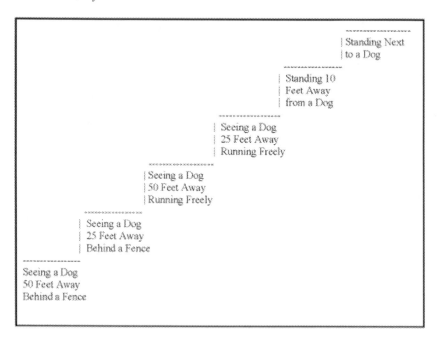

In covert systematic desensitization, we first break down the feared event into steps and then create an ordered list or "hierarchy" from least feared to most feared. Relaxation is paired with visualizing each step. A person does not move on to visualizing the next step until he or she is comfortable visualizing the current step.

In this example, the person would begin imagining himself being fifty feet away from a dog that is behind a fence. As the person imagines this, he would keep calm through progressive relaxation as with the rational visualization described earlier. When the person feels comfortable imagining this scene, he then would move to the next most-feared aspect, which in this case would we seeing a dog twenty-five feet away behind a fence. He would *not* move to the next level until he felt comfortable with imagining the current level. Once a person feels comfortable with imagining the highest, most-feared level, he or she is then ready to begin "in-vivo" systematic desensitization, which is discussed later.

(2) Physical Practice

While mental practice is an excellent way to help you learn new reactions and behaviors, being physically able to perform the action you desire is what your ultimate goal will be for most situations. Sufficient "mental practice" will enable you to perform your desired behaviors *comfortably*. As a result, the next step is to begin regular physical practice of your desired behavior by acting on what you mentally rehearsed. If your problem was feeling anxious while giving speeches, begin to give speeches. If your problem was making yourself angry in reaction to your mother-in-law's comments, begin visiting her while thinking and acting out your new, mentally-rehearsed desired thoughts and behaviors.

Sometimes people suffer from "From Missouri-itis," which means that they refuse to believe something until they actually see it. In these cases, a person might continue to feel uncomfortable when physically practicing the new behavior or reaction. If you find that there continues to be some uncomfortableness, you could begin using "in-vivo" systematic desensitization, which is actually physically practicing the desired behavior in successive steps, as in the "covert" systematic desensitization just described. Therefore, you physically act out the same steps that you mentally rehearsed until each step feels comfortable to you.

A Willingness to Act "As If"

A willingness to act "as if" is extremely important in emotional and behavioral change. Every time we engage in a new behavior, we are acting as if it is something that we do.

For example, I recently hung a new door in my home that was not already "pre-hung." I had experience with installing pre-hung doors, but I had never installed one that was not pre-hung. To install this door, I had to install the hinges myself, trim the side of the door to fit the opening, and make certain that the door was level. After installing the door, my wife said to me, "I am glad that you know how to do these things." I chuckled because I had an *idea* of how to do it, but I had never *actually* done it to know that my understanding was correct. So I faked it! But I did not fake it to deceive people. I faked it for the purpose of practicing. I acted "as if" I knew what I was doing, and I acted "as if" well enough to do a pretty good job. If I had to wait until I knew with absolute certainty that I could install the door well, I would never have installed it. If someone were to look at the door, they probably would be surprised that this was the first time I had installed a door in this manner.

One way to act "as if" is to pick a role model—someone who is good at what you want to do or who has the attributes that you wish to develop. For a young man wanting to be more comfortable and effective at asking girls for a date, I would encourage him to select a role model—someone who is confident and effective at asking girls for a date. Next, I would ask the young man to study that person to learn how he approaches girls— what he says and does. Then, as the young man approaches women, he would become the person he picked, acting just as he does.

A willingness to act "as if" also can be helpful in getting through personally difficult situations. If you wake up in the morning not feeling well, and you know that you have a long day ahead of you at work or school, *acting as if* you feel wonderful will help you to get through the day. The more you act as if you feel happy, the happier you will feel. Even if you do not believe that you have a single reason to be happy, *acting as if* you are happy will make it more likely that you will find reasons to be.

What Makes a New Thought "Grow"?

As I am sure you have discovered by now, the most important aspect of "getting better" is to change your thinking. If we liken a new, rational thought to a seed that we are planting, we want to water this seed, give the seedling plenty of fertilizer, and nurture it until it becomes a full-grown, healthy plant.

There are four factors that will make your new thought grow. These four factors are like fertilizer for your new, rational thoughts.

Desirability of a thought means that a person can see that there are advantages to thinking it, even if he or she does not currently believe it. This occurs often in counseling and psychotherapy. The client does not believe a word of what the therapist is saying but will admit that there are advantages to thinking the way that is being suggested.

If it were not for desirability of thinking, gambling would not exist. There would be no such thing as a state lottery. What causes people to stand in line for hours to purchase a lottery ticket when the jackpot is very high? Most people realize that there is a very low probability of winning the lottery. What causes them to stand in line for hours is the thought, "If only I were to win the lottery, how much better my life would be!" That is desirability of thinking.

So a person might think of herself as unintelligent. Her therapist works at helping her to see that she is much brighter than she has always thought. She does not believe a word of what is told to her, but she will admit that she probably would be happier and pursue more goals if she were to think the way the therapist is suggesting. Realizing the advantages of thinking that she is intelligent will help her to look for evidence that supports that belief—to give it a chance.

Repetition is achieved by simply repeating the new rational thoughts daily as described earlier in this chapter. The more that people repeat thoughts to themselves, or the more a message is repeated to them, the more likely it is that they will come to believe them. I am sure you have heard people say things like, "He lies so much, after a while he comes to believe his own lies." That is due to repetition.

Evidence is very important in developing long-term thoughts. Many people think thoughts that have a very weak foundation, like a house built on sand. As a result, the thoughts are not durable enough to be helpful in tough times. We want our new, rational thoughts to have a solid foundation.

Sometimes people tell me, "I tried to think that everything would be okay, but I just could not keep thinking that way." When I ask them what evidence they had to support this idea that everything would be "okay," they say, "Well, none really." This is an example of a thought with a weak foundation. Instead, if a person said, "The reason I will be okay is because I have gone through this before and survived, and others like me have dealt with similar situations," he or she will be more likely to continue thinking this new thought.

To build a solid foundation for your new, rational thoughts, look for evidence every day that supports them.

A related issue is *Expert Voice*. The more knowledgeable a person believes the source of information is, the more likely he or she is to take seriously what the source says. Unfortunately, it is the *perception* that the source is knowledgeable that matters, not whether or not the source actually is! While it is a good idea to seek advice from people who have demonstrated that they do have knowledge with something that concerns us, it does not hurt to investigate what they tell us to make certain that they are correct. For example, my medical doctor and cardiologist are excellent physicians. I trust them. After all, they saved my life by recognizing that I had advanced cardiovascular disease. Despite that fact, if they prescribe a medication for me, I make certain that the medication does not interact with other medications that I am taking.

Emotional Insight is the result of practice (i.e., repetition, visualization, and physical practice as described earlier in this chapter). Recall that emotional insight is the perception that a thought "feels right." If a thought feels right to a person, he or she is more likely to think and believe it. As was mentioned in this chapter, this gut thinking is unfortunate in that just because a thought feels right does not mean that it is accurate. Regardless, we want to make this new, rational thought feel right through practice.

The following is another format that I developed to help you practice your new thoughts that is based on these four factors.

Thought to Practice

__Goal:__ *To feel calm when seeing my ex-girlfriend and to treat her kindly.*

__Thought:__ *Anything that is physically present is "something." Therefore, it is impossible for me to be a "nothing." What I am is a human being. I need no one or nothing for me to be a human being. I was born with the same human worth as everyone else, and no one or nothing can take that away from me!*

I didn't need my ex-girlfriend—I only wanted her. Therefore, I'll feel appropriately sad as I think of losing her as a disappointment, not something that is terrible or that I can't stand. Certainly I can stand her breaking up with me, because I am!

The sooner I calmly accept the fact that we ended this relationship, the sooner I will find happiness in another relationship or with something else.

__Desirability__: *When I think this way, I'll be much more likely to react calmly when I see my ex-girlfriend.*

__Evidence__:

__Repetition__: *I shall repeat this thought to myself at least five times per day for the next month. I shall practice this thought at the following times:*

__Emotional Insight__: *Practicing my thought will make it "feel right" to me eventually. Therefore, I shall practice it every day.*

The *first step* is to write out your goal statement. This will be the reason to practice the new thought.

The *second step* is to write out the new, rational thought to practice.

The *third step* is to look for evidence every day that supports your new belief. Even if you are uncertain whether or not something is evidence that supports your new belief, write it down.

The *fourth step* is to lay out a schedule to practice (read aloud to yourself) this new belief. Schedule certain times of the day to practice it.

The *fifth step* is to make a statement concerning the fact that the new thought will feel comfortable eventually after sufficient practice.

The next chapter discusses another outstanding method of acquiring new thoughts—rational hypnotherapy.

Chapter 12 Summary

1. The stages of emotional re-education remind us of the experience of cognitive-emotive dissonance and the fact that practice is required to develop a habit.

2. Cognitive-emotive dissonance is experienced any time we do, think, or feel something that is the opposite of what we are accustomed. It is normal and to be expected.

3. Acting "as if" helps a person to experience the benefits of new thinking before he or she completely believes it.

4. Rational visualization is a very helpful technique because the human brain does not know the difference between an image that is produced from external stimuli and an image that is produced internally. That is why dreams are so real to us.

5. Supporting your new belief with evidence will give the belief a solid foundation and make it more durable.

13

Rational Hypnotherapy

By now, you clearly understand the fact that our thoughts cause our feelings and behaviors. It is also important to know, however, that we acquire our thoughts several different ways. We learn our thoughts by observing how other people think, which is called *observational learning*. If you listen to first-grade children during election years, they will tell you who "should" be president. How do they arrive at their opinions? By hearing their parents, they come to express the same views.

We also learn our thinking through *operant conditioning*, meaning that we are rewarded or punished in some way for thinking our thoughts. When we are rewarded for thinking a certain way, we are more likely to continue thinking that way. When we are punished, we are less likely to think that way again. An example of a thought being punished is a person discovering that his thought, "This machine will give me a can of soda pop," is incorrect when he loses his money to the machine. As a result, he is less likely to think that thought about that machine in the future.

Another way that we acquire thoughts is through *hypnosis*. Now, you might be thinking to yourself, "Maybe some people acquire thoughts through hypnosis, but I have never been hypnotized. So I must have never acquired thoughts through hypnosis." It is important to understand, though, that we all go through states of hypnosis naturally throughout every day. We go through states of hypnosis as we wake up and as we fall asleep (which happen to be the two best times to learn something). We also go into states of hypnosis when we daydream. Have you ever traveled somewhere, had your mind on something, and found yourself surprised that you arrived at your destination? If so, you have experienced hypnosis. People also go into a state of hypnosis when they experience sudden shock and trauma. If confusion is also experienced during the incident, a person will experience an even deeper state of hypnosis.

One of the best, but most unfortunate, examples of "accidental" hypnosis is what most Americans experienced on September 11, 2001. I remember that day vividly. I was at a hotel in Appleton, Wisconsin, conducting a seminar for mental health professionals. The seminar began at 8:30 a.m. About ten minutes after the commencement of the seminar, someone entered the room and notified us that an airplane had hit the World Trade Center in New York City. Given our pre-9/11 mentality, we assumed that the plane must have been a small-engine plane that had experienced mechanical problems. During the break at 10:00 a.m., we went into the lobby of the hotel and quickly realized that our assumption was way off the mark.

The hotel had a very large projection television in the lobby, and everyone in the hotel must have been in that lobby. Despite that fact, it was so quiet that I am sure we could have heard a pin drop. Everyone was glued to the television screen in a rather deep state of hypnosis. What caused the hypnotic state? The traumatic nature of what we witnessed (the death and destruction) along with the confusion we experienced (we could not believe what we were witnessing—people do not intentionally fly planes into buildings) encouraged us to go into that deep state of hypnosis.

When we are in a state of hypnosis, what is said to us, what we think, and messages to which we are exposed are more likely to be taken as a fact, although we might not entirely believe the information. The deeper the state of hypnosis, the less the issue of believability is relevant to whether or not a person acts on that message.

For example, one female client of mine had a problem with social phobia—she was very afraid of being around other people, especially crowds. As a part of her therapy, we elected to do Rational Hypnotherapy. One post-hypnotic suggestion that I gave her (after she was in a good state of hypnosis) was, "Seeing people causes you to relax, and each time that you see people, you do relax twice as quickly as the time before."

During the following week's appointment, I asked her how she was doing. She said, "You know, it is the strangest thing. Do you remember last week that you told me that seeing people would cause me to relax? When you told me that, I thought that that was the biggest bunch of nonsense I had ever heard in my life! But I'll be darned if I'm not relaxed around others!" She had no explanation for why she was relaxed around people even though she had not *believed* the suggestion when it was presented to her. The reason the suggestion worked was that she was in a good state of hypnosis during the hypnotherapy session, and she did not reject the suggestion. In other words, as I gave her the suggestion, had she said to herself, "No, I do not want to be relaxed around people," the suggestion would not have worked.

Therefore, the main reason Rational Living Therapists use hypnotherapy with their clients (with their permission and informed consent) is because *the client does not have to believe the suggestions or messages presented* for those suggestions to become a part of the way the client thinks and behaves. Often psychotherapy or counseling clients *wish* that they believed the positive, rational ideas that their therapists encourage them to believe. They seem to have a hard time doing so at times, though, usually because they see no reason to believe them. With hypnotherapy, the client does not have to *believe* those positive messages for those messages to have a positive effect.

Another reason Rational Living Therapists use hypnotherapy with their clients is that research has shown that the deeper the state of hypnosis, the fewer repetitions of the information presented are needed for a person to acquire the knowledge and to act on it. Therefore, it is not necessarily the case that a person will be relieved of his or her problem with one session of hypnotherapy (although I have seen dramatic results often after one hypnotherapy session). However, hypnotherapy will require fewer repetitions of the information for problem resolution to occur than it would with other approaches.

As a result, Rational Hypnotherapy is an excellent technique to speed the process of getting better. Therefore, Rational Hypnotherapy is just another way to help people to change the way they think. But the main difference between it and the other thought-changing approaches described in this book is that a person does not have to believe the new thoughts and that the thoughts are learned more quickly through hypnotherapy.

There are many myths and misconceptions concerning hypnosis and hypnotherapy. Following is a list of the most common myths, along with their factual counterparts.

Common Myths About Hypnosis and Hypnotherapy

1. **Myth:** A person is asleep during hypnosis.

   Fact: A person is totally awake while in a hypnotic state.

2. **Myth:** People in a hypnotic state do not know what is going on around them. They totally tune out the surroundings.

   Fact: During hypnotherapy people can hear every sound that they would ordinarily hear. They are aware of their surroundings. They are asked to close their eyes though.

3. **Myth:** The hypnotist can make me do things that I don't want to do, like rob a bank or take my clothes off.

   Fact: An ethical hypnotherapist would not ask a person to do these things to begin with. People can and do reject any suggestion that is contrary to their morals, desires, or survival.

4. **Myth:** A person can get stuck in hypnosis.

   Fact: A person cannot get "stuck" in hypnosis. You go through a semi-hypnotic state every time you wake up and fall asleep. You simply open your eyes.

5. **Myth:** The hypnotist hypnotizes people.

   Fact: People hypnotize themselves. The hypnotist just guides them through it.

6. **Myth:** People lose control of themselves when hypnotized.

   Fact: People maintain total control of themselves.

7. **Myth:** I have never been in a hypnotic state.

   Fact: We experience hypnotic states, to some degree, every day.

8. **Myth:** Hypnosis is the work of the Devil. Hypnosis puts you in a vulnerable state that makes it likely that you will be possessed.

   Fact: No evidence of this whatsoever. Many ministers and priests use hypnotherapy.

Hypnotherapy is a very safe, effective technique to help people to rid themselves of old, irrational thoughts and to replace them with new, rational thoughts. Hypnosis is not sleeping. You do not "go under" like when you are under general anesthesia for surgery. There is no feeling associated with being in a state of hypnosis. Most people expect to feel some strange, unique feeling that they have never felt before. When they do not, they have the "I wasn't hypnotized" syndrome.

Additionally, note that not only do you *not* lose control of yourself during hypnotherapy, but, in fact, you can have greater-than-usual control of yourself. For example, if someone were to ask you right now to make your right hand completely numb so that a surgeon could operate on it, would you be able to do that? Probably not. But you could make it numb, warm, cold, and heavy as a boulder, or a whole host of other sensations while in a state of hypnosis. The possibilities are virtually endless.

There are many ways to perform hypnotherapy. I recommend Rational Hypnotherapy, a technique that I developed that is consistent with the rational philosophy you have been learning in this book. Contact the National Association of Cognitive-Behavioral Therapists at 1-800-853-1135 and we will be glad to inform you of our self-hypnosis programs or possibly refer you to a Rational Hypnotherapist in your area.

Chapter 13 Summary

1. Hypnotherapy is just another way to help people change their thoughts.

2. When people are in a sufficiently deep state of hypnosis, they do not need to believe the ideas to which they are exposed.

3. The deeper the state of hypnosis, the fewer repetitions of the information presented are needed for a person to acquire the knowledge and to act on it.

4. Not only do you not lose control of yourself in a state of hypnosis, you actually have better control over your body and behavior.

5. People can learn self-hypnosis and apply it to many different situations and problems.

14

More Rational Techniques

There are eight additional rational self-counseling techniques that I believe are important to include in this book: (1) Breaking Response Chains, (2) Environmental Manipulation, (3) Contingent Reinforcement, (4) Reinforcement of Incompatible Behavior, (5) Putting Things into Perspective, (6) Time Distancing, (7) "Life Is Too Short" Philosophy, and (8) Positive/Negative Imagery. I encourage you to utilize these techniques to make your self-counseling even more successful.

Breaking Response Chains

If we view behavior or reactions as a sequence or chain of events, the earlier in that chain we disrupt it, the more successful we will be in preventing the behavior. Let's take as an example a man (let's call him Paul) who says that he sometimes feels anxious at work, and when he does, he usually stops at a bar on the way home and gets drunk.

The *first step* in breaking response chains is to notice a pattern. When do you act or react in the way that you want to change? What tends to remind you to act or react in the undesired way? Knowing the answer to these two questions will help you to know when to implement your new strategy. In this example, Paul gets drunk in reaction to the anxious feelings; therefore, until he learns how to eliminate the thoughts that cause him to feel anxious at work, he will want to use the anxious feelings as a signal that he needs to implement a plan to keep himself from getting drunk.

The *second step* is to plan a course of action that will prevent the undesired behavior or reaction. It is important to develop a plan that will make it nearly impossible to engage in the undesired behavior while implementing it. An excellent strategy for Paul would be to call his wife when he feels anxious and ask her to pick him up or to follow him home after work.

The *third step* is to begin acting on the plan. Make a sincere statement to yourself that you refuse to act or react in the old, undesired way and instead will put the plan into action. When Paul feels anxious at work, he tells himself, "I refuse to drink on the way home, and, instead, I will call my wife and have her follow me home."

There are many situations in which breaking response chains can be very helpful. If, for example, you know that discussions of certain unimportant topics tend to lead to arguments, find a way to change the subject early in the discussion. Think about how breaking response chains could benefit you.

Environmental Manipulation

Environmental manipulation is creating an environment for yourself that will make it more likely that you will succeed. Environmental manipulation is particularly helpful for, but not limited to, habit control. For example, when working with people who want to lose weight, I encourage them to seek an appropriate diet plan that their physician has approved. Once they understand the diet plan and what they are to eat, I encourage them to remove any food items from their home that are not on the plan (unless there are others in the home that intend to eat them). The reason for removing these items from their home is not because they have no ability to refuse to eat them (of course they do), but because there is no rational reason for a person to place herself in a position to tempt herself.

When people seek to quit smoking gradually by weekly reducing the amount that they smoke, I encourage them to keep in their home only as many cigarettes as they intend to smoke for the day. Obviously, people have the ability to purchase more; but if it takes some effort to travel to a store to purchase them, they have time to talk themselves out of smoking more cigarettes than they had intended.

Alcoholics Anonymous encourages people who have had a habit of drinking irrationally to avoid places where alcohol is served, particularly bars and nightclubs. I often encourage people to surround themselves with people who have achieved what they want to achieve, who are rationally positive and optimistic, and avoid those who are irrationally pessimistic.

Remember, though, that we maintain total control over our thoughts, feelings, and behaviors. So we need not concern ourselves that we necessarily will think pessimistically if we are around others who do so. We do stand a greater chance of *talking ourselves* into thinking pessimistically, though, if the people around us do so.

Contingent Reinforcement

A reinforcer is anything that increases the likelihood that a behavior will be repeated. Reinforcement is using a reinforcer to encourage a behavior, like a reward for doing well. Contingent reinforcement means that for someone to receive the reward, they must do something to earn it. Contingent reinforcement is often used in child rearing with much success. Adults, though, are on contingent reinforcement schedules as well. An employer is unlikely to pay an employee if the employee does not work. Spouses are less likely to do kind things for each other if there is not some amount of reciprocity.

Sometimes contingent reinforcement is intentionally self-imposed. For example, a person working at motivating herself to read her homework assignment might make watching her favorite television show contingent upon reading it—if she does not read the assignment, she will deny herself the pleasure of watching the program. This approach certainly does require some self-discipline. However, self-discipline only means that a person has clearly defined goals that are very important, that he or she is keeping mindful of those goals, and that he or she realizes that a strategy like contingent reinforcement is an important part of achieving those goals.

Reinforcement of Incompatible Behavior

An important fact about the human brain is that it does not like a vacuum, meaning that if we eliminate a behavior but do not replace it with a different behavior, we tend to revert to the old behavior. So developing a replacement behavior is very important. As long as we are going to develop a replacement behavior—a new way to act and react—why not make that replacement behavior incompatible with the original? An incompatible replacement behavior is one that would make engaging in the original behavior difficult.

You might have seen the public service announcements that make statements like, "It is hard to smoke marijuana while playing a tuba." These announcements encourage replacement behaviors to using drugs that are incompatible with using them. If you want to eliminate a habit, develop replacement behaviors that are incompatible with that habit. If you tend to bite your fingernails while watching television, place your hands in your pockets whenever you watch your favorite shows, at least until the habit is broken. If you tend to smoke while driving, make a concerted effort to keep both hands on the steering wheel. If you tend to drink alcohol excessively in the evenings, find an activity, like a martial arts class, to fill the time.

Putting Things into Perspective

Whether we intend to or not, we make comparisons on a daily basis. We rate people, for example, in terms of attractiveness, cooperativeness, intelligence, willingness to listen, and other traits.

When we say, "That person is not very intelligent," we are rating that person by some standard of intelligence. This is why we do not think of everyone as equally intelligent. In psychology, we call this a **figure-ground comparison**. For example, a person might say, "President Clinton is a terrific president compared to President Carter, but a lousy president compared to President Reagan." The perception of the situation depends on what it is being compared to. It is important for us to rate our problems as well, rather than treating every personally negative situation as being equally bad, and, therefore, having the same negative emotional reaction to all problems.

For example, one day I was traveling to my office with a long day ahead of me. I knew I was going to have a very busy schedule. What made matters much worse for me was the fact that I had a very bad headache. I was stopped at a traffic light when I happened to notice a man getting out of a car at a grocery store. He seemed to struggle to get out of the car, and when he was out of it, I realized why—he was disabled. He needed braces to walk, which he used with a lot of effort to get into the store. Seeing this man's situation made me realize that my headache and schedule for the day really were not so bad. I am sure the man would have loved to have traded places with me.

Sometimes people get the impression, though, that they do not have a right to be upset about their situations because others have it worse than they do. Putting things into perspective has nothing to do with denying yourself the right to be upset. You always have the option of exercising your biological right to make yourself as upset as you want to be. However, putting things into perspective helps you to be only as upset as you want to be.

Time Distancing

If you upset yourself about something, ask yourself, "Is it likely that I will be as upset about this situation tomorrow, or next week, or next month, or next year as I am right now?" If your answer to this question is no, then it does not make any rational sense to be as upset about it now. However, if you believe that you will be just as upset next week as you currently are, that is not proof that your thinking makes rational sense.

Ask yourself, "Why will I not be as upset about it tomorrow as I am now?" The usual answers include these:

- I will not be as tired tomorrow as I am today.

- I probably will not have the headache tomorrow that I have today.

- This has nothing to do with what is happening tomorrow or any other day.

- I will probably have come up with a solution by then.

- I will not have as much going on tomorrow, so that will give me a chance to work on this better.

- I know that I am only thinking this way because I am already upset about something else that happened today.

- I will be used to it by then.

Remember that "time" does not heal wounds. Time only gives us the opportunity to talk ourselves out of feeling miserable. So if a person does not feel as upset a week later as she currently feels, that would only mean that she found a way to talk herself out of it. If she can do it now, she will save herself a week's worth of misery!

"Life Is Too Short" Philosophy

Existential psychologists and philosophers say that life means nothing without death. If there were no ending to life, living would not be worth much because there would be an endless supply of days.

Of course, everyone must die at some point. Acknowledging and accepting that fact helps us to appreciate the life we do have. Therefore, should you make yourself consistently upset about anything, ask yourself, "Is this how I want to spend my days, feeling this miserable?" or "If I knew that I would die tomorrow, would I be as upset about this as I am now, or would it seem trivial?"

Positive/Negative Imagery

Positive/negative imagery is another technique that is helpful to eliminate problem behaviors and to replace them with rational actions.

Positive imagery encourages positive, rational behavior. It is visualizing a positive outcome that results from rational behavior. Negative imagery is the opposite—it discourages irrational behavior through visualizing a very negative outcome that results from irrational behavior. I recommend that you first practice the negative imagery and then immediately move to the positive imagery.

For example, I mentioned earlier that I had heart bypass surgery. My doctors tell me that my arteries were blocked because of very high cholesterol and that it was important for me to adhere to a very strict low-fat, low-cholesterol diet. However, I loved the foods that partially caused my cholesterol to be so high—cheese, red meat, hamburgers, and the like.

To develop an aversion for these foods and an appetite for heart-friendly food, I performed practice sessions during which I first imagined myself eating a hamburger and immediately dropping dead from a heart attack! I also imagined myself eating cheese and red meat and immediately pictured myself lying in a hospital bed as I had following my surgery. After I upset myself with those images, I then calmed myself through progressive relaxation and imagined myself as a healthy, vibrant eighty-year-old eating pasta and vegetables and enjoying them. After a while, the artery-clogging foods certainly lost their appeal, while the heart-friendly foods became very appealing.

Chapter 14 Summary

1. The Breaking Response Chains technique is very helpful to prevent unwanted behavior.

2. To increase the chances that you will achieve your goals, create an environment of success.

3. One way to change your behavior is to do things that make it difficult to engage in the old, unwanted behavior.

4. Time distancing is a great way to reduce or eliminate your current unpleasant feelings about a specific situation.

5. Imagery, both positive and negative, can be a very emotive way to discourage old, irrational behavior and to encourage new, rational behavior.

15

Change Your Body, Change Your Emotions

Science has yet to improve on Mother Nature at her best—the human brain. This is a point that Maxie C. Maultsby, Jr., MD (1984) has stressed throughout his career. The brain is capable of triggering very painful emotional reactions. Conversely, the brain is also capable of triggering very pleasant emotions. Since the brain is the organ that controls our emotions, it makes sense to learn how to use our brain in a way that makes us feel good.

Practice the following proven stress-reducing, mood-enhancing techniques daily, and you will very likely begin noticing an improvement in your emotional state.

The Universally Calming Perspective

Dr. Maultsby (1984) developed the following poem to help keep you focused on rational acceptance of undesirable situations:

> Even though this is not what I wanted to see
> Until I make it more the way I want it to be
> I shall keep myself pleasantly calm, naturally.
> With a warm, soft smile on my face
> I'll continue to breathe in this slow, relaxing pace
> Until I am pleasantly calm, naturally

As I now think it is best to be.

I recommend that you memorize this poem so that you can carry it with you wherever you go; thus, you will be able to obtain almost instant relief in any situation by using it.

Why the "warm, soft smile?" Research experiments have shown that facial expressions trigger chemicals in the brain that produce emotional states. Frowning encourages sadness. Smiling encourages happiness, even if it seems as though there is nothing to be happy about. Although you might not *feel* like smiling, you probably could at least *squeeze* a "Mona Lisa" smile on your face. Doing so will make a positive emotional difference.

Rational Progressive Relaxation

My CD, "Rational Progressive Relaxation," is a great way to learn to relax quickly and deeply. I recommend that you purchase this CD either by calling 1-800-853-1135 or by visiting http://nacbt. americommerce.com.

Your Physical Health: Take Care of It!

Your emotions are the result of chemical and electrical processes occurring in your body, and these chemical and electrical processes are affected by many factors. As you have learned in previous chapters in this book, you, in effect, direct your brain to produce the chemical changes that result in how you feel and in what you do.

Taking care of your body helps you to have a "sound mind." The following is a list of vitamins, herbs, and physical techniques that can assist your body in helping you feel good emotionally. *However, I strongly urge you to talk with your medical doctor about these supplements before taking them, especially if you already are taking psychiatric or other medications.*

Vitamins and Herbs

As you know from reading this book, the healthy, undrugged brain has all the chemicals that it needs to make you feel and act better. Therefore, although physicians often prescribe them, psychiatric medications usually are not necessary. This is *not* to say that psychiatric medications are not helpful at times, particularly when a person has difficulty benefiting from self-counseling due to fatigue or concentration problems, or he or she has a problem such as schizophrenia or bipolar disorder.

While the following vitamins and herbs usually are not necessary either, it does make sense for us to do what we can to help keep the brain and body healthy so that we are in the best possible position to use them to counsel ourselves effectively.

Research has proven that the following vitamins, herbs, amino acids, and other supplements are as effective as (and sometimes more effective than) their pharmaceutical counterparts, without the negative side effects usually associated with prescription drugs. These supplements can be obtained at your local health food store. Also, most of these supplements can be found at the NACBT's online store at http://nacbt.americommerce.com.

The "B" Vitamins: Essential for Proper Nerve Functioning

The "B" vitamins (including B_1, B_2, B_3, B_5, B_6, B_{12}, and folic acid) are essential for proper nerve functioning. "B" vitamins also play a role in metabolism. However, emotional distress tends to deplete the body of the "B" vitamins, which sometimes leads to nervousness and decreased appetite. Therefore, most holistic health physicians recommend "B" vitamin supplementation (usually as a B-Complex) for people who are experiencing emotional distress consistently (Whitaker, 1995).

Antioxidant Vitamins, Minerals, and Herbs

Antioxidants are substances that prevent damage to the body from free radicals. Free radicals are molecules that are very reactive and bind to body tissue and damage it. This damage is called oxidation. Cut an apple in half and let it sit on your counter for an hour. When you return, you will see evidence of oxidation—the once-white apple has turned brown. That is what happens to one's body when it is not protected sufficiently with antioxidant nutrients.

Research has shown that free radicals are responsible (at least in part) for causing (and worsening) the two major health problems of our day—heart disease and cancer. While much of the attention with heart disease has been on cholesterol, some research suggests that cholesterol is more likely to do its damage to artery walls if it (the cholesterol) is first altered by free radicals. Therefore, protecting cholesterol and arteries from free radical damage is important in the prevention of cardiovascular disease (Whitaker, 1995).

Our bodies are exposed to free radicals daily from both internal and external sources. Free radicals are the byproducts of many normal body processes that we cannot avoid. However, we can reduce our exposure to many sources of free radicals, such as alcohol, cigarettes, secondhand cigarette smoke, electrical fields (including electric blankets), pollution, fried foods, and stress. "Emotional stress" causes a reaction from one's body that produces a large amount of free radicals. This is why, most researchers believe, stress affects our body. If you look at someone who tends to be anxious and smokes regularly, he or she usually will look somewhat older than his or her same-aged peers. Just as they turn the apple brown, free radicals seem to affect our skin by causing wrinkles.

The main antioxidant nutrients are vitamins C and E. While we get these nutrients from the foods we eat, the amount we receive in our food is not enough to protect us from free radicals. Therefore, most holistic health practitioners recommend taking antioxidant supplements (usually 500 milligrams of vitamin C and 400 international units of vitamin E) daily and avoiding sources of free radicals (Whitaker, 1995).

Omega-3 Fatty Acids

Omega-3 fatty acids have become popular in recent years for their positive effects on the cardiovascular system and their apparent ability to raise HDL ("good") cholesterol. However, omega-3 fatty acids also appear to improve our emotional health as well.

Omega-3 fatty acids are effective in treating symptoms of depression in patients who remain depressed despite being on standard antidepressant medication therapy (Peet and Horrobin, 2002). In fact, Schmidt (1997) reports that omega-3 fatty acids can raise a natural antidepressant brain chemical called "dopamine" by 40 percent.

The two most popular sources of omega-3 fatty acids are fish and flax oil. While my preferred way of obtaining omega-3 fatty acids is through flax seed oil capsules, flax oil is helpful *in the brain* for only about one-third of us (Ross, 2002).

Ross (2002) recommends taking two grams of fish oil supplements a day.

Natural Help for Depressive Symptoms

Note that the following natural substances are not substitutes for learning the rational self-counseling skills detailed in this book. They can, though, be helpful in providing relief from depressive symptoms.

L-tyrosine

L-tyrosine is an amino acid (a building block of protein). While clinical studies (Werbach, 1991) have demonstrated L-tyrosine's effectiveness at reducing symptoms of depression, it is particularly helpful in reducing the potential side effects of antidepressant drugs known as SSRIs (Selective Serotonin Reuptake Inhibitors). Commonly prescribed SSRIs include these:

SSRI Antidepressants	
Prozac	Cipramil
Seromex	Emocal
Seronil	Sepram (Generic: Citalopram)
Fontex (Generic: Fluoxetine)	Luvox
Paxil	Fevarin (Generic: Fluvoxamine)
Seroxat	Lexapro (Generic: Escitalopram)
Opitar	Wellburtin (Generic: Bupropion)
Aropax (Generic: Paroxetine)	Effexor (Generic: Venlafaxine)
Celexa	Zoloft (Generic: Sertroline).

L-tyrosine helps with the common SSRI side effect of low energy (Korf et al., 1983). Serotonin is a neurotransmitter that is the biochemical counterbalance to your brain's natural stimulants, the catecholamines. Physicians prescribe SSRI antidepressants to raise serotonin levels in the patient's brain. *However, raising serotonin levels via SSRIs can deplete levels of catecholamines by as much as 60 percent.* The result of this decrease in catecholamines is low energy, apathy, twitches, tics, and sexual dysfunction.

According to Julia Ross (2002), L-tyrosine appears to restore the balance by improving the level of catecholamines. She recommends a dosage of 500 to 1000 milligrams to be taken in the morning to mid-afternoon (by 3:00 p.m.). Amino acids are best absorbed on an empty stomach.

Make certain to discuss L-tyrosine with your physician, especially if you are experiencing SSRI-induced side effects. Also note that there is a possible negative interaction between L-tyrosine and MAO inhibitors (another type of antidepressant).

St. John's Wort

St. John's Wort is a well-researched herb with antidepressant properties. It has been found to be just as effective as Prozac for mild to moderate symptoms of depression (Schrader, 2000) and more effective than Zoloft for mild to moderate depressive symptoms (Brenner et al., 2000). Another benefit of St. John's Wort is that it appears to have antiviral properties.

The recommended dosage (Ross, 2002; Whitaker, 1995) is 300 mg, three times a day. Hypericum is the active antidepressive ingredient in St. John's Wort, so make certain that the supplement states on its packaging that it is standardized at .3 percent Hypericum.

Make certain to discuss St. John's Wort with your physician before taking it. Known interactions include birth control pills (it decreases the effectiveness of oral contraceptives), blood thinners (St. John's Wort thins the blood as well), and other antidepressants. It can also make a person sensitive to sunlight.

5-HTP

Supplementation with 5-HTP can provide rapid improvement in mood, sometimes within a matter of hours (Ross, 2002). Its ability to raise serotonin levels is what makes 5-HTP a potent antidepressant. In fact, the manufacturer of Prozac, Eli Lilly, conducted a study in which they combined 5-HTP with Prozac. Serotonin activity was increased by 150 percent with Prozac, but it increased to 650 percent when 5-HTP was added!

Another study comparing 5-HTP to the powerful antidepressant Luvox found that 5-HTP improved depressive symptoms in 68 percent of patients compared to 62 percent of those on Luvox (Poldinger et al., 1991).

Ross (2002) recommends starting with 50 milligrams in mid-afternoon. Add another 50 milligrams in an hour, if you do not receive much benefit. If needed, add a third 50 milligrams for maximum effect one hour later. Whichever level provided the desired result, repeat the dose at 9:30 p.m. (50–150 milligrams).

As for safety and side effects, 5-HTP is associated with zero sexual dysfunction (Benkert, 1976, 1975) while SSRI antidepressants are associated with 50–70 percent sexual dysfunction. Other studies (Ross, 2002) have shown that 5-HTP has had fewer side effects than placebos!

Of course, discuss 5-HTP supplementation with your physician before using it. There is a possible negative interaction with MAO inhibitors.

Natural Help for Anxiety Symptoms

Although medical science has developed very potent drugs that reduce symptoms of anxiety, there is a significant price to pay for using most of them—addiction! The following natural substances are nonaddictive and can be very potent as well. Be certain to discuss these substances with your physician before taking them, especially if you already are taking psychiatric medications or are taking any medication that causes drowsiness, such as beta-blockers for the heart or antihistamines for allergies.

Calcium

Calcium is a muscle relaxer and pain reliever. It helps to produce general relaxation and can encourage sleep in those who have suffered from insomnia. While many claims have been made about the superiority of certain types or brands of calcium, they essentially are all the same. Ross (2002) recommends 500–1000 milligrams daily. Again, seek physician approval before beginning calcium supplementation.

Also note that supplemental calcium might interfere with the absorption of other nutrients and with medication. Therefore, take calcium at least four hours before or after taking medication or vitamins.

GABA

GABA (gamma-aminobutyric acid) has been described as your brain's natural Valium (Ross, 2002). Valium is a well-known anti-anxiety medication. In fact, Valium, along with other anti-anxiety medications, was designed to mimic or amplify GABA's naturally calming effects.

GABA is both an amino acid and an inhibitory neurotransmitter. It decreases production of adrenaline. Adrenaline is a hormone that causes the increase in heart rate, breathing rate, and nervousness that we experience when something threatening confronts us. GABA supplementation can help to turn off stress after we upset ourselves, and it can help to prevent stressful responses when taken before an expected ordeal.

Ross (2002) recommends taking 500–1000 milligrams, one to three times a day. Again, talk with your doctor before taking GABA.

Valerian Root

Valerian Root is a rather foul-smelling herb that packs quite a calming punch. It is an excellent anti-anxiety agent with a very good safety profile (Bloomfield, 1998). One Utah woman in 1995 attempted suicide by taking twenty times the recommended dose of valerian root. She was discharged from the hospital the next day unharmed.

Valerian root is also very good for inducing sleep, and it appears to decrease the incidence of nightmares.

As a sedative, Bloomfield (1998) recommends 300–900 milligrams taken one hour before bedtime. For general anxiety relief, the effects are dose-dependent. Therefore, follow the manufacturer's directions on the label until the desired effects are produced.

Chamomile

Chamomile is another excellent, safe anti-anxiety herb (Bloomfield, 1998). This herb is ingested most often in the form of tea.

Besides having excellent anti-anxiety properties, chamomile is an antispasmodic and can help to alleviate menstrual cramps. Chamomile also is very effective in treating gastrointestinal discomfort, including nausea. A warm cup of chamomile tea before going to bed can help you fall asleep.

Again, the effects of chamomile are dose-dependent. You might need to experiment to determine whether using one or two tea bags produce the desired effect. On a cautionary note, avoid chamomile if you have a ragweed allergy. Also, do not use chamomile for more than seven consecutive days because a ragweed allergy might result.

Sometimes Allergies Cause Psychiatric Symptoms

Dr. William Crook's book, *Solving the Puzzle of Your Hard-to-Raise Child,* "should be" required reading for all mental health professionals. In his book, Dr. Crook clearly establishes the fact that allergies can, and often do, cause a host of symptoms that are often mistakenly believed to be indicative of a psychiatric disorder.

Crook (1987) suggests that allergies (both food and airborne) cause symptoms of anxiety (psychomotor agitation, vertigo, nausea, confusion), symptoms of depression (fatigue, lethargy), and neurological symptoms, like tics, tremors, and Tourette's syndrome. Allergies also can cause inattention and hyperactivity and encourage the misbehavior that often coincides.

According to Dr. Crook, symptoms of allergies include

- a pale color
- dark circles under the eyes (allergic "shiners")
- a congested nose
- allergic gape (person tends to keep the mouth open because the nose is stuffed)
- headaches (especially in the forehead)
- fatigue or drowsiness
- inability to concentrate
- short attention span
- hyperactivity
- nausea or other stomach discomfort
- muscle aches

These symptoms can give a person the impression that he or she is depressed, anxious, or both. Considering these symptoms is important, especially if it seems to you that you are depressed or anxious, but are not particularly upset about anything.

If you experience these symptoms, ask your physician about getting tested and treated (if necessary) for allergies. Even if you are reacting to something in your life, and that is what encouraged you to read this book, allergies might be making matters worse for you.

Sleep

Anyone who has ever been around a person who consistently loses sleep knows the main effect of it—fatigue, irritation, and anger. Sound sleep is a necessary part of good mental and physical health. Without it, many physical problems can develop. The resultant fatigue makes otherwise small problems seem catastrophic as the person simply does not have the energy to handle things well.

Many people think that they do not have to take their sleep schedule seriously. But sleeping recharges our batteries, so to speak. Just like an electronic device, eventually we too slow down and stop when our batteries get too low.

Often, people have difficulty sleeping when they have excessive worries or fears. They might have difficulty falling asleep. They might wake up intermittently throughout the night. Often, they experience both.

To get quality sleep, try this:

- Make certain that you get between six and eight hours per night.

- Maintain a regular sleep schedule so that your body will know that it is time to sleep.

- Realize that there is no point in thinking about your concerns in the middle of the night unless you can do something about them then. So allow yourself to be distracted by something else, like music, until you fall asleep.

- With your physician's approval, make use of chamomile or valerian root to help you sleep soundly, naturally.

Refrain from Excessive Alcohol, Tobacco, and Caffeine Use

Alcohol is a central nervous system depressant. If you are already depressed or otherwise sluggish, alcohol can make you feel worse. Granted, many people try to make themselves feel better by getting drunk. However, the good feeling of being intoxicated is often replaced with a hangover, fatigue, and possible social, legal, and work-related problems as well. It is in your best interest to have all of your resources available to you to deal with your problems. Excessive alcohol consumption interferes with your ability to take care of business.

Avoid tobacco and caffeine if you are experiencing anxiety consistently. Using these two substances when anxious is like pouring gasoline onto a fire. Cigarette smoking produces carbon monoxide, a gas that robs your body of oxygen. Whenever we are deprived of oxygen, we feel lethargic. Cigarette smoking also produces cyanide—the gas used in gas chambers.

Routine

In the late 1960s, Holmes and Rahe (1967) undertook a series of stress management studies to determine what events in life cause the greatest stress effects. Because of this research they concluded that it may be possible to anticipate stress crises and assist people in overcoming their stress.

Holmes and Rahe asked research subjects to rate common life events by "Life Crisis Units" (LCUs) and then ranked their responses. This is how the subjects responded:

Event	LCU's	Event	LCU's
Death of spouse	100	Change in responsibilities at work	29
Divorce	73	Son or daughter leaving home	29
Separation	65	Trouble with in-laws	29
Jail term	63	Outstanding personal achievement	28
Death of close family member	63	Spouse begins or stops work	26
Personal illness or injury	53	Begin or end of school or college	26
Marriage	50	Change in living conditions	25
Fired at work	47	Change in personal habits	24
Marital reconciliation	45	Trouble with boss	23
Retirement	45	Change in work hours or conditions	20
Change in health of family member	44	Change in residence	20
Pregnancy	40	Change in school or college	20
Sex difficulties	39	Change in recreation	19
Gain of new family member	39	Change in church activities	19
Business readjustment	38	Change in social activities	18
Change in financial state	38	A moderate loan or mortgage	17
Death of close friend	37	Change in sleeping habits	16
Change to a different line of work	36	Change in number of family get-togethers	15
Change in number of arguments with spouse	35	Change in eating habits	15
A large mortgage or loan	30	Holiday	13
Foreclosure of mortgage or loan	30	Christmas	12
		Minor violations of law	11

Ranking of Amount of Change Produced by Various Life Events (Holmes and Ruch, 1971)

Holmes and Rahe defined stress as the body's adaptation to change. The more that a person has to adapt to a life event, the more stress the body experiences. It does not matter as much whether the life event is viewed as positive (like getting married) or negative (like getting divorced) as it does the amount of adaptation required to adjust to the event. In other words, it usually takes more time and effort to adjust to getting married than it does to getting a traffic ticket.

Holmes and Rahe discovered that the likelihood of people developing physical illness varies with how much change they experience in a given time frame. The more stress one experiences, the greater is the likelihood that one will experience a physical illness.

The human body thrives on regularity, and it attempts to adapt to change. Whether the change is seen as being good (winning $1 million) or bad (death of one's spouse), the body must adapt to it regardless.

Even minor changes in one's daily routine cause stress. Going to work a different route is stressful. Waking up at different times is stressful. Therefore, the more *irregularity* that we have in our daily living, the more stress we experience.

I encourage you to maintain a regular schedule of sleeping, eating, exercising, bathing, working, relaxing, and anything else you do regularly. Your body will thank you for it. Feeling good physically will make it easier to feel good emotionally.

Chapter 15 Summary

1. The healthy, undrugged brain is Mother Nature at her best.

2. There are various natural ways to help keep the brain and body healthy.

3. Stress is the body's adaptation to change. The nature of the change is not as important as the amount of change to which the body must adapt. Maintaining a regular schedule of eating, sleeping, and working is important to reduce stress.

4. Sleep is an underappreciated factor in emotional health.

5. Allergies can cause emotional and neurological problems.

16

Conclusion

Well, there you have it—my guide to feeling the way you want to feel, no matter what! With practice and at least occasional reminders, there is every reason to believe that you can utilize these rational self-counseling skills for the rest of your life.

I hope that you found this book informative and inspiring. I would love to hear from you about your experience with it. Please feel free to contact me at

National Association of Cognitive-Behavioral Therapists
Attention: Aldo R. Pucci
P.O. Box 2195
Weirton, WV 26062

You may e-mail me at aldo@nacbt.org. Also, please feel free to visit the NACBT Web site at http://www.nacbt.org. On the main page there is a section that allows you to enter your e-mail address to receive free updates on rational self-counseling.

Additionally, if you would like to be on our mailing list to be informed of products, services, and workshops we offer, simply contact us by any of the means listed here. Therapists wishing to learn more about Rational Living Therapy may visit our Web site at http://www. rational-living-therapy.org.

It has been my pleasure to share with you the philosophy and techniques that I have described in this book. I certainly wish you well.

Camera Checks

This is a list of common expressions used in our society that do not pass the camera check of perceptions as they are typically used. If you think of other expressions that you would like to share, please send them to NACBT, P.O. Box 2195, Weirton, WV 26062 or e-mail them to me at aldo@nacbt.org.

1. Fell all to pieces	22. Moron
2. Dirty rat	23. Idiot
3. Blew up	24. Dummy
4. End of my rope	25. It's killing me
5. Trapped	26. Beast
6. End-of-the-world	27. Ugly as sin
7. Scared to death	28. I died
8. Nervous breakdown	29. Splitting headache
9. Lost my mind	30. Doesn't have the guts
10. Crapped on me	31. Jumped down my throat
11. Blimp, Whale	32. Get off my back
12. Jerk	33. Loser
13. S.O.B.	34. Worked myself to death
14. "A" hole	35. Gutless mouse
15. Tore me apart	36. He rode me
16. Apart at the seams	37. Eating me up
17. Broken heart	38. Cold hearted
18. Jerk my chain	39. Went off the deep end
19. Floored me	40. Cracked up
20. Pain in the butt	41. Went nuts
21. Stole my heart	

References

Babyak, M., Blumenthal, J., Herman, S., Khatri, P., Doraiswamy, M., Moore, K., Craighead, E., Baldewicz, T., Krishnan, R. (2000). Exercise treatment for major depression: Maintenance of therapeutic benefit at 10 months. *Psychosomatic Medicine,* 62(5), 633–38.

Beck, A.T. (1976). *Cognitive Therapy and the Emotional Disorders.* New York: International Universities Press.

Benkert, O. (1975). Studies on pituitary hormones and releasing hormones in depression and sexual impotence. *Progress in Brain Research,* 42, 25–36.

Benkert, O. (1976). Effect of parachlorophenylalanine and 5-hydroxytryptophan on human sexual behavior. *Monographs in Neural Sciences,* 3, 88–93.

Bloomfield, H. (1998). *Healing Anxiety Naturally.* New York: HarperCollins.

Blumenthal, James A., Babyak, Michael A., Moore, Kathleen A., Craighead, W. Edward, Herman, Steve, Khatri, Parinda, Waugh, Robert, Napolitano, Melissa A., Forman, Leslie M., Appelbaum, Mark, Doraiswamy, P., Murali, and Krishnan, K., Ranga. (1999). Effects of exercise training on older patients with major depression. *Archives of Internal Medicine,* 159, 2349–2356.

Breggin, P. (2000). *Your Drug May Be Your Problem: How and Why to Stop Taking Psychiatric Medications.* New York: HarperCollins.

Brenner, R., Azbel, V., Madhusoodanan, S., Pawlowska, M. (2000). Comparison of an extract of hypericum and sertraline in the treatment of depression: A double blind, randomized pilot study. *Clinical Therapy,* 22(4), 411–19.

Burns, David (1980). *Feeling Good: The New Mood Therapy*. New York: Signet.

Crook, William G. (1987). *Solving the Puzzle of Your Hard-to-Raise Child*. New York: Random House.

Dunn, A., Trivedi, M., Kampert, J., Clark, C., Chambliss H. (2005). Exercise treatment for depression: Efficacy and dose response. *American Journal of Preventive Medicine*, 28(1), 1–8.

Ellis, Albert (1988). *How to Stubbornly Refuse to Make Yourself Miserable About Anything—Yes, Anything*. New York: Carol Publishing Group.

Ellis, Albert (2002). *Overcoming Resistance: A Rational Emotive Behavior Therapy Integrated Approach*. New York: Springer Publishing Company.

Holmes, T.H., and Rahe, R.H. (1967). The social readjustment rating scale. *Journal of Psychosomatic Research*, 11, 213–18.

Holmes, T.H., and Ruch, L.O. (1971). Scaling of life change: Comparison of direct and indirect methods. *Journal of Psychosomatic Research*, 15, 221–27.

Korf, J., Van den Burg, W., and Van den Hoofdakker, R.H. (1983). Acid metabolites and precursor amino acids of 5-hydroxytryptamine and dopamine in affective and other psychiatric disorders. *Psychiatria Clinica* (Basel), 16(1), 1–16.

Maslow, A. (1954). *Motivation and personality*. New York: Harper.

Maultsby, M.C. (1975). *Help Yourself to Happiness*. New York: Institute for Rational Emotive Therapy.

Maultsby, M.C. (1984). *Rational Behavior Therapy*. Appleton, WI: Rational Self-Help Aids/I'ACT.

Maultsby, M.C.(1990). *Coping Better, Anytime, Anywhere: The New Handbook of Rational Self Counseling.* (Second Edition). Appleton, WI: Rational Self-Help Aids.

Peet, M. and Horrobin, D. (2002). A dose-ranging study of the effects of ethyl-eicosapentaenoate in patients with ongoing depression despite apparently adequate treatment with standard drugs. *Archives of General Psychiatry,* 59, 913–19.

Poldinger, W., Calanchini, B., and Schwarz, W. (1991). A functional-dimensional approach to depression: Serotonin deficiency as a target syndrome in a comparison of 5-hydroxy-tryptophan and fluvoxamine. *Psychopathology,* 24, 53–81.

Ross, Julia (2002). *The Mood Cure.* New York: Penguin Putnam, Inc.

Schmidt, Michael A. (1997). *Smart Fats: How Dietary Fats and Oils Affect Mental, Physical and Emotional Intelligence.* Berkeley, CA: Frog Ltd.

Schrader, E. (2000). Equivalence of St. John's wort extract and fluoxetine: A randomized, controlled study in mild-moderate depression. *International Journal of Clinical Psychopharmacology,* 15(2), 61–8.

Werbach, M. (1991). *Nutritional Influences on Mental Illness.* Tarzana, CA: Third Line Press.

Whitaker, Julian (1995). *Dr. Whitaker's Guide to Natural Healing.* Rocklin, CA: Prima Publishing.

Yerkes R., and Dodson, J. (1908). The relation of strength of stimulus to rapidity of habit-formation. *Journal of Comparative Neurology and Psychology,* 18, 459–82.

About the Author

Aldo R. Pucci, PsyD, is president of the National Association of Cognitive-Behavioral Therapists, an association that he formed in 1995. Dr. Pucci was trained originally in cognitive-behavioral therapy by one of its pioneers, Dr. Maxie C. Maultsby, Jr. Dr. Maultsby, who recently retired from Howard University as the chairperson of the Department of Psychiatry, is the originator of Rational Behavior Therapy. Dr. Pucci modified Dr. Maultsby's approach to include original techniques and philosophies (like the replacement of "self-esteem" with the "Four A's") and hypnotherapy. The result is what Dr. Pucci calls "Rational Living Therapy."

He is president of the Rational Living Therapy Institute. He has served as an adjunct faculty member in the Graduate Counseling Program at Franciscan University of Steubenville. He has taught cognitive-behavioral therapy and Rational Living Therapy to thousands of mental health professionals throughout the United States. His seminars and workshops receive rave reviews.

Dr. Pucci has extensive experience with the application of cognitive-behavioral therapy both in community mental health centers and in private practice. He has helped people with a wide range of problems and concerns to help themselves through rational self-counseling. The NACBT's Board of Advisors awarded Dr. Pucci the Diplomate in Cognitive-Behavioral Therapy. He also is a Licensed Professional Counselor, a Certified Clinical Hypnotherapist, and a Certified Medical Hypnotherapist.

Dr. Pucci lives in Weirton, West Virginia (a suburb of Pittsburgh, PA), with his wife, Sandy, and their two children, Aldo Jr. and Maria.

Mental Health Professionals

If you are interested in obtaining certification in Rational Living Therapy, visit the Rational Living Therapy Institute's Web site at

http://www.rational-living-therapy.org

Rational Living Therapy is a very systematic approach to cognitive-behavioral therapy, which means that the Rational Living Therapist knows where he or she is at any given point in the process of therapy.

Rational Living Therapy is highly motivational. If you dislike giving up on clients and wish that there were some way to encourage any client to make changes, Rational Living Therapy is ideal for you. It is designed to tap into the client's desires by utilizing Rational Motivational Interviewing techniques.

Rational Living Therapy is very instructive. The instructive nature of RLT helps produce long-term results for the client.

Rational Living Therapy also focuses on underlying assumptions. By doing so, therapy is much "deeper," thus making the results more long term.

Rational Living Therapists are very concerned with irrational labeling. For this reason, we disagree with the labeling that results from mental health professionals' use of the *Diagnostic and Statistical Manual of Mental Disorders*. Many of these "diagnoses" actually are only labels for a set of behaviors. However, these labels often create a perception that the client "has" or "suffers from" a "disorder." This perception can become very problematic for the client, leading to a great deal of hopelessness. Rational Living Therapists help clients to avoid irrational labeling and hopelessness.

Rational Living Therapy takes the best of Rational Emotive Behavioral Therapy, Rational Behavior Therapy, and Cognitive Therapy and integrates knowledge and research findings in the areas of cognitive development, learning theory, general semantics, brain functioning, social psychology, perception, and linguistics. Rational Living Therapy takes advantage of special brain states to facilitate learning and progress.

Rational Living Therapy also rejects the common concepts of self-esteem and self-confidence and also departs from the traditional CBT emphasis of "self-acceptance." RTL's replacement to these concepts (the "Four A's") is much more practical and useful.

National Association of Cognitive-Behavioral Therapists'
Online Store

For a great selection of cognitive-behavioral therapy self-help books and audio programs, visit the NACBT's Online Store at

http://nacbt.americommerce.com

Our secure site offers self-help books, as well as self-help audio programs, such as

- Rational Progressive Relaxation
- Self-Hypnosis for Insomnia
- Rational Eating
- Pain Management

As well as supplements for emotional health, such as

- St. John's Wort
- L-Tyrosine
- 5-HTP
- Valerian Root
- Super Stress Formula
- DHA

For mental health professionals, our site offers the Rational Living Therapy Certification Self-Study Programs Levels One–Three, as well as the Rational Hypnotherapy Certification Program.

Our online store accepts VISA, MasterCard, Discover, and American Express. We accept international orders.